A Dirty, Filthy Book

A Dirty, Filthy Book

Sex, Scandal, and One Woman's Fight in the Victorian Trial of the Century

MICHAEL MEYER

WH
ALLEN

WH Allen, an imprint of Ebury Publishing
20 Vauxhall Bridge Road
London SW1V 2SA

WH Allen is part of the Penguin Random House group of companies
whose addresses can be found at global.penguinrandomhouse.com

Copyright © Michael Meyer 2024

First published by WH Allen in 2024

www.penguin.co.uk

A CIP catalogue record for this book is available from the British Library

ISBN 9780753559925
Trade Paperback ISBN 9780753559932

Typeset in 13.5/16pt Garamond MT Std by Jouve (UK), Milton Keynes
Printed and bound in Great Britain by Clays Ltd, Elcograf S.p.A.

The authorised representative in the EEA is Penguin Random House Ireland,
Morrison Chambers, 32 Nassau Street, Dublin D02 YH68

Penguin Random House is committed to a sustainable future
for our business, our readers and our planet. This book is made
from Forest Stewardship Council® certified paper.

For Frances and Benji,
always along for the ride

Contents

Oh! It is absurd to have a hard and fast rule about what one should read and what one shouldn't. More than half of modern culture depends on what one shouldn't read.

– Oscar Wilde, *The Importance of Being Earnest*, 1895

It's the one thing they won't let you be, straight and open in your sex. You can be as dirty as you like. In fact, the more dirt you do on sex the better they like it. But if you believe in your own sex and won't have it done dirt to: they'll down you. It's the one insane taboo left: sex as a natural and vital thing. They won't have it, and they'll kill you before they'll let you have it.

– D.H. Lawrence, *Lady Chatterley's Lover*, 1928

Neither my birth-control discussion nor Margaret Sanger's efforts were pioneer work.

– Emma Goldman, *Living My Life*, 1931

Prelude

'This Battle Must Be Won'

Westminster, 23 June 1880. We open at the Houses of Parliament, where on an otherwise uneventful early summer Wednesday, the prison room inside Big Ben's clock tower holds two unrepentant rebels. One, the newly elected Liberal MP Charles Bradlaugh – age 46, tall, clean-shaven, with long grey locks combed back from his icebreaker brow – has refused to swear the required seat-taking oath that ends 'so help me God'. When Midland labourers voted in Bradlaugh, they had also elected Parliament's first professed atheist. To rousing applause from the House of Commons' green-leather benches, the Serjeant-at-Arms had marched the barrel-chested Bradlaugh – disparaged by Queen Victoria in a series of diary entries as 'horrible', 'immoral', and 'repulsive looking' – up the clock tower stairs and into the smallest jail cell in the largest city in the world.[1] But Victorian London, seat of an empire upon which the sun never sets, cannot cage Bradlaugh for long. Not with Annie Besant at his side.

Upon hearing the news of her confidant's arrest, Besant – petite, chestnut-haired, 32, and still legally married to the abusive Anglican vicar she had walked out on seven years before – rushed in a one-shilling hansom cab from her rented house near Primrose Hill and down through the capital's coke-flecked murk to the tower beside the Thames. The era is one of high Victorian politesse; the visitor is allowed to join the prisoner for supper.

'The Prison in the Clock-Tower of the Palace of Westminster' – *The Illustrated London News*, 3 July 1880

In the cell's high-ceilinged, oak-panelled sitting room – pulsing from the gallows-drop thud of Big Ben's hammer and the bell's reverberating E note – Annie Besant plots their next move. Once again, the pair are up against Church and Crown. Once again, Bradlaugh counts on Besant to take the lead. Not for nothing would a smitten George Bernard Shaw once marvel: 'There has never been an orator to touch her.'[2]

In an era when British society could not have been more gendered – men sporting bushy sideburns known as Piccadilly Weepers, bonneted women squeezing their crinolines sidelong through doorways – Annie Besant had thrown herself into public life in the same manner that Big Ben announces the hours: loudly, and with a resonance that can still be felt today.

This is not the first time that Besant and Bradlaugh have shared a cell. Three years before, City of London constables had arrested the duo for publishing and selling the first popular birth control manual. Called *Fruits of Philosophy*, the American doctor Charles Knowlton's pathbreaking booklet put safe methods of 'checking' pregnancy in the hands of women, and argued that reproductive health should be frankly discussed in physiological, rather than moral, terms. Annie had priced her reprint of the pamphlet's pulpy pages at sixpence to better reach the working-class men and women packing the terraced brick lowlands of London's East End.

Besant and her partner Bradlaugh's crime, officially, was obscenity. The sensational trial that followed dragged debate over sex, censorship, marriage and morality onto the front pages of newspapers gracing breakfast and dinner tables across the United Kingdom. The coverage spawned more coverage; a prosecution meant to silence insubordinate voices instead broadcast them further than ever before.[3]

Nothing like it had ever happened, and the proceedings took place on a stage that would not be seen again. Trimmed in ermine and wigged with horsehair, Britain's highest judge had moved the proceedings to the palatial splendour of the Court of Queen's Bench. The since-razed courtroom was attached to hallowed Westminster Hall; the sounds of Big Ben and the bells of Westminster Abbey seeped through its soot-stained, sandy limestone walls. Here, at the very heart of the British Establishment, Annie Besant had bravely asserted a woman's right to bodily autonomy.

'It will be no exaggeration of Mrs. Besant's speeches,' Charles Bradlaugh wrote after the verdict, 'to say that they are unparalleled in the history of English trials.'[4]

Until then few men, and no women, had dared to publicly

advocate for, let alone teach, sexual education and safe methods of birth control. (The latter term would be coined decades later in the United States by Margaret Sanger, who, like her British counterpart Marie Stopes, had yet to even be born when Annie Besant stood in the dock.) In a century scored by steaming, clanging, sparking progress – hear the trains, feel the blast furnaces, smell that smoke – the teaching or sale of contraception not only remained socially taboo, but also became technically illegal. While birth control remains a contentious subject today, in the Victorian era, as one journalist later put it, open discussion about sex and reproductive health 'was not even controversial. It was nothing but asterisks.'[5]

Annie Besant not only spoke and spelled out shushed and censored ideas, but willingly courted her prosecution as a test case. 'If we go down in this struggle,' she wrote after her arrest, 'there are many London publishers who, when their turn comes, will regret that they failed to do their duty at this crisis.'[6]

She chose active over passive resistance. 'So many people boast on the platform of what they are going to do,' she continued, 'and then quietly subside when the time for doing comes, that it seems to startle them when platform speeches are translated into deeds. Falstaff is so easy a character for an actor to play.'

Besant felt the kingly duty to lead. 'We do not want our libraries to be chosen for us by detectives,' she asserted, 'nor do we intend to acknowledge that [the Crown] is the best judge as to what we may read. A very decided stop must be put to this tyrannical interference with our rights.'[7]

The worst that could happen to her, she claimed, were fines and prison. But as a near-bankrupt single mother estranged from a rapacious husband itching to seize custody of their children, Annie Besant knew that a guilty verdict would mean so much more.

For decorum's sake, she was the only woman allowed to attend her own trial. The adage holds that anyone who acts as their own lawyer has a fool for a client (and a jackass for an attorney), but still Besant and Bradlaugh opted to represent themselves, using the courtroom as a megaphone. Forty-five years before Helena Normanton became the first British woman allowed to be called to the bar and practise as a barrister, the novice Annie Besant stood in a courtroom packed with lofty men – judge and jury, prosecutors and press – and eloquently made the case against book banning, and for the free discussion of contraception and a woman's right to its use.

'We have not the smallest intention of posing as meek and melancholy,' she promised. 'We well know that if we can upset the proceedings, our enemies will think twice before they begin again, and we shall probably go on our way undisturbed, and the right to discuss will have been made . . . To lose all, save honour, is better than to lose honour and gain all.' *The Queen v. Charles Bradlaugh and Annie Besant* made her one of Britain's most famous women, surpassing Florence Nightingale, and coming in second only to her nominal prosecutor, Queen Victoria. Emerging from a Miss Havisham-like decade of mourning for her late husband, Prince Albert, Her Majesty's fortieth year on the throne had begun fortuitously, when on New Year's Day in 1877 the Conservative Prime Minister Benjamin Disraeli had finally overcome parliamentary opposition to proclaim her the Empress of India.

By this time, Annie Besant and Charles Bradlaugh were as inseparable as the widowed queen and her Scottish servant, John Brown. But unlike Victoria, who relished signing her letters 'R & I' – *Regina et Imperatrix*, Queen and Empress – Besant was a common married woman. Her own embossed stationary may have showed her motto 'Be strong', but by law she was weak, with the same rights as a dependent child – only without the possibility of escaping the home upon maturity. A British wife was chattel, subservient to her husband's desires and expected to be a tender mother and spotless wife. Coverture laws forbade her to own property, sign contracts, keep her own salary, maintain custody of her children, or love on her own terms.

After rejecting marriage in favour of nursing, but before making her name in the Crimean War, Florence Nightingale had wondered 'Why have women passion, intellect, moral activity, and a place in society where no one of the three can be exercised?'[8] A quarter-century later, Annie Besant seized that place for herself in the seat of the world's largest empire. In an unpublished memoir donated to the British Library, her niece Freda Fisher – writing 50 years after the trial, when, among other rights, women could vote, strike, divorce and be economically autonomous – realised that 'A large portion of the history of female emancipation is bound up in the story of her doings.' The journey extracted many tolls. 'The bill my aunt paid for her independence,' Fisher wrote, 'was a very heavy one.'[9]

After her prosecution and, three years later, her dinner with Charles Bradlaugh in the prison cell below Big Ben, the hands of Annie Besant's own life-clock will sweep across nearly every major political and intellectual movement of her time. In addition to leading the vanguard in the long march for reproductive rights, she will preach, organise, and – at the first 'Bloody Sunday' – bleed for suffragism, fair pay, meals for malnourished schoolchildren, religious freedom, and the independence of colonial Ireland and India.

Her agitation against the Raj (though not her trailblazing trial or promulgation of birth control) will be remembered with Indian street names, postage stamps and even, in 2020, a Coast Guard patrol ship launched as the *Annie Besant*. Mahatma Gandhi will admire her 'amazing energy and courage', and never forget 'the inspiration I drew from her in my boyhood'.[10] The Mahatma, like George Bernard Shaw and nearly every other friend and fellow fighter with whom Besant will forcefully fall out, will remain magnanimous to the end. Long after their courtship crashed, the future Nobel laureate in literature will write her into his plays as the strongest woman on his stage.

Her closest confederate, Charles Bradlaugh, will not take their own split so well.

But that fissure, so unthinkable as their tea is poured in Parliament's prison on this mild June night in 1880, remains in the future tense. As does the short cul-de-sac in London's East End named Annie Besant Close, and the small plaque in Spitalfields noting the building's pre-gentrified life as the location where Annie Besant helped found the British Trade Unions. Such paltry memorials would not surprise Virginia Woolf, who, after surveying the shelf of gendered biographies recording Britain's nineteenth century, concluded, 'The Victorian age, to hazard [a] generalization, was the age of the professional man.'[11]

In our more equitably enlightened times, Annie Besant's pioneering advocacy remains overshadowed by her erstwhile allies. In Northampton, the base of the towering statue of Charles Bradlaugh recalls him as 'A sincere friend of the people. His life was devoted to progress, liberty, and justice.' From his perch atop a busy roundabout, today he looks devoted to directing traffic. Up Earl Street at the busy Charles Bradlaugh pub, a framed lithograph depicting his arrest in the House of Commons hangs on the wall back by the toilets. The owner and bar staff draw a blank when asked what they know about Annie Besant, and their trial over birth control.

Her name does not appear once in the door-stopping two volumes of the *Cambridge Social History of Britain, 1750–1950*, even as its pages note, without surmising a reason (which could be legion), that the nation's birth rate was halved, to three children per couple, in the years starting from 1877.

That happened to be the year when Annie Besant first popularised contraception in print.

In London's Parliament Square, you won't find her name among the 59 early supporters of women's suffrage chiselled onto the plinth of Millicent Fawcett's statue.* Nor is she among the 75 names carved onto the Reformer's Memorial, the Victorian activist roll of honour standing tall in the capital's Kensal Green Cemetery. The granite obelisk has room to add her, too; one blank space remains beneath the likes of Charles Bradlaugh, William Morris, Robert Owen, Lydia Becker, Harriet Martineau, Mary Carpenter and Henry Fawcett, the Liberal MP who in 1877 had shamefully dodged Besant's summons to testify on her behalf.

In 2022, English Heritage – 'We bring the story of England to life' – replaced an unofficial marker commemorating Annie's role in London's Matchgirls' Strike of 1888 with an official one that omits her name. The old sign's outline remains stained into the red brick wall; as with her life, if you know where to look, you can see her trace, still. Besant's lone Blue Plaque, affixed to the white stucco bungalow she briefly

---

* In fairness, this roll of honour somehow also omits – among many others – Josephine Butler, Anne Clough, Eliza Sharples, Harriet Taylor and her husband, John Stuart Mill, and Bertrand Russell's father, Viscount Amberley.

rented near the Crystal Palace in south London after fleeing her husband, curtly sums her up in two words: 'Social Reformer'. Which, if you know the totality of her achievements, is a bit like defining Victoria as merely 'A Queen'.

The past does not fit neatly into memory, let alone onto a plaque. But like that official marker – cloaked by overgrown vines at 39 Colby Road in a city where only 14 per cent of its Blue Plaques celebrate women – Annie Besant hasn't been written out of history so much as obscured by it. You can sometimes spot her in the thick tomes surveying the Victorian era, although her fleeting appearance on a page or two – a fraction of Bradlaugh's mentions – usually belies her outsized, if correct, depiction as 'the leading female radical and secularist' and 'the mirror of her age'.[12] In these tellings, Besant wasn't born so much as hatched. And just as soon as she enters the story – cue the 'sex radical' – she's gone, never to return.[13]

You know it's time to write a book when the one you want to read doesn't exist. The seeds of this one were planted after taking a wrong turn passing through Northampton one hot summer day, and wondering why the town had erected a statue to Marlon Brando, looking leaner and taller but simmering, even in stone, with purposeful intensity. Who was Brando's Victorian lookalike, Charles Bradlaugh? More interestingly – turn the smartphone screen from the sunlight's glare, and keep clicking link after link – who was his 'close associate' Annie Besant?

A badass. A battering ram. A woman who braved the opprobrium and stones (actual stones!) hurled at her, inspiring the next generation of social reformers and suffragists. No matter one's politics, who among us would not want to live so bold? This story focuses on the decade-plus when this unhappy housewife of a clergyman took aim at and subverted such seemingly intractable Victorian tenets as the Church, marriage, sex, class and imperialism. Rather than waiting for change to happen, the audacious Annie Besant had liberated herself.

As we will see, she was no saint (though it had been a childhood ambition), which makes Annie all the more interesting. This is not a hagiography, arguing for her beatification. Nor is it a comprehensive dual biography of her and her colleague's large and long lives. Besant and Bradlaugh have, separately, been the subject of now mostly out-of-print books; the most recent monograph sketching the outline of their trial dates back nearly 50 years, before the digitisation of source materials led to new discoveries. There remained a richer, more focused tale to tell, one pulling the camera back to reveal their late-Victorian London, and zooming in to examine the voices and forces arrayed against them. This story is a reclamation, pruning back those obscuring vines to shine full light on a particularly gripping period of Annie Besant's activism and its repercussions, for her, and for us. Her causes and ideals remain relevant today.

As an early salvo in the ongoing battle over birth control, Besant and Bradlaugh's arrest for publishing a prophylactic primer predated the prosecution of other (in)famous campaigners, including Emma Goldman, by nearly 40 years. In a priggish era when a woman's place was expected to be beneath her husband in every position, Charles Knowlton's *Fruits of Philosophy*, and Annie's subsequent editions, also intimated that intercourse could be pleasurable and enjoyed without such life-altering consequences as ostracism, loss of work, and dependence upon a man's salary, home and rules. From her own experience, and interviews with and letters from women across Britain, Besant knew that choosing if, and when, to have children would lead to women's social, sexual and economic freedom.

Her partner Charles Bradlaugh's arrest for violating the Obscene Publications Act was the next in a line of dogged acts of civil disobedience that endeared him to the Northampton electorate who would send him to Parliament – and into the clock tower prison cell. But for a 29-year-old single mother of two young children with no savings and a reputation as a radical, this defiance was everything. As a woman, Annie Besant had far more to lose.

Outwardly, she didn't flinch. Uniquely, we can hear her story largely in her own words. Fifty years before Virginia Woolf argued that a female writer needed 'a room of her own', Annie Besant owned her own press and publishing company. Unlike most accused criminals shuffling mutely into court or jail and off the page, she recorded the run-up to her arrest, the trial and its aftermath in a series of unabashed columns, pamphlets and speeches. She also penned a searing memoir, which, for reasons which will become clear, she later decided to pulp. It lives again here, as do her muckraking articles and archly witty editorials accessible only on the stationary-grade Victorian newsprint where they first appeared, now mouldering in a small London archive open only a few hours one day each week. (For consistency and ease of reading, some of the punctuation in this transcribed material has been standardised.)

Far ahead of her time, Annie Besant foresaw that reproductive rights were worth fighting for, codifying in law, and unceasingly defending. Across the years, her voice still rings as clearly as Big Ben. Birth control remains the most cost-effective intervention in health care, just as access to it remains under threat.[14]

'By this time next week I shall be on my trial,' Annie wrote in June 1877. 'One word only I say in conclusion: Let the verdict be what it may, my mind is made up. I believe the question of [checking] population to be a vital one, and discuss it I will. I believe that the discussion will be put down if Knowlton is suppressed by force, and therefore I mean to publish his pamphlet. A verdict, a sentence, do not alter these facts, and therefore do not alter my determination. Come what may, this battle must be won, and, having taken up the sword, I will not lay it down again until the victory is won.'[15]

Her 12 special jurors (of course, all male) had been drawn from the Establishment she sought to subvert. They lived in smart London townhouses that subscribed not to Bradlaugh and Besant's small, secularist and republican weekly the *National Reformer*, but to the staid daily *Times of London*, whose readers supported the primacy of Church and Crown.

To scoop his competition (19 other morning London papers, and 9 evening ones) *The Times'* owner ordered his son and heir apparent to serve on the jury as its foreman. The Establishment's mouthpiece would have a front seat for *The Queen v. Charles Bradlaugh and Annie Besant*. Initially, however, the paper, like the rest of the British press, did not realise the public's piqued interest in the case, and in its defendants. One defendant, in particular. A woman, standing in the centre of political power, asserting her right to educate, to speak freely, to choose.

No prison cell, or judge, or jury sitting beneath a tolling Big Ben could silence her. Turn those storied clock hands back to 1877; the end of the old world has just begun.

PART I

'FIRST, CATCH YOUR HARE'

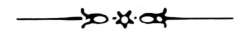

I

THE TIMES OF LONDON

The first lines that a Victorian saw in the United Kingdom's daily paper of record were those heralding the new additions to the empire. Birth announcements ran topmost in *The Times*. Their dense column of type crowded onto a front page that looked as packed as Fleet Street. Horse-drawn hackneys and omnibuses clomped and rattled through the heart of the City of London, powdering bustles and frock coats in straw and dust. The clatter of hooves and iron wheels interrupted criminal trials inside the Old Bailey and arraignments at Guildhall. Wooden cobbles replaced the granite setts paving the roads outside the courtrooms to dampen the din and keep the metropolis at bay. But London was incessant, and London always won.

By the 1840s, the British capital had surpassed Beijing as

the largest city in the world; Paris was barely half its size. (For a people supposedly squeamish about sex, Victorians were shagging like rabbits.) In the next two decades, steam trains trundled rural migrants to London, shovelling them into the industrious city like coal at new railway stations including Paddington, Victoria, King's Cross and St. Pancras. The world's first underground metro line opened here in 1863. A map from this time – one of the two dozen competing, ever-updating versions on sale at the platform newsagent W.H. Smith & Sons – looks like it was inked by a startled octopus. Tentacles of railways encircle the city; empty dots resembling sucker-circles mark a multitude of stations. Three hundred and eighty-seven, to be precise. And the Victorians were very precise. All this chaos required control.

Several maps charted the tamed but still dangerous River Thames for oarsmen, anglers, ferry passengers and spectators of the annual Oxford and Cambridge Boat Race. Another map depicted the world's largest docklands, whose inlets and canals made streets paved with ships. Up to 6,000 vessels could moor at once. Their three-masted riggings stretched a vast spiderweb across the London sky.[1] Gas lamps illuminated new parks such as Battersea and Victoria, as well as public spaces cleared from former dumping grounds, like Leicester Square. Arterial roads with wide carriageways including Victoria Street and Shaftesbury Avenue levelled former slums. One of London's last palatial Jacobean townhouses was razed so Northumberland Avenue could connect the river to Trafalgar Square. Joseph Bazalgette's world-beating sewer works began to cleanse the fetid water; a reporter standing on the new Victoria Embankment excitedly reported that 'a fine salmon, on the lookout for fresh clean water, made its appearance in the Thames'.[2]

By the 1870s, approximately one of every eight residents

of the British Isles – some 4 million people – lived in London. Arriving to join them was the daughter born to Lady Mary Powys, announced on the front page of *The Times* on 6 April 1877. In the column printed beneath the lion and the unicorn that still crowns the broadsheet today, *Times* readers also learned that the Countess of Coventry – wed to a Conservative politician – delivered 'a son, stillborn'. The paper did not record these children's names. Nor did it reveal the monikers of the other 25 women who birthed the day's *Times*-worthy arrivals. These new mothers were not individuals. They were wives.

And so readers gleaned that on Easter Sunday, 'at 23 Prince's-street, the wife of Henry Richardson' delivered a boy. The next day, 'the wife of James Peters' gave birth to a son in Surbiton. Also in the 6 April *Times* came news that 'the wife of Walter Hills' delivered a stillborn girl. The family's Regent's Park townhouse was a short walk from 23 Gloucester Crescent, where 'the wife of Frederick Oxley' delivered a stillborn boy. Did the women know one another, and share their grief? Had this been their first pregnancy, or, following the era's average, their sixth? The reticent *Times* did not say; the next line of type reported that 'the wife of Edgard Henry Fitch' gave birth to a son in Brixton. The emotionless, transactional tone carries a whiff of husbandry, as if delivering the latest news from the barn.

Unknown to her subjects at the time, their monarch also viewed childbirth in these terms. 'What you say of the pride of giving life to an immortal soul is very fine, dear,' Queen Victoria privately wrote to her namesake daughter, the Princess Royal, 'but I own I cannot enter that; I think much more of our being like a cow or a dog at such moments, when our poor nature become so very animal and unecstatic.'[3]

The offspring being delivered by London's underclass of course did not warrant mention in *The Times*. But they are there, if unseen, cutting, carrying and creating the fine silks, pure milk and window curtains whose adverts filled its back pages. (The act forbidding factory work for children under ten would not be passed until the following year; compulsory schooling up to that age would not be required until 1880.)

The plump columns of theatre and concert times also conjure up the capital's prepubescent workforce, including the bootblacks and beggars calling out to patrons entering the newly opened Royal Albert Hall, hosting a Wagner Festival this April of 1877. The 60-year-old German – his jaw furred by whiskers in a new style called the Newgate frill, after the noose at London's notorious prison – would be conducting his best-known operas. Under the quivering light of gas street lamps, girls sold steel pens, shirt buttons and lucifer matches outside the Haymarket and Royal Court theatres, the Piccadilly seances at Maskelyne and Cooke's, and the Crystal Palace exhibition of a new technology called the 'bicycle'. The prematurely aged faces of 'guttersnipes', 'urchins' and 'sprogs' – as Victorians called them – crowded the broughams pulling up to Madame Tussauds, whose latest waxworks included likenesses of 'HRH Princess Beatrice, H.M. Stanley (the African explorer) and Rev. Josiah Henson (Uncle Tom).' The dummies were better cared for.

In stave three of Charles Dickens's *A Christmas Carol*, Ebeneezer Scrooge is appalled to see 'yellow, meagre, ragged, scowling, wolfish' street children. When he asks the Ghost of Christmas Present why the kids have 'no refuge or resource', the phantom repeats the cold-hearted imprecation that Scrooge had shouted at the story's start: 'Are there no prisons? Are there no workhouses?' In 1877 these 'jugs' – including Pentonville, Millbank and Holloway – as well as London's 52 workhouses were packed full. Children as young as seven were sentenced to hard labour for petty crimes.[4]

The city teemed with sticky fingers. Earning honest pennies for selling playbills and primroses did not stave off starvation. Ads for missing items fill a front page column of the 6 April 1877 *Times*. One Londoner sought to recover the 'journal of the late Arctic expedition by an officer of H.M.S Alert', another a 'large pair of white opera glasses'. One unlucky sod managed to misplace his white terrier. The purse containing a five-pound note, the silver brooch, the gold pocket watch, another gold pocket watch, and many chains – all gone, and unlike the wayward Thames salmon, never to return. The newspaper ran no column titled FOUND.

The rookery that inspired Fagin's lair in *Oliver Twist* had recently been cleared, but the Dickensian drear of slinking thieves in crowded hovels still pulsed at London's core. In 1852's *Bleak House*, Tom-All-Alone's warren made a mottled scab of barnacles clinging to the sleek steamship of grand offices running the empire. 'It might be better for the national glory that the sun should sometimes set upon the British dominions,' Dickens wrote, 'than that it should ever rise upon so vile a wonder as Tom.'

In 1877, the slum's actual equivalent – acres of shanties pressed against the four Inns of Court – was also gone, as was Charles Dickens, who had died seven years earlier. The poverty remained. The writer's first-born son, Charles Dickens, Jr., fixed a familiar, penetrative eye on Victorian London's great paradox: as the city's modernizations increased, so, stubbornly, did its penury. In *Dickens's Dictionary of London*, the younger writer described Seven Dials – today encircled by profitable theatres and posh boutiques – as 'the heart of one of the poorest districts in London'.

Dickens, Jr. noted that 'various improvements have been made in the neighbourhood, and the Dials are now traversed by omnibuses, and have made considerable progress towards civilisation'. But once you walked past the shops selling pet fish, bullfinches, blackbirds and terriers (*that white one looks familiar*) to the point where the neighbourhood's seven streets still meet, you could see, spilling before its rag-and-bone shops, destitution and disarray.

'These streets,' the younger Dickens wrote,

> swarm with children of all ages ... Children sit on door-steps and on the pavement, they play in the gutter, they chase each other in the road, and dodge in and out of houses. It is evident that the School Board has not much power in the neighbourhood of the Dials. Public-houses abound, and it is evident that whatever there may be a lack of in the Dials there is no lack of money to pay for drink. At night the public-houses are ablaze with light, and on Saturday evenings there is a great sound of shouting and singing through the windows, while the women stand outside and wait hoping against hope that their husbands will come out before the week's money is all spent.[5]

Under B, *Dickens's Dictionary of London* included an entry for 'Black Eye'. Should the afflicted be obliged to go into society, the author recommended a make-up artist in Marylebone 'equal to concealing the most aggravated case'. For five shillings, the man would even visit you at home. Progress, of sorts, from the remedy the elder Dickens had recommended four decades earlier, in *The Pickwick Papers*, of standing in the open street and pressing your wounded face against a cold lamp post for half an hour.[6] London was not a place for the meek.

Letters to the Editor of *The Times* on 6 April 1877 complimented the paper for its series documenting 'the big blot' of

overcrowding in the world's 'most wealthy, the most powerful, and so styled the most civilized' metropolis. 'Herded
together in tenements unfit for beasts to inhabit,' wrote one
Fenchurch Street resident, 'deficient in any adequate supply
of ventilation, light or water,' the working class lived 'under
conditions, arising from the intermingling, day and night, of
men, women, and children, in the same rooms, which render
morality or even decency almost an Impossibility.'

With typical Victorian demurral, the writer was likely
referring to sex, either forced or paid. While an enduring
image of the lives of Victorian women is one in which, as
one biographer joked, 'Everyone had headaches, and lay
about on sofas', it belies the sexual ignorance, repression and
violence simmering beneath that scene.[7] Rectitude and reserve
shaped many Victorian psyches to view the base, mutual
pleasures of intercourse as a stain on a proper wife's purity,
and their tame, domesticated (literally, *house-broken*) lives.
Prostitution was rife in a city filled with soldiers, sailors and
married men. This was the era when the journalist W.T. Stead
would compare London to the Minotaur's Labyrinth, a trap
where maidens and youth were doomed to be devoured by 'a
foul product of unnatural lust'.[8]

In *The Times*, the Fenchurch Street correspondent's letter
lamented the 'half starved, half clothed, filthy children, the
bane of our elementary schools, the reproach of our Christianity and civilization – children whose frequent deaths so
swell the bills of mortality . . . the springs of life poisoned at
the very beginning of life's journey. This is, unfortunately, no
new tale, yet we must be thankful to you and all others who
aid in keeping the subject before the public, till for very
shame some remedy is found.'[9] Like *The Times*' reporters –
and unlike Charles Dickens's fairy-tale endings, or Karl Marx,
then writing as usual in seat G7 inside the British Museum's

Reading Room – this concerned Londoner did not suggest what a possible solution might possibly be.

Against this backdrop, Annie Besant's advocacy for birth control was both novel and needed. It was also a crime.

※

The past might well be a foreign country, but in old newspapers, London feels familiar. So much of it – streets and tube stops, churches and museums, Harrods and Liberty's – remains in place. The ads for Schweppes and Nestlé could run today; the ones for inkstands and hat boxes sharply evoke the Victorian-era films and programmes that now fill our screens. The news of the day can also read like an early draft of a familiar script. In the spring of 1877, Parliament weighed its response to Russia's invasion of a neighbouring land. (Then, it was the start of the Russo-Turkish War.) The passage of time also provides unearned wisdom. Knowing how things turn out, you can tsk and grimace at the omissions and attitudes, and smile at the facts that, in retrospect, read wryly. In an era where fashion began to favour the tall and slim, one of the few female names in the dense 16 pages of the 6 April *Times* was the winner, by a neck, at the Warwick races: a filly, named Fasting Girl.

The queen did not make her appearance in this edition until page nine, in a single line of Victorian reserve, *par excellence*. The day's Court Circular reported that at Osborne House, 'Her Majesty walked this morning'.

In fairness, Victoria's often engaging diary adds little more to *The Times'* account. 'A very fine, but rather windy morning,' she wrote. 'Walked with Beatrice down to the sea, & picked up shells on the beach . . . The primroses everywhere quite marvellous.'[10] Some days are not as exciting as others;

behind one door a child is being born, behind another a world is falling apart. Directly below Victoria's doings, *The Times* reported a 'wife murder'. The killer was a coachman named Starkey. And her? Who had she been? His name was inked into history; his unnamed victim vanished like the smoke of a snuffed-out candleflame.

On the newspaper's eleventh page, a letter from a reader in Devon reported that overcrowding was not endemic to London and the northern industrial hives. In the fields around Sidmouth, diphtheria was sweeping like a scythe through lean-to's whose only supply of water came from 'a brook polluted, as my eyes have seen, with all manner of abomination'. This concerned citizen 'in vain gave remonstrance' to inspectors and the Local Board, only to be told it was someone else's problem. In fact, he warned, it was every Briton's affair, for soon a bill would come due for our 'utter indifference to the lives of those who are hovelled'.

On the same page of *The Times* – printed below the shipwrecks and drownings and the times of sailings to Sunderland, the Straits Settlements, and Sydney – appeared a glimpse of the London that would inspire Arthur Conan Doyle to create a heroic detective to prowl this 'great cesspool into which all the loungers and idlers of the Empire are irresistibly drained'.[11]

The day's police records recounted that a snapped rope required an injured, condemned prisoner to be hanged, minutes later, for a second time. Other Londoners had been arraigned for perjury; for obstructing traffic by taking bets on horse races in front of King's Cross; for being 'drunk and implacable' in public; for burgling in Belgravia; for cruelty to a pony; for neglecting to maintain a wife and child; for attempted 'murder by revolver'. Running alongside this grim, felonious news appeared notice of an unusual case. Seeing it today, tucked way back on page 11, makes it look like the criminals had successfully dropped themselves behind enemy lines. Readers did not then know that this raid on the Establishment was going exactly to their plan.

At the GUILDHALL, MR. CHARLES BRADLAUGH, 10 Portland-place, St. John's-wood, publisher, and Mrs. ANNIE BESANT, Oaklands, Mortimer-road, St. John's-wood, journalist, were brought before Alderman Figgins on a warrant charging them with publishing an obscene book on the 24th of March last. Williams Simmonds, a City detective constable, said he went to the publishing office of *Free Thought*, at 28, Stonecutter-street, about 20 minutes to 5 o'clock. It was an open publishing shop. He saw the two defendants in the publishing office, and asked Mrs. Annie Besant for a pamphlet called 'The Fruits of Philosophy.' Mrs. Besant gave him the book, and he paid her 6d. for it.

Five days later, the officer bought another sixpence copy. This three-pence edition of *The Times* did not detail anything else about the pamphlet, although a Victorian reader would likely know that the 'fruits' and 'philosophy' of its title were bywords for 'procreation' and 'science'. There was no reason, then, to suspect that *The Times*, like the rest of the British press, would soon reveal the core of its contents, and give its publisher a platform she could never have erected alone.

With a search warrant in hand, the story related, a detective sergeant named Robert Outram had returned to Besant and Bradlaugh's small printshop near the new Holborn Viaduct and Central Criminal Court, nicknamed for its location beside the City of London's old bailey, or wall. This would not be Outram's only walk-on role in the capital's history. Eleven years later, he will don a disguise and prowl Whitechapel's fog-slicked cobblestones in search of the murderer known as Jack the Ripper.

Outram's quarry on Stonecutter Street proved an easier collar. 'In cross-examination,' *The Times*' story continued, the 'witness said he was aware that Mr. Bradlaugh had given notice to the chief office of the City Police that he would attend the shop on the 24th of March and sell the book from 4 to 5 o'clock.' After DS Outram returned to the shop a second time and 'bought a copy of the book from the defendant Besant', he next appeared with his warrant, and marched the pair across Fleet Street to Bridewell Police Station. They were under arrest for violating the Obscene Publications Act, a law enacted 20 years earlier to quash pornography.

The Times omitted the fact that the accused were already minor public figures, as president and vice president of the National Secular Society, which campaigned to curb organised religion's clench on public life. The paper did note that 16 people (NSS members, in fact) had promised to help post Bradlaugh and Besant's bail of £200 each, an exorbitant sum in an era when a working-class Londoner labouring ten hours for six days usually earned £1 weekly. William Booth, who would found the Salvation Army the following year, estimated that a family needed £50 a year to just get by, and £60 to be comfortable. *Dickens's Dictionary* said that in Notting Hill, a fair-sized house could be had for £75 to £120.

After being led past the statues of the mythical City guardians Gog and Magog, Besant and Bradlaugh had stood in Guildhall's courtroom, whose stained-glass windows and chandeliers illuminated the oil portraits of wizened, wigged men staring solemnly from the wainscoted walls.

'Alderman Figgins thought they had gone as far as they could at present,' *The Times* reported, and granted an 11-day adjournment, until 17 April. 'Mr. Bradlaugh said he maintained, whether rightly or wrongly, that the book was not an obscene book, and he wished to have the case properly tested.'

The story included no quotes from the woman in the dock beside him, identified only as 'Mrs Besant'. A reader could well have assumed that she was just an unsuspecting house-wife earning a bit on the side in a printshop that turned out to be selling dirty books. Little they did suspect that she had walked out on an Anglican minister husband, and that it had been her idea to publish and print *Fruits of Philosophy* and invite arrest. This was, after all, but the first time that Annie Besant's name had appeared in Britain's paper of record. Across her activist career – spanning two oceans, three monarchs, and 56 years – more than 600 stories would follow.

Coincidentally, another first, undertaken by another brave woman, appeared in this same edition of *The Times*. The front page carried a notice from the Royal Aquarium, the 'Most central place of amusement and pleasantest lounge in London'. Since its opening a year earlier in a prime location facing Westminster Abbey – 'Omnibuses and Underground Rail from all part of London set visitors down at the very door' – the cavernous aquarium had struggled to stay afloat. With tanks largely empty of fish, and a revival staging of *Great Expectations* as scripted by W.S. Gilbert (on the eve of his more lucrative partnership with Arthur Sullivan) failing to draw crowds, 'the Aq' had turned to bread and circus.

You could partake from a cheap *table d'hote*, as Victorians called a *prix fixe* menu, featuring soups, joints and sweets, and then, for only one additional shilling – the same price as an entrance to the Tower of London's old and cold exhibits – enjoy 'the most marvellous combination of attractions ever offered the public'. The roster for 6 April 1877 included acrobats, 'Atherton's Dogs, from Vienna', a comic troupe, 'the Man Flute', tightrope walkers, and – making history – the 'first appearance of the marvellous Zazel, fired from the cannon'.

As a hush fell over the full house of a thousand spectators, and the orchestra conductor's baton quivered with expectancy, the match was struck, the cannon boomed and a young woman blasted into the London night.

Besant's own daring performance would soon take place just across the street, inside the Court of Queen's Bench at Westminster Hall. Admission would be free, but good luck squeezing into the throng eager to see the spectacle. The defendant's trajectory looked just as fixed as that of the world's first human cannonball. What goes up, invariably, must come down. But unlike the amazing Zazel, Annie Besant was working without a net.

2

ICONOCLAST – CHARLES BRADLAUGH

At first, it had not been her fight.

Eleven years earlier, Charles Bradlaugh had founded the National Secular Society to promote the separation of religion and state in a nation where the very name of the established Church combined the two. His mutiny against the Church of England, with Queen Victoria as its Supreme Governor, had begun in a chapel off the Hackney Road, when as a pious teen studying for his catechism, Bradlaugh discovered, and voiced, the discordances between the four gospels and the Anglican *Book of Common Prayer*. Suspended by his vicar from Sunday school teaching, Bradlaugh further angered his father, a longstanding clerk at a City law firm, by pledging himself teetotal, an abstemious vow then associated with 'freethinkers', the social movement that appealed to logic and empiricism over dogma and authority.

As an errand boy for his father's Cloak Lane employers, Bradlaugh saved money by traipsing London's street-web on foot, rather than riding omnibuses. In addition to strengthening his lanky frame into an athletic – and, in time, pugilist – build, Bradlaugh pocketed the halfpenny fares. With his formal school finished at the age of 11, he spent those coins – embossed with the profile of a fresh, slender-necked Victoria – on books. Bradlaugh's first purchase was a

A young Charles Bradlaugh

copy of the *People's Charter*, the 1838 manifesto of the working-class, republican Chartist movement. Its struggle to expand voting rights (for men) and abolish the requirement that MPs own property prefigured his own (then unimaginable) election to Parliament and his (easier to foresee) imprisonment.

Haunting Cannon Street's second-hand bookstalls in the 1840s, Bradlaugh discovered the works of Ralph Waldo Emerson, the first of the two American writers (Dr Charles Knowlton being the other) who would bend his life's path. The teenage Bradlaugh clandestinely copied into a notebook Emerson's personal declaration of independence, the essay *Self-Reliance*. 'Insist on yourself, never imitate,' the transcendentalist urged. 'To be great is to be misunderstood.'

'Trust thyself: every heart vibrates to that iron string.' What today sounds like platitudes was then distinctive and disrupting, especially to a young, rebellious East Ender. The lines also warned Bradlaugh what lay ahead, and foretold his own strength. 'For nonconformity,' Emerson promised, 'the world whips you with its displeasure. It is easy enough for a firm man who knows the world to brook the rage of the cultivated classes.'

In 1849, Bradlaugh's obsequious law clerk father (imagine *Bleak House*'s Mr Guppy in middle age) gave the stubborn 16-year-old three days to apologise to the vicar and return to church under the penalty of losing his job and bed. The boy wasted no time walking out. Bradlaugh found lodging at the shabby Spitalfields home of the feminist lecturer and fellow freethinker Eliza Sharples, who had grown increasingly destitute since the death of her partner, Richard Carlile. The pre-Chartist, republican Carlile once had been jailed three years for blasphemy and seditious libel for publishing, among other tracts, Thomas Paine's incendiary *Common Sense*, which railed against the 'crowned ruffians' of the monarchy, and *Age of Reason*, which criticised the Church of England. Carlile had, however, evaded punishment in 1826 (when George IV sat on the throne) for writing, printing and selling a pamphlet purporting to teach the 'most important instructions for the prudent regulation of the principle of love and the number of a family'.

Emerson felt that 'Society is a wave', ever-moving onward, but, like the churning surf, constantly re-forming with different particles of water. 'Its unity is only phenomenal,' he wrote. 'The persons who make up a nation to-day, next year die, and their experience with them.'

But do they? Or do vestiges of their form, of their wavelength, transmit across time? This is a London story; those second-hand stalls that sparked an alienated 1840s teen to flee from guppydom will morph into Soho's book and music shops, Shoreditch galleries and punk hang-outs along the Kings Road. After becoming president of the London Republican Club, Bradlaugh – like the Sex Pistols a century hence – will also snidely sing the words 'God Save the Queen', making him another link in the capital's long-running chain of cussed dissenters.

But if Emerson is correct, then it is just an interesting coincidence that, three decades before his arrest for publishing a birth control manual, the teenage Charles Bradlaugh had found refuge in the home of the man who had written one of Britain's first.

It is not a good book. Before meeting and falling for Eliza Sharples, and in between prison sentences for seditious libel, Richard Carlile's *Every woman's book, or What is Love?* attacks matrimony. It was, he wrote, 'a system of degradation and slavery, and consequently of fraud and discomfort'. In an observation that foretold Charles Bradlaugh and Annie Besant's own mismatched marriages, Carlile – failing to mention the loyalty of his wife, Jane, who served two years in prison for publishing his *Republican* newspaper – declared that married people 'are frequently unhappy, and sometimes hate each other soon after marriage'.

Far ahead of his time, Carlile also lobbied for gender equality, although not in voting, wages, or household management, but in the bedroom. In an era where a private act of Parliament was necessary to obtain a divorce (an advancement, of sorts: Henry VIII never officially divorced, but dispatched his wives via an archbishop's annulment, and the executioner's axe), he argued that both spouses should be free to find new partners without censure from society. '*Let us take our fill of love*,' Carlile wrote, 'is one of the best exhortations in the Bible, one of the best ever made by woman to her lover.' He does not finish the proverb, however, wherein Solomon explains to his son the sin of adultery. Carlile was an avowed atheist, and arguments like these opened him – as they would Bradlaugh and Besant – to charges that a pamphlet teaching contraception was in fact a Trojan horse aimed at toppling marriage, and morality.

Sex, Carlile declared, 'is an affair of pleasure and happiness, and should be a matter of common conversation, as other simple pleasures are, every one of which, when reasonably indulged in, produces happiness. Why should we not speak out freely upon this?' If parents spoke plainly to their children, then 'all ignorance, and what is worse, all hypocrisy upon the subject, which leads to so many disasters, would be abolished'.

In the tone of a conspiracist relating the truth that the authorities *just don't want you to know*, Carlile – who had no medical training – repeated the canard that 'the proximate cause', in nine out of ten ill women, 'was the want of sexual commerce'. This sort of male-spurted quackery, still circulating a half-century later, will compel Annie Besant to ask contemporary physicians to vet *Fruits of Philosophy* before she published its teachings.

Carlile may have been seminal in his audacity, but his tract offered little effective advice. Of its 48 pages, only two mention contraception, and only anecdotally. Across the Channel, he said, pessaries (a forerunner of diaphragms) were as common as handkerchiefs. 'French and Italian women wear them fastened to their waists, and always have them at hand,' he wrote. British aristocrats preferred the vaginal sponge. 'An

English Duchess was lately instanced to the writer, who never goes out to a dinner without being prepared with the sponge.'[1] Men, Carlile instructed, could don 'the *skin*, or what, in France, is called the *baudruche*, in England, commonly, the *glove*'. Condoms, then made from sheep's guts, were not cheap, easy to produce, or widely employed.[2] Nor were they particularly effective, as they were often rinsed and reused. (Even after the mid-century's vulcanisation of rubber mass-produced condoms, Victorians would associate these 'French letters' more with preventing diseases in prostitution than with birth control.[3])

Carlile also recommended withdrawal. Continental women, he confided, 'look upon the man as a dishonest brute who does not attend to it'. Finally, he described the technique of 'emitting semen in the cavity below the womb', which required a woman to elevate her pelvis as her partner climaxed. This method, he unhelpfully added in these dark ages of sex education, 'can only be understood by anatomists or explained by anatomical plate. It seems questionable.'

⁂

Aside from this last morsel none of Carlile's information was new. For as long as humans have understood the effects of intercourse, they have tried to prevent it. Contraception appears in writings from ancient Egypt, Rome, Persia, India and China; Homer describes condoms in *The Iliad*.[4] The *Book of Genesis* famously depicts *coitus interruptus*. After being commanded by his father Judah to impregnate his widowed sister-in-law, Onan defiantly 'spills his seed' not inside her, but upon the ground. For this cunningness, 'the Lord slew him, because he did a detestable thing'.

Hermeneutic scholars, and compunctious teens, have

wrestled with the propriety of onanism ever since. The Victorian era's rise of public schools – social instruments that codified class and propriety – fuelled the popularity of novels that described their misery for outsiders, including Jane Eyre at Lowood, Nicholas Nickleby at Dotheboys and Tom Brown at Rugby. But did any pubescent pupil suffer more than the well-meaning Eric, who, in the 1862 best-selling novel *St. Winifred's, or The World of School*, commits sin after sin before succumbing to the worst one of all, named only as 'it'? The author, Dean Farrar, was then a master at Harrow and later the head of Marlborough. 'May every schoolboy who reads this page,' he wrote, 'be warned by the warning of their wasted hands from that burning marle of passion where they found nothing but shame and ruin, polluted affections and an early grave.' To the Victorians, masturbation equalled death.[5]

Elizabethans had not been so squeamish; Shakespeare's plays, of course, are filled with vulgar innuendos, including 'French withered pears' for syphilitic vaginas, and 'porridge' and 'pie' for healthy ones. 'Fist' became a verb for male self-pleasure.[6] In perhaps the stage's first 'your mum' joke, in *Titus Andronicus* a character retorts, 'Villain, I have done your mother.' In a play presumably representative of innocent romance, the laddish Mercutio tells his buddy Romeo, of Juliet, 'O, that she were an open-arse, or thou a popp'rin pear!' The fruit both resembled male genitalia, and punned upon 'pop her in'. The audience laughing along at the Globe theatre likely would have known that the teen lovers should take precautions in the bedchamber; information about birth control circulated freely.

Elizabethan women relied on the rhythm method, beeswax cervical caps, and tried pessaries of ground, bitter almonds and an unguent made from the glandular secretions

of a beaver. As conception was thought to require both partners to experience an orgasm – or 'paroxysm', as it was
called – women also numbed their privates with herbal elix-
irs. Men took vinegar penis baths. They attempted withdrawal,
and wore amulets made from weasel testicles. As semen was
believed to be blood made white by the heat humour, bloodletting was also prescribed. One physician recommended
opening a vein until the patient was 'ready to fall downe for
faintness, and losse of blood'.[7] So much for spontaneity. Or
consciousness.

This era of hot nights in cold bedrooms proved short-
lived. Oliver Cromwell's revolution put censorious English
Protestants – dubbed 'Puritans' – in control of Parliament,
which, among other strictures, closed the Globe and other
theatres. (Sodden vegetables presumably went back onto
dinner plates instead of being hurled at the stage.) Even after
the English civil wars and restoration, the Puritan primacy of
the Church, and its teaching that contraception contravened
scripture, reigned supreme. During the English Enlighten-
ment it was considered daring when the Utilitarian social
reformer Jeremy Bentham advocated the use of the 'spunge'.
But he did so indirectly, couched in a paragraph of a 1797
essay arguing for the reduction of the poor rates.[8] The nudg-
ing puns – 'gap' for *vagina*, 'Marcus Curtius' for *semen* (the
mythological Roman had hurled himself into a chasm) – may
not have impressed Shakespeare, but Bentham predated, by
a year, the publication of Thomas Malthus's book, *An Essay
on the Principle of Population*, which predicted that the rising
birth rate would outstrip the resources needed to support it.

Malthus – one of eight children, but the father of only
three – argued that to maintain our subsistence, humans
could not rely on 'positive' checks (including war, disease,
famine and natural disasters), and so needed to practice

'preventive' checks. As a devout Anglican curate, however, Malthus did not endorse contraception. Instead, he called for delayed marriage, celibacy and self-control. Charles Dickens makes the childless Scrooge a Malthusian mouthpiece when, at the story's start, he refuses to donate to charity, barking that he pays his taxes so the destitute may be cared for in workhouses and prisons. Told that many can't go there, and many would rather die, Scrooge retorts, 'If they would rather die, they had better do it, and decrease the surplus population.'[9]

Unlike Scrooge, who has a turn of heart (yet remains childless), Thomas 'Misery' Malthus has not aged so well. First, he failed to foresee the Industrial Revolution, and that technology and trade would increase the food supply. Second, he did not imagine that humans, like all living things, were adaptive. After voyaging on the HMS *Beagle*, a budding naturalist wrote that he 'happened to read for amusement Malthus on *Population*'. The essay sparked a 25-year-old Charles Darwin to consider the struggle for existence, and the preservation of favourable traits over time. 'Here, then,' he wrote, 'I had at last got a theory by which to work.'[10] Reverend Malthus would not have been pleased to know that he helped to inspire *On the Origin of Species*.

When Darwin's theory of evolution was published in 1859, Malthus had been dead 25 years. Yet in his lifetime he had to endure the rise of 'neo-Malthusians', social reformers who trumpeted his dire predictions to help spread their gospel of birth control. In 1822, the social reformer Francis Place, in his Malthus-sounding pamphlet *The Principles of Population*, recommended that before intercourse women insert a sponge 'as large as a green walnut or a small apple'.[11] (Readers may well have questioned his authority; Place had fathered 15 children.) He wrote his book not to celebrate sex, but to spare ill and abused wives from their husband's predations. At his Charing Cross tailor shop Place saw how his female customers endured repeated pregnancies caused by men whose desire they could not legally refuse.

'The monster comes to claim his marital rights,' one such London wife, Caroline Norton, would write in an open letter to Queen Victoria in 1855. 'He comes in the name of the English law, and who shall resist or gainsay him?'[12] The times would not change quickly enough to spare Annie Besant from learning the unfortunate answer. (Marital rape would not be made a crime in the United Kingdom until 1991.)

No matter his benevolent intentions, Francis Place, like Richard Carlile, was branded a 'bold, bad man' and shunned alike by religious and Radical Londoners. ('I am ashamed,' Emerson wrote in *Self-Reliance*, 'to think how easily we capitulate to badges and names, to large societies and dead institutions.') But no constable seized the men's work, and no warrant called for their arrest, even after the formation of the Metropolitan Police in 1829, and the passage of a statute, called the Vagrancy Act, under which they could have been charged.

Both men moved on to other causes and concerns. Francis Place co-authored the *People's Charter* that would magnetise the moral compass of a teenage Charles Bradlaugh. Richard Carlile left Jane Cousins and their five children (she supported them independently as a successful, and rival, London bookseller) to enter a 'moral marriage' with Eliza Sharples, who bore him four more children, and would take in the disowned and homeless Bradlaugh.[13] These were his mentors.

In a silent protest against civic corruption through capitalism and cant, Richard Carlile had once hung in the window of his printshop the effigies of a broker and bishop. After an angry crowd gathered outside, he refused to remove the display, even after being found guilty of causing a public disturbance. A KFC now occupies the site, at 62 Fleet Street. After enduring their own prosecution, Annie Besant and Charles Bradlaugh will honour Carlile by moving their own publishing company to number 63, across the street from, and thus mirroring, his former freethinking redoubt.

⁂

Although now recognised for their daring originality, Richard Carlile and Francis Place's contraceptive tracts did not warrant multiple printings. Their work sank into the vast sea of print that spelled England's Paper Age, an epoch hastened by the Victorian propensity to document even the smallest of life's transactions.[14] This creamy ocean of pamphlets, periodicals and petitions, of plea rolls, affidavits and writs, of books and letters sent through the new penny post, of scandal sheet tabloids known as 'rags', and 'commonplace' scrapbooks in which diarists collected favourite clippings, was printed on fibrous paper often made from cast-off clothing. (Britain's ever-increasing number of bank notes originated in a mill dubbed 'Rag Hall'.) Demand outstripped supply; as a monthly serialised author and weekly magazine publisher, Charles Dickens (who in *Bleak House* kills off the foolscap-hoarding Krook in a vindictive, if improbable, fireball of spontaneous combustion) monitored the fluctuating price of paper like a nervous broker watching changes in shares.

Given this glut of printed matter, consumers were spoiled for choice. In his guidebook to the city, Charles Dickens, Jr. listed 406 weekly London publications, including recognisable titles like *Punch*, *Vanity Fair* and the *Economist*, alongside trade organs such as the *Sewing Machine Gazette*, *Livestock Journal* and *Perruquier*, the bulletin for wig-and-toupee makers. In a ratio likely since reversed, religious readers could choose from 32 weeklies; gardeners only three. Dickens, Jr. boasted that 'Fleet-street and its neighbourhood take good care that Londoners shall find London all the world over', but at home readers both cosmopolitan and labouring shared fickle taste.[15] Henry Mayhew, the Victorian chronicler of London's under-classes, reported how the capital's booksellers and railway platform newsstands reaped the greatest sales from 'the class best known as "light reading"'. It included novels, stories in instalments and poetry, 'but rarely political or controversial pamphlets'. One vendor explained how a tract 'about the Pope sold at first; but in a month or six weeks, people began to say, "A shilling for that! I'm sick of the thing."'[16]

So it was not surprising that, back in the 1830s, on the heels of Richard Carlile and Francis Place's booklets, the appearance of a more extensive, and better-sourced, work also did not inflame English passions at either extreme. Its neo-Malthusian American author had first printed its 50-odd pages anonymously, with the intention of giving it freely to his patients in the mountainous Berkshires region of west-ern Massachusetts. His anodyne title, *Fruits of Philosophy*, belied its content, and the fact that it was one of the United States' first treatises on family planning. From the start he took precautions: the first edition was printed on 3 by 2½ inch pages, making it easily concealable behind a counter or up a dress sleeve.

In 1832 a Boston printer enlarged its format and added Dr Charles Knowlton's name to the cover, along with the sub-title *The Private Companion of Young Married People*. Knowlton soon drew abuse from pulpits from Taunton to Cambridge (Massachusetts), as well as a $50 fine – plus $27.50 in court costs – for publishing an obscene book, followed by a three-month sentence of hard labour for intending to 'debauch and corrupt, and to raise, excite and create ... inordinate and lustful desires' in impressionable youth. The judge's unintentional endorsement, however, led to sensational sales of the forbidden *Fruits*.[17]

Its publisher next took aim at the overseas English market. But Dr Knowlton's work made a faint impression in the heaps and drifts of printed paper piling up across Victorian London. For the next 44 years, including the first 39 of the queen's reign, the pamphlet freely circulated but attracted little attention – an old post on the vast inter-net of British publishing. Everything changed on 8 December 1876, when police officers suddenly arrested a National Secular Society bookseller in Bristol on the grounds that he 'unlawfully, wilfully, maliciously, and scandalously' had published this 'indecent, wicked, and obscene book'.[18]

Its American author had been dead for 26 years. An unknown Annie Besant would leap to his defence. 'I faced a storm of obloquy,' she later reflected, 'fiercer and harder to bear than any other which can ever touch me again. The long suffering that followed was a splendid school for the teaching of endurance.' At the time, a British woman could matriculate at no other institute of higher learning. Annie Besant could have written its curriculum.

❈

Amid the hundreds of publications for sale on London's straw-sprinkled streets, only one before this had been seized for selling too cheaply. In 1868, the Crown issued a writ against the 35-year-old Charles Bradlaugh, publisher of the *National Reformer* newspaper, under an outdated statute that had been passed in 1819 to tamp down the passions of the French Revolution and England's Peterloo Massacre. The law decreed that any pamphlet or paper selling for less than sixpence required the publisher to file a surety for the princely sum of £400. 'If our price was 6d we should not be prosecuted,' Bradlaugh wrote then. 'It is only cheap blasphemy and sedition which is liable to be suppressed.' The key word was *cheap*: the *National Reformer*, mouthpiece of his republican and atheist National Secular Society, sold for just two pence.

Since we last saw him browsing second-hand bookstalls and moving in with Richard Carlile's widow, Bradlaugh had been tutored in freethinking and public speaking by George Jacob Holyoake, the publisher and coiner of the modern use of 'secularism'. In humiliating debt (totalling £4 15s), Bradlaugh had enlisted in the British Army at the age of 17. Hoping to be sent to the warm, spice-laden air of India, he was instead shipped to cold, damp barracks in Ireland. His lifelong support of Home Rule was cemented after being mustered to guard a land agent evicting tenants from their meagre homes. Into the icy driving sleet, soldiers carried the bed holding an ailing old man, where he died in front of Bradlaugh.

Following the passing of Charles Bradlaugh's own father – whose 22 years of clerking without a raise earned a short death notice in *The Times* – his aunt put up the £30 to purchase his release from the military. Bradlaugh left the army as he had entered, as an undistinguished private.[19]

Upon his return to the incubator of 1850s London, he rose through the ranks of a City law office with the rapidity of a Dickens character. It was a fortuitous time to enter the profession, as a series of reforms streamlined the grinding, circular complexities that the author, himself a former clerk, had parodied in *Bleak House*'s interminable probate suit, *Jarndyce v. Jarndyce*. Bradlaugh mastered the new civil and criminal procedures, and was trusted to argue them before masters and judges in chambers.

This on-the-job legal education informed the 21-year-old's penchant for public speaking, including his sermons – under the *nom-de-guerre* Iconoclast – at the secular Sunday school held for London's working class at the Hall of Science on Old Street. A plasterer who admired Bradlaugh's talks introduced him to his daughter, Susannah Hooper, two years his elder. The pair wed in early summer 1855, when Bradlaugh was 22.

One month later, in July, he counted himself among the estimated 200,000 people who thronged the banks of Hyde Park's Serpentine to protest a proposed law prohibiting shops from opening on Sundays. The Sabbath-protecting bill unduly affected the working class, who used their one weekly day off to buy provisions. After the demonstration grew violent, Bradlaugh was called to give evidence to the Royal Commission investigating the 'Sunday Trading Riots'. He felt proud to be praised by the commissioners for his exacting testimony, and vindicated when the bill was withdrawn.

Bradlaugh and Susannah set up house in Hackney, on the northern edge of Victoria Park, a lively, beautiful swath of greenery that, advised *Dickens's Dictionary*, 'no student of London life should miss seeing'.[20] On weekends, Bradlaugh made the short stroll from his terrace to the park's clearing, called Bonner's Fields, where he publicly lectured against religion and the monarchy.

The Bradlaughs soon welcomed a daughter, called Alice, and a second, Hypatia, named after the Alexandrine astronomer and philosopher who had been torn to pieces by a Christian mob in the year 415. The moniker was likely Bradlaugh's choice, in homage to Richard Carlile and Eliza Sharples, who had also given their daughter the name. (It was also the eponymous title of one of Victoria's favourite historical novels, pronounced by a leading Anglican cleric as, 'Not a fit book to be read by our mothers and sisters.' That didn't stop the queen from reading it aloud to her husband, Albert.)[21]

At the age of 24, Bradlaugh succeeded his mentor Holyoake as president of the London Secular Society. At 25, Britain's ever-spinning web of railroads allowed Bradlaugh to network with like-minded freethinkers across the nation. On Saturdays, after ending his law office shift at midday, he often hopped on a cheap, slow train to travel third-class to the industrial north to speak. He began drawing crowds. One debate, with a pugnacious Congregationalist, entertained and enflamed 1,500 people over four nights. Bradlaugh emerged triumphant.

In 1860, his circle of London radicals raised £1,000 to start a publication to promulgate their philosophy. At its founding, the *National Reformer* purported to be a secular newspaper. Soon it became apparent that it was really a broadsheet broadcasting its editor, Charles Bradlaugh, across Britain. George Jacob Holyoake and other early supporters abandoned the enterprise after Bradlaugh branded the paper 'an advocate of atheism'. They also blanched at his review praising the book its many critics were calling 'the Bible of the brothel'. Published anonymously in 1855, *The Elements of Social Science* promoted birth control and prostitution as a means of preventing over-population and premature marriages. Privately, the otherwise prim Bradlaugh – whose third child, Charles, Jr., had recently been born – supported neither idea, only the right to publish them.

W.H. Smith and Sons, Britain's largest newsagent, banned the *National Reformer* from its stands. After his partners withdrew their backing, Bradlaugh took full ownership of the newspaper. He abandoned his dream of qualifying as a solicitor after one with whom he was apprenticing fled London under suspicion of fraud. Instead, Bradlaugh began dreaming of one day entering Parliament. His next move did not portend its success: in 1866, he founded the National Secular Society.

He first attracted the Establishment's attention, and much-needed *Reformer* sales, in articles arguing for the expansion of voting rights to all men over 21, as well as the appointment of an independent commission to investigate English misrule in Ireland. The first was granted, and the second ignored, although the Liberal leader, William Gladstone, wrote to Bradlaugh in praise of his proposal.

The *National Reformer*'s support for the Irish republican Fenian Brotherhood, however, rankled Benjamin Disraeli's Conservative government. Inland Revenue agents charged Bradlaugh under a Newspaper and Stamp Duties Act that had been all but forgotten. 'With all humility,' Bradlaugh replied to the government in print,

> I am obliged to bid you defiance; you may kill the *National Reformer*, but it will not commit suicide. Before you destroy my paper we shall have to fight the question, so far as my means will permit me. I know the battle is not on equal terms: you have the national purse, I an empty pocket; you have the trained talent of the Law Officers of the Crown, I my own wits; but it would be cowardly indeed to shrink in 1868 from a contest in which my gallant predecessor, Richard Carlile, fought so persistently more than a quarter century since.[22]

Bradlaugh represented himself; the Crown sent its Attorney-General, a knighted Harrow graduate with over two decades of courtroom experience. In the first hearing, the upstart outmanoeuvred the master over procedural matters. Outside the courtroom, the Liberal Westminster MP John Stuart Mill — Utilitarian apostle of Jeremy Bentham, and, in works including *On Liberty*, Britain's fiercest protector of free speech — carried a petition in support of Bradlaugh into the House of Commons and argued for the repeal of the act under which he was being prosecuted. To the banner of the *National Reformer,* the unbowed Bradlaugh added: PUBLISHED IN DEFIANCE OF HER MAJESTY'S GOVERNMENT.

Mill also supported Bradlaugh's attempt to ride the notoriety into Parliament, donating £10 for his quixotic campaign to capture a seat in Northampton, where crowds of boot and shoemakers had flocked to his lectures calling for the disestablishment of the Church of England, and reform of the House of Lords. (Mill's endorsement likely cost him his own seat, which he lost to the pious W.H. Smith.) A vitriolic Queen's Counsel named Hardinge Giffard, running as a Conservative in Cardiff, travelled to Northampton to rail against the Liberal Bradlaugh. Both men would lose this vote. Little did they suspect that soon they would clash again, in court, over birth control.

The case against Bradlaugh and his *National Reformer* collapsed before being revived after the election, by the Liberal William Gladstone administration. Smarting from betrayal, Bradlaugh finally gave in. 'Fighting the Crown is a luxury to be indulged in by the rich,' he admitted. 'I have fought from necessity, and retire at a loss I am ill able to bear.'

But three months later came a storybook reprieve: the government struck down the 1819 law, along with eight other statutes restricting the freedom of speech. 'You gained a very honourable success,' John Stuart Mill wrote to Bradlaugh, 'in obtaining a repeal of the mischievous Act by your preserving resistance.'[23] But he did not think, he added, that the Crown would reimburse Bradlaugh for his considerable legal expenses. He was correct.

Yet now Charles Bradlaugh's name became currency. To raise money for his newspaper and its cause he accepted almost every invitation. In one 1870 month alone he delivered 26 lectures, declining to postpone or cancel even after scarlet fever killed Charles, Jr. at the age of ten. Bradlaugh refused to talk about the loss, and expanded his speaking circuit to the Continent, leaving Susannah and their daughters behind. Following a speech (in English) in republican France in 1871, the revolutionary Paris Commune – remembering his public support for Felice Orsini's assassination attempt on Napoleon III – entered his name in the city's mayoral contest. Next Bradlaugh travelled to Spain to speak in favour of republicans clashing with Carlists. In 1873, he sailed for the first time to the United States, where his lectures calling for the 'impeachment' of the monarchy – but only *after* Victoria, he cagily added – would play well in a country that had seen off George III.

British public opinion, to be sure, ran against him. In Parliament, MPs threatened charges of treason, and London editorials argued that the royal line of Germanic Hanoverians who Bradlaugh had branded 'useless foreigners whom the English pay to perpetuate a pauper prince race' in fact ruled over an empire whose freedoms allowed him to print and say what he pleased. The long-sequestered Victoria was also enjoying an upswell of public sympathy following her bedside vigil for the Prince of Wales, who in February that year recovered from a bout of typhoid fever that doctors presumed would kill him. In her diary that April, the 53-year-old queen marvelled at the reception she received from crowds lining her carriage's route from Buckingham Palace through Bradlaugh's borough to Victoria Park on a rare outing to express gratitude for her subjects' support. 'I received the most kind & enthusiastic greetings from the very very poorest,' Her Majesty wrote. 'There were many kind expressions of "God bless you", "Come again", & nothing could have been more hearty or cordial than my reception by those poorest of the poor. It was really touching.'[24]

Rapturous crowds greeted her critic in America. After disembarking from the 11-day ocean crossing, Charles Bradlaugh was given the pleasure of jumping the customs queue by a New York City agent who told him, 'Mr. Bradlaugh, we know you here.' Reporters flocked to interview him. In their story headlined 'A Rabid Radical Republican', the *New York Herald* breathlessly said that his appearance, at 'over six feet in height, with a loose swinging gait, and his chest like the breast of an oak; his large blue eyes, brown hair, which thickly clusters back of his ears; his fair ruddy skin, and his thoroughly athletic proportions bespeak him as the pure-blooded franklin who, from the days of Runnymeade, has been habitually creating trouble for the oppressor and the bloated aristocrat'.[25] In a review of his first speech, on (what else?) republicanism, another newspaper proclaimed him 'the greatest of living orators', superior to any in America, and 'the future President of England'.

Before his arrival in Boston, a Protestant newspaper warned its readers away. 'You have heard of Mr Bradlaugh,' its editorial began. 'Mr Bradlaugh is a creature six feet high, twenty inches broad, and about twelve thousand feet of impudence. He keeps a den in a [London] hole-in-the-wall, dignified by the title of the "Hall of Science," in which he holds forth Sunday after Sunday to a mob of ruffians whose sole hope after death is immediate annihilation.' The writer branded Bradlaugh 'uneducated' and 'a vagabond'. Back in England, another paper claimed, 'Practical politicians among the advanced liberal party avoid him as honest men avoid a felon, as virtuous women avoid a prostitute.'[26]

Could there have been better publicity? Working-class Irish immigrants packed the hall in Boston, where the master of ceremonies called Bradlaugh a modern Samuel Adams, and quoted the Liberal MP Charles Dilke, who said he 'does the thinking for more minds, has more influence, than any other man in England'.[27] Like many British radicals, Bradlaugh was an early supporter of a woman's right to vote, and so among the suffragists who also thronged to his speech was Victoria Woodhull, who a year earlier had become the first woman to run for the American presidency. That night, Bradlaugh shared the stage with the old abolitionists Charles Sumner and William Lloyd Garrison, 'who cheered him repeatedly'.[28]

Bradlaugh steamed from speech to speech, trailing clouds of words as he puffed from Buffalo to Cincinnati, and St Louis to Kansas City. In Chicago, Richard Carlile's daughter, now in middle age, came out to see her former loser lodger turned sought-after star. At the invitation of the American vice president, Bradlaugh returned to Boston to attend a reception honouring Ralph Waldo Emerson. In London a poor teenage Bradlaugh had copied down and re-read the writer's inspiring ode to self-reliance. Twenty-six years later, his finances remained tenuous (rebellion did not then pay), but the self-made Bradlaugh now sat as the guest of honour beside his boyhood hero.

If this were a play, the curtain could fall there; a circle has closed. But in real life, Charles Bradlaugh was called upon to speak. 'Now I stood in the presence of the great preacher,' he wrote. 'After my tribute of respectful and earnestly thankful words to Emerson as one of the world's teachers, I could not refrain from using the spirit of his lines to ground a comparison between the public opinion of Boston in 1773 and 1873.'

Bradlaugh – who could lapse into bouts of becoming a know-it-all bore – did not record what he said, only that it 'called forth quite a lively debate' in the room. No less than a half-dozen Boston dignitaries weighed in. If he felt the sinking feeling that he should have remained silent, his lines do not show it. 'I fully expected,' Bradlaugh continued, 'that Mr. Emerson, who had listened with marked attention and evident interest to the conflicting statements, would give some opinion; but as the oracle remained silent, I was obliged to be content with his pleasant personal words of promise to seek me out for another meeting before my departure for England.'[29]

He did not. Perhaps it was here, after this polite brush-off, that Charles Bradlaugh first learned to turn down every opportunity to open his mouth, to let someone else address the room. His writings show no such self-awareness. But in 1874, upon his return to London, and a second defeat in his windmill-tilting quest to join Parliament, his actions do. For here, at last, onto the stage, and into his life, walked Mrs Annie Besant.

3

AJAX – MRS BESANT

'When I was asked to give a lecture in this hall,' began the young woman at the lectern, 'I hesitated a little what to select for the subject of it. But it so happened that this is my first lecture in any public hall, and a feeling of loyalty to my own sex made me determine that my first speech should be dedicated to the assertion of its rights; and I, therefore, choose as my subject, "The Political Status of Women."'

The 26-year-old standing on stage at London's Co-operative Hall – centrally located at the nexus of Fleet Street and the Strand – was dressed fashionably for 1874, shunning a tight short-waisted basque bodice for a two-piece dress, topped by a less-restricting tunic. If she was nervous, she did not show it. 'She was very fluent,' recorded an attendee, 'with a great command of language, and her voice carried well; her throat, weak at first, rapidly gained in strength, until she became a most forcible speaker.'[1]

From the first, she displayed a barrister's mind. 'I divide what I have to say,' Annie Besant continued, 'under distinct heads, choosing as these heads the arguments I desire to destroy.' These included the opinion that women were 'naturally unfit' for voting, that they were indifferent about the matter, and that 'political power would withdraw them from their proper sphere' of domesticity.[2] She echoed the arguments of

Annie Besant after her arrival in London. Her short hair made a marked
contrast with the era's fashion of long, braided tresses.

the nascent suffrage movement's earliest representatives,
including John Stuart Mill, who seven years earlier – on the
back of the activism of his wife and daughter, Harriet and
Helen Taylor – had attempted to replace the word 'man' with
'people' on the expanded electoral register. From the House
of Commons Ladies' Gallery, Millicent Fawcett had witnessed its defeat. Like Fawcett, Annie Besant was born in
1847, the year when the Brontë sisters were compelled to
publish *Wuthering Heights* and *Jane Eyre* under male pennames.
In London some three dozen statues commemorated great
Britons; only two depicted women – the queens Anne and
Victoria. In 1869, when Fawcett had addressed the first meeting of the London Society for Women's Suffrage, *The Times*
did not bother to send a reporter. Five years later, it remained
remarkable to see any woman addressing a crowd from a
stage, let alone one as young as Annie Besant.

In the first act of her life, she had perfectly played the role assigned to her by polite society. Born Annie Wood, within earshot of the bells of St Mary-le-Bow church (making her a Cockney, or 'true Londoner'), she was actually three-quarters Irish. The only daughter of Emily Morris inherited her mother's dark curly hair, and from her father a connection to royalty. William Wood's English side of the family included his uncle Sir Matthew, who had been the Sheriff, Lord Mayor and reformist Whig MP for the City of London. In 1820, he had managed the unpopular Princess of Wales's return from exile on the Continent, and steadfastly and publicly supported her unhappy, short-lived reign as Queen Caroline. He had also helped to pay the debts of Edward, Duke of Kent, so the heir to the throne could be born in England. In 1837, that grown child made Matthew Wood a baronet, after she was crowned Queen Victoria.

Annie's side of the Woods moved to Ireland, where her father was born and raised in Galway. After qualifying as a doctor at Trinity College Dublin, William instead accepted a relative's offer of a commercial post in London. Annie's earliest memories were of waiting to pounce joyfully on her father when, at the end of the workday, he returned to their handsome home in St John's Wood. From their garden on Grove End Road, Annie could hear the cricket bats cracking balls at Lord's. (Today, she might also hear Beatles fans snapping selfies at the zebra crossing near Abbey Road Studios.)

Annie's idyll shattered at the age of five, when her father – soaked after riding on the top of an omnibus in the rain – caught that dreaded Victorian affliction: a cold. A physician diagnosed William with 'a galloping consumption', and gave him six weeks to live. Annie remembered being lifted to his bed to 'say good-bye to dear Papa'. Looking at her with startled eyes, her father made her promise to be 'a very good girl to darling Mamma, as Papa was going right away'. He died the next day. Like Queen Victoria, whose father passed away when she was one, Annie would grow up without paternal love, or restrictions. She keenly absorbed the scene, earlier that week, when, after her mother had summoned a priest to her father's deathbed, he had wrathfully ejected this 'messenger of a creed he detested'. Annie also fumed when, at the funeral, her older brother Henry got to ride, as chief mourner, in the first carriage following the hearse. She, however, was ushered back inside the house to sit on a sofa amid an unkindness of raven-cloaked spinster aunts.

Her grief-stricken mother's black hair turned white overnight. In a patriarchal society, she had been left with no income, and three young children to support. Her Anglicanism was spiced with Celtic mysticism, and so when her husband appeared in a vision to claim he needed their youngest son to be with him, she was unsurprised when the three-year-old boy also died, of consumption. In the span of five months, Annie had lost both her father and baby brother. She channelled her feelings into the protection of her mother, who called the exuberant girl 'Sunshine'.

The family placed their hopes on Annie's brother Henry. One of Sir Matthew Wood's sons, a successful Queen's Counsel and a Liberal MP for Oxford, offered to pay for Henry's education at a city school, and then place him in business. (No one seems to have given Annie a second thought.) Her mother's 'Irish pride rebelled,' she wrote, 'against the idea of her son not being a University man,' and so – cutting herself off from their monied relations – she moved the family to Harrow. Its famed public school, founded under Queen Elizabeth I's Royal Charter, offered comparatively low fees for town residents. After renting a neglected, ivy-covered former vicarage at the top of Harrow Hill, Annie's mother gained the headmaster's permission to lodge boys, along with a house-tutor. The arrangement lasted for the next ten years, until Henry enrolled at Cambridge. It had been, Annie later wrote, 'a bold scheme for a penniless widow, but carried out to the letter; for never dwelt in a delicate body a more resolute mind and will than that of my dear mother'.

Annie loved the house, which backed onto a garden whose sunny slope held gooseberry bushes and fruit trees. She picked apples and fell into books. Her favourite was *Paradise Lost*. 'I liked to personify Satan,' she recalled, 'and to declaim the grand speeches of the hero-rebel.' She was eight years old.

In town, her mother befriended the sister of the naval officer and popular novelist Captain Frederick Marryat, who had counted Charles Dickens among his many admirers. In his dotage, Marryat had lived with his sibling Ellen, and after his passing, 'Miss Marryat' — as Annie would know her — felt the chill of an empty house. Annie's mother, meanwhile, tended over one brimming with adolescent boys. 'In truth,' Annie recorded, 'I was as good a cricketer and climber as the best of them.' One morning, not realising that a visitor had called, Sunshine danced into the drawing room babbling about books. Charmed, Ellen Marryat offered to educate her, free of charge, at Fern Hill, her Dorsetshire country house (today a charming hotel), located near the Jurassic Coast. Annie moved in with Marryat's niece and a clergyman's son named Walter Powys, who would go on to become a first-class cricketer at Cambridge.

No such road was open to a British schoolgirl of the 1850s and 60s. (Although Emily Davies would make history by establishing Girton College at Cambridge in 1869, it would not be permitted to grant its first degree until 1948, honorarily, to the Queen Mother.) But Annie's life had taken a felicitous turn. Miss Marryat, she wrote, 'had a genius for teaching, and took in it the greatest delight'. The children called her 'Auntie', and studied composition, recitation, French, German and music. Instead of using an English grammar — 'that torment of the small child' — Ellen Marryat took her charges on walks through the Devonshire countryside and for picnics on the sand and shingle beaches at Lyme Regis and Charmouth. 'We wrote letters, telling of the things we had seen,' Annie remembered, which Marryat then corrected for grammar and spelling, and made them rewrite. She also developed her attention to style. 'A clumsy sentence would be read aloud, that we might hear how unmusical it sounded.' On Sundays, when the Evangelical Marryat allowed the reading of no books other than the Bible, Annie found that its 'dignified cadences' pleased her ear, and 'were swiftly caught and reproduced' when she recited the pages. What commentators would later call her 'natural talent' for public speaking had been honed through years of work, under the tutelage of a never-married woman who had chosen to live free of men.

Ellen Marryat brought her niece and Annie, now 13, to Germany to practise their language with native speakers. (If the matron ever told her charges that her income derived from her hated father, dead for four decades, who had been an MP and West Indies slaver, Annie did not say.) The girl once called Sunshine was changing into 'a very slight, pale, black-haired girl, alternating between wild fun and extreme pensiveness'. Her hazel eyes — brown, flecked with emerald sparks — made her stand out. 'I have a theory,' she later told an admirer, 'that eyes with green lights in them generally go with strong magnetism.'[3] German boys, cheeks gashed with duelling scars, flirted with her, as did the sons of expatriate dukes and marquises. Miss Marryat, who forbade the reading of romances, then decamped to the city dubbed the capital of love.

Under Napoleon III, Baron Haussmann was sculpting imperial Paris into its recognisable shape, with wide boulevards lit by gas streetlights and lined by cream-coloured buildings of uniform height. Massive new train stations opened, as did Les Halles produce market, covered by a great canopy of iron and glass. It was all almost as interesting as London. Annie studied in the Louvre, strolled in the Tuileries Garden and knelt inside Notre Dame. For the first time, she also fell in love – with the Church.

When Miss Marryat arranged for her to be confirmed, Annie felt awed by the solemn pageantry of her preparation, whose prolonged prayers would end with the laying on of the hands. 'I could scarcely control myself,' she remembered, 'as I knelt at the altar rails, and felt the gentle touch of the aged bishop.' As an adult, she wondered if, by denying a teenager sex education and dating, there was anything easier 'than to make a young and sensitive girl intensely religious'.

At 14, Annie returned to her mother. 'A very pleasant place was Harrow to a light-hearted serious-brained girl. The picked men of Oxford and Cambridge came there as junior masters, so that one's partners at croquet and archery could talk as well as flirt.' She did not tell her mother. 'She had a horror of sentimentality in girls,' Annie wrote, 'and loved to see them bright and gay, and above all things absolutely ignorant of all evil things and premature love-dreams.'

Unsurprising, perhaps, for a woman who had been widowed so young. Annie, meanwhile, became more and more devout, repeating prayers expressing her love for Christ – declarations, she later realised, that were far more erotic than anything in the novels she had been banned from reading.

'That passionate love of "the Saviour",' she reflected, 'really is the human passion of love transferred to an ideal – for women to Jesus, for men to the Virgin Mary.' This chapter of her memoir could be titled 'Fifty Shades of Pray.' Across her puberty, Annie breathily whispered, 'O Jesu, beloved, draw me after Thee with the cords of Thy love', and 'It may be my greatest desire to please Thee', and 'Oh, that I could embrace Thee with that most burning love of angels.' In one of her favourite orisons she incanted, 'Let Him kiss me with the kisses of His mouth; for Thy love is better than wine. The king has brought me into his chambers. Let my soul, O Lord, feel the sweetness of Thy presence. May it taste how sweet Thou art. May the sweet and burning power of Thy love, I beseech Thee, absorb my soul.'

To prove her fidelity – or, like those bloodletting Elizabethans, to cool her passions – Annie began fasting. It did not curb her hunger to become a great religious leader. Closing the cover on a book of the lives of martyrs, she recalled, brought her with a shock back to earth, 'where there were no heroic deeds to do, no lions to face, no judges to defy. And I used to fret to that I was born so late, when all the grand things had been done, and when there was no chance of preaching and suffering for a new religion.'[4]

On official holidays (Easter, Whit Monday, Lammastide and Christmas) Annie decamped to her maternal grandparents' south London terrace. When she was 18 – in 1865, the year *Alice's Adventures in Wonderland* was published – a pretty, steep-steepled Anglican church opened near the home close to the Oval cricket ground, in Albert Square.

St Stephen's Catholic-borrowed High Church pomp enticed her like the bottle labelled DRINK ME tempted Alice. Annie was 'a very attractive girl, rather highly strung, and full of life,' her niece (brother Henry's daughter) wrote, relaying the recollections of their relatives. 'With her long curling hair held up by the then fashionable black silk net, a lace collar fastened at the throat with a brooch containing her father's hair, and her skirts billowing around her . . . she was just a happy English girl devoted to her mother, and bubbling over with high spirits and youth. She had a more serious side, and at that time there was only one outlet for her emotions, and that was the Church.'[5]

During Passion Week, as the innocent Annie Wood decorated the St Stephen's altar with white geraniums, she met the new curate, just down from Cambridge. His name was Frank Besant.

Reader, she fell for his robes. 'To me,' she confessed, 'a priest was a half-angelic creature.' Soon she would find that under his surplice, Frank Besant was a wholly Victorian man. Her descriptions of his pedantic liturgies evoke the better one, in *Middlemarch*, when the bland Reverend Casaubon, courting the quick-witted Dorothea Brooke, is described as having 'no good red blood in his body . . . Somebody put a drop under a magnifying-glass, and it was all semicolons and parentheses.'[6]

That summer of 1866 – when a Charles Bradlaugh-led demonstration for electoral reform violently uprooted the railings of a locked Hyde Park – the Wood family decamped on holiday to St Leonards-on-Sea. Frank Besant tagged along uninvited. Following a week of chaperoned walks and horseback riding, the curate called on Annie en route to catching his return train to London. With all the emotion of stopping to purchase a newspaper, he proposed marriage. Startled, Annie stood mute. 'I hesitated,' she wrote, and 'did not follow my first impulse of refusal but took refuge in silence.' Embarrassed, he fell upon convention, accusing her, in that paternal Victorian phrasing, of 'trifling with his affections'.

He commanded Annie not to tell her mother before he could speak to her first. Then he left to board his train, leaving Annie 'the most upset and distressed little person on the Sussex coast'.[7]

After reading Dorothea's passionless betrothal to Reverend Causabon, Harriet Beecher Stowe protested to her friend George Eliot that others would share her disbelief, puncturing *Middlemarch*'s verisimilitude. However, she wrote to Eliot, 'I understand that girls often make a false marriage and plight their faith to an unreal shadow who they suppose inhabits a certain body.'[8]

Annie made the same mistake. Most middle-class girls married between the ages of 20 to 25; to wait any longer risked being put on the shelf, and a life outside Victorian norms. Annie was only 18 when she found herself engaged. She did not pretend to love Frank Besant, but imagined that as a clergyman's wife she could serve the Church and poor with a zeal to match the female saints. 'She could not be the bride of Heaven,' the journalist W.T. Stead later observed, 'and therefore became the bride of Mr. Frank Besant. He was hardly an adequate substitute.'[9]

In the 14 months before their wedding, Annie only saw her fiancé intermittently. In that period, the House of Commons roundly rejected John Stuart Mill's motion to extend the right to vote to women, Queen Victoria laid the foundation stone of the Royal Albert Hall and a Fenian uprising rocked colonial Ireland. Annie, visiting Manchester with her mother, for the first time felt the political become personal. The city had taken sectarian sides during the trial of a trio of men who had – unintentionally, they argued – killed a policeman while attempting to free a fellow member of the Irish Republican Brotherhood. Outside the courthouse, Annie found herself trapped between an English and Irish mob, and then came face-to-face with the distraught fiancée of one of the prisoners. The men were quickly found guilty and hanged, before a crowd of 10,000, outside Salford gaol.

In her diary, Queen Victoria recorded, 'Heard before 12 that those wretched men had been executed & that all was perfectly quiet at Manchester. I prayed for these poor men last night.'[10]

To Karl Marx, Friedrich Engels wrote, 'So yesterday morning the Tories accomplished the final act of separation between England and Ireland.'[11]

Annie shared the Irish outrage – to nationalists, they became the 'Manchester Martyrs' – as did her future partner in crime. 'I have found, with a keen sense of pleasure,' she later wrote, 'that Mr. Bradlaugh and myself were in 1867 to some extent co-workers, although we knew not of each other's existence.' As he pleaded for the Irishmen's lives on Clerkenwell Green, she was 'only giving such poor sympathy as a young girl might, who was only just awakening to the duty of political work'.

The next month, she married a hidebound Anglican priest. 'We were an ill-matched pair from the very outset,' Annie acknowledged, 'he, with very high ideas of a husband's authority and a wife's submission . . . I, accustomed to freedom, indifferent to home details, impulsive, very hot-tempered, and proud as Lucifer.' Her own paradise was lost, irretrievably, on her wedding night.

'Many an unhappy marriage dates from its very beginning,' she wrote, 'from the terrible shock to a young girl's sensitive modesty and pride, her helpless bewilderment and fear.' Like most Victorian mothers, Annie's had not told her what to expect in the bridal bed. 'No more fatal blunder can be made,' Annie fumed, 'than to train a girl to womanhood in ignorance of all life's duties and burdens . . . That "perfect

innocence" may be very beautiful, but it is a perilous possession, and Eve should have the knowledge of good and evil
ere she wanders forth from the paradise of a mother's love.'
Her ignorance of 'all that marriage meant' – sex – 'was as
profound as though I had been a child of four'.

Reverend Besant did not try tenderness, or exercise
restraint. By law, he did not need her consent. Annie was his,
with flesh to penetrate, not caress. Her elided outline of the
evening still steams with shocked embarrassment and pain.
'No mother,' she charged, 'should let her daughter, blind-
fold, slip her neck under the marriage yoke.'[12]

Mrs Besant's harrowing account of consummation stands
in sharp contrast to that of her future nominal prosecutor's.
Like Annie, Queen Victoria had also married at age 20. But
she had won the bridegroom lottery. 'I *never, never* spent such
an evening!!' she confided in her diary after her wedding
night in 1840. 'My *dearest dearest dear* Albert sat on a footstool
by my side, and his excessive love and affection gave me feelings of heavenly love and happiness, I never could have *hoped*
to have felt before! He clasped me in his arms, and we kissed
each other again and again! His beauty, his sweetness and
gentleness, – really how can I ever be thankful enough to
have such a *Husband*! . . . At 20 m[inutes] p[ast] 10 we both
went to bed; (*of course* in *one* bed), to lie by his side, and in his
arms, and on his dear bosom, and be called by names of tenderness, I have never yet heard used to me before – was bliss
beyond belief! Oh! this was the happiest day of my life! –
May God help me to do my duty as I ought and be worthy of
such blessings!'[13]

Ironically, the reign of Elizabeth I – 'the virgin queen' –
was one of sexual frankness; the monarch whose name
became the byword for sexual circumspection herself very
much enjoyed making love.

Inside the queen's bedroom at Windsor Castle, Victoria awoke for the first time as a wife. 'When the day dawned (for we did not sleep much) and I beheld that beautiful angelic face by my side, it was more than I can express! He does look so beautiful in his shirt only, with his beautiful throat seen.'[14] That was just Tuesday. On Wednesday, she wrote, 'Already the 2nd day since our marriage; *his* love and gentleness is beyond everything, and to kiss that dear soft cheek, to press my lips to his, is heavenly bliss. I *feel* a purer more unearthly feel than I ever did. Oh! was ever woman so blessed as I am!' The conjugal delight continued that night, after Victoria found Albert asleep on the sofa: 'I touched his cheek with my hand, but it did not wake him, and then I woke him with a kiss. He took me in his arms (in bed) and kissed me again and again, and we fell asleep arm in arm, and woke so again.'[15] On Thursday morning, 'My dearest *Albert* put on my stockings for me.'[16]

Back in the real world, the Revered Besant led his new bride 100 miles northwest, to Cheltenham. Annie found herself marooned 'in a strange town, among strangers, with a number of ladies visiting me who talked only of servants and babies – troubles of which I knew nothing – who were profoundly uninterested in everything that had formed my previous life, in theology, in politics, in questions of social reform, and who looked on me as "strange" because I cared more for the great struggles outside than for the discussions of a housemaid's young man', or the amount of butter used by the cook. She did not have a recipe for seedcake, and did not want one. For the first time in her life, Annie felt 'timid, dull, and depressed'.[17]

She gamely tried to write her way out of it, first penning a pamphlet that she herself wanted to read, sketching the lives of what she termed the black-letter saints, those martyrs not remembered with official, red-letter days on the Church of England's calendar. Next, she wrote a secular short story that in retrospect reads like a vision board. The fantasy had a newly married woman, like Annie nicknamed 'Sunshine', thrown from a horse shortly after marrying. Crippled and confined to her bed, and doted on by a loving (and, presumably, chaste) husband, she lived out her days as a Lady Bountiful, showering charity upon the townsfolk.

Without telling her husband, Annie submitted 'Sunshine and Shadows' to a London magazine named *The Family Herald*, whose cover promised 'Select Reading for Leisure Moments. Interesting to All – Offensive to None'.[18] A few weeks later, when she opened the editor's reply, from the envelope fell an acceptance cheque of 30 shillings. It was the first money Annie had ever earned – and, totalling one and a half pounds, more than most labourers made in a week. A wave of independence washed over her. Then she realised that under British law, her earnings wholly belonged to her husband.

They would remain so in perpetuity, even after the statute was at last struck down by the Married Women's Property Act of 1870, which applied only to marriages after its passage. Among other rights, the law allowed women for the first time to have their own bank accounts.

Her Majesty was not pleased. 'The Queen is most anxious,' she wrote to a friend,

> to enlist every one who can speak or write to join in checking this mad, wicked folly of "Women's Rights," with all its attendant horrors, on which her poor feeble sex is bent, forgetting every sense of womanly feeling and propriety . . . It is a subject which makes the Queen so furious that she cannot contain herself. God created men and women

different – then let them remain each in their own position . . .
Woman would become the most hateful, heartless, and disgusting of human beings were she allowed to unsex herself;
and where would be the protection which man was intended
to give the weaker sex?[19]

When Annie's short story appeared in print, an already-
displeased Reverend Besant discovered that his wife, in a
further stab at autonomy, had signed it with the initials of
her maiden name: A.W.

Soon after, her literary career was 'checked' (she wrote,
punning on contraception) by pregnancy. In a portrait taken
that year, 1869, the expectant Mrs Besant looks downright
miserable. The baby boy, Arthur – called Digby – was followed, in short order, by a daughter, Mabel. She 'was delicate
from birth,' Annie wrote, 'suffering from her mother's unhap-
piness, and born somewhat prematurely in consequence of a
shock'.[20]

Her husband had assaulted her. After pleading with him that
she never wanted to become pregnant again, he had hit her, on
the shoulder. Rather than asking forgiveness, this man of the
cloth told her to leave his house and return to her mother.

Cruelly, Frank Besant knew that was impossible; the Wood
family's trusted lawyer had slowly embezzled her mother's savings, leaving the elderly woman penniless. Annie now found
herself trapped in a physically abusive marriage – in a field, he
angrily seized her by the arm and dragged her home; after
refusing him in bed, he bruised her body by shoving her to the
floor – with two sickly infants and no path of escape. Once,
she tipped a bottle of chloroform to her lips, surrendering to
the release of suicide. Only the thought of her motherless
children caused her to hurl the toxin out the window.

She sought the counsel of other priests, who told her this

was her cross to bear. A crisis of faith followed; her religious past became the enemy of her suffering present. Like Milton's Lucifer, Mrs Besant chose to rebel. 'All of the hitherto dormant and unsuspecting strength of my nature rose up,' she wrote. 'I did not yet dream of denial, but I would no longer kneel.'[21]

Gossip burbled through cloistered Cheltenham like the mineral springs that ceaselessly fed its spas. Seeking a fresh start, Annie appealed to her late father's cousin, the Oxford MP since elevated to Lord Chancellor of Great Britain and raised to the peerage as Baron Hatherley. For the Besants he arranged a crown-living – a church posting paid by the state – in southern Lincolnshire, outside of Boston. (And, for Annie's brother, freshly finished at Cambridge, a plum posting at what will be named the Royal Society of Arts, where he will work as its longstanding secretary. In 1890, he will be knighted by Victoria, becoming Sir Henry Wood.)

Reverend Besant was installed as vicar at the eleventh-century St Margaret's church, whose square Norman tower rose from the wheat and barley fields surrounding the village of Sibsey. Mabel and Digby loved the open space, and their father fell into his duties to his flock of farmers and began translating, from Latin, parish records dating back to the early Elizabethan age. The work, whose slow and long pace matched the receding of his hair and the growth of his snowy, ascetic beard, would happily occupy him for the rest of his life. In Annie's telling – the only side of the story we have – Frank Besant never thanked her for securing for him this comfortable pastoral life. The reverend only threatened that if she ever told a soul, he would kill her.

The stone walls of their prim churchyard cottage made a prison. For the next two years, Annie threw herself into charity work in the Fens, visiting crowded, unventilated hovels to nurse ailing farm labourers and children stricken with typhoid. 'I learned then some of the lessons that I was able in after years to teach from the platform,' she wrote. 'The political education progressed while the theological strife went on within.'[22]

Out of respect for her mother, then living in London with Henry, Annie sought outside counsel, taking her questions about the Church's teachings to a well-regarded Oxford priest. 'It is not your duty to ascertain the truth,' he scolded. 'It is your duty to accept and believe the truth as laid down by the Church.' She politely parried. He shut her down. Finally, with despairing resignation, Annie replied that she had no choice but to face her problems alone. The dean responded in fury, crying, 'I forbid you to speak of your disbelief!' But she was already out the door.

Back in Sibsey, the 25-year-old discovered what her contemporary Emily Dickinson herself felt, in a poem that begins 'One need not be a Chamber – to be Haunted'. In the 'lonesome place' of an abbey whose stones echoed with the protagonist's own footsteps, the speaker at last finds not a fearsome ghost, but the freeing release of 'ourself behind ourself, concealed'.[23]

Locked inside the church to practise the organ alone, 'a queer whim took me,' Annie recalled, 'that I would like to know how it felt to preach, and vague fancies stirred in me that I could speak if I had the chance. The longing to find outlet in words came upon me, and I felt as though I had something to say and was able to say it. I ascended the pulpit steps.' Facing the empty pews, Annie was revealed to herself. 'I shall never forget,' she wrote, 'the feeling of power and delight — but especially of power — that came upon me as I sent my voice ringing down the aisles.'

☙

She told no one. Annie continued to attend her husband's sermons but refused to take Holy Communion. He demanded that she conform or leave. 'In other word, hypocrisy or expulsion,' she summed up. 'I chose the latter.'[24]

Centuries after the Magna Carta curbed the Divine Right of Kings, one early British feminist, Frances Power Cobbe, decried her country's adherence to the 'Divine Right of Husbands'.[25] Even the queen, usually conservative in all things domestic, was sympathetic to a betrothed's fate. 'All marriage is such a lottery,' Victoria wrote to her eldest daughter. 'The happiness is always an exchange — though it may be a very happy one — still the poor woman is bodily and morally the husband's slave. That always sticks in my throat. When I think of a merry, happy, free young girl — and look at the ailing, aching state a young wife generally is doomed to — which you can't deny is the penalty of marriage.'[26]

The Victorian invention of the marriage certificate (yet more Victorian paper) listed the husband's occupation, as well as that of his father and his wife's father — but left no space for her own, since her place was in the home.[27] Although as monarch Victoria had been the only married British woman who held her own property and income, she also unquestioningly accepted her true standing with Albert. 'Men are very selfish,' she warned the Princess Royal, 'and the woman's devotion is always one of submission which makes our poor sex so very unenviable. This you will feel hereafter — I know; though it cannot be otherwise as God has willed it so.'[28] Divorce may have been a Victorian reform, but at first it strongly favoured men. After years of public pressure from campaigners like Caroline Norton – whose husband had blocked her from seeing their three children, and from a divorce, after she left him – in 1857 new civil courts, replacing ecclesiastical ones, were created to hear divorce petitions. Victoria, Supreme Governor of the Church of England and Defender of the Faith, had given Royal Assent to the law. That summer, a torpid heat wave engulfed the Houses of Parliament in the sewage stench of the pre-Embankment Thames. Lime-soaked sheets hanging in the building's windows did little to repel the vapours. British women who read the text of the Matrimonial Causes Act also had reason to hold their noses. Despite the bill's intentions, the all-male Parliament had made it all but impossible for a woman to legally leave her husband.

The law decreed that a man could rather easily divorce his adulterous wife. She was a danger to bourgeois society; bearing another man's child could upset clear lines of paternity, succession and inheritance. On the other hand, a woman cuffed to an unfaithful husband would have to prove his guilt of an additional, rather more felonious offence, including incest, bigamy, bestiality, or desertion for more than two years. Annie – like Charles Dickens's long-suffering wife Catherine – could not obtain a divorce on the grounds of physical and emotional abuse until Parliament passed an amendment. It would not do so until 1937.

In the autumn of 1873, after threatening to expose Reverend Besant's behaviour, which could ignite that Victorian powder keg marked SCANDAL, Annie's brother secured for her a legal separation. Frank Besant would pay a quarter of his annual salary, or about £10 monthly, for the maintenance of his wife and three-year-old Mabel. The amount, Annie wrote, was 'sufficient for respectable starvation'.[29] She counted herself lucky to retain custody of her daughter; by law, both children belonged to their father.

Annie's firstborn, Digby, about to turn five, would remain with Reverend Besant. She could see her son only for one month each summer, when the children temporarily traded parents. Annie was barred from taking any furniture; from Sibsey she carried away only her personal effects and her hated husband's surname. She would later sell most of her sundry possessions to make ends meet, but her married name was a brand burned onto her very self. On the podium, in the press, in the courtroom and in history she would forever be known as Mrs Annie Besant. But already she was thinking of a way to make the moniker her own.

Her upright brother Henry, a *Times* reader and member of the Oxford and Cambridge Club on Pall Mall, offered to take her in — on the condition that she abandon her 'heretical ideas'. His memoirist daughter Freda later recounted, 'My Aunt, who wanted freedom, and an intellectual outlet for her brain and immense energy, refused.'[30]

In south London's Gipsy Hill neighbourhood, Annie rented a cottage near the Crystal Palace and took in needlework, the Victorian low-paying service job for women in reduced circumstances.

Her mother, the woman who had fondly dubbed her 'Sunshine', moved in but needed more care than she could give. In the spring of 1874, Annie relented and took Communion for the last time, at her mother's deathbed. 'I am leaving you alone,' the elder Wood sighed to her daughter, a parting line that could be interpreted as a lament, a promise or a curse. She was buried next to her husband and infant son in Kensal Green. Annie returned to her rented cottage, whose bare walls amplified her echoing sobs. She held her daughter and watched the shadows creep in. This was the turning point in her life, she wrote, when with the chilling clarity of a clock-strike she truly understood, 'You are all alone.'[31]

�֍

Facing poverty, she relied on the kindness of an ever-widening circle of radicals including Moncure Conway, an American abolitionist who preached in a nonconformist chapel in Camden Town. Conway's wife urged her to attend a talk by the best orator she had ever seen, a man named Charles Bradlaugh. Annie demurred, having heard he was 'rather a rough sort of speaker'.

The Conways and their activist peers fed Annie a lifeline writing handbills and tracts espousing their 'Freethought' beliefs, which urged Britons to rationally weigh laws and regulations instead of blindly obeying authority. As a sitter watched Mabel, Annie worked in the British Museum's Reading Room. She became the Dickens of pamphleteering, prolifically churning out paper paid by the piece.

After finishing her shift one hot July day, she stopped at the High Holborn shop owned by the freethinker publisher Edward Truelove to buy something to read – and fan herself – on the long commute south of the Thames to her rented home. For sale on the counter was a copy of Charles Bradlaugh's *National Reformer*. 'Attracted by the title, I bought it,' Annie wrote. 'I read it placidly on the omnibus on my way to Victoria Station, and found it excellent.' The issue contained a long letter from a Northampton reverend, explaining why he could not support Bradlaugh's third attempt to become an MP, as well as an article explaining the purposes of the National Secular Society. '[I] was sent into convulsions of inward merriment,' Annie wrote, 'when, glancing up, I saw an old gentleman gazing at me, with horror speaking from every line of his countenance. To see a young woman, respectably dressed in a cape, reading an Atheistic journal, had evidently upset his peace of mind, and he looked so hard at the paper that I was tempted to offer it to him.'[32]

It was an era of taking sides, of joining-up, of belonging to a club, if you were rich, or a social union, if you were poor. (Earlier that year, a group of Salon-rejected painters, including Claude Monet and Paul Cézanne, had staged their own Paris exhibition, where an unimpressed critic derisively dubbed the gang Impressionists.) After writing to Bradlaugh that August 1874 to confirm that there was no requirement to declare herself an atheist, Annie, with little else to lose, decided to join the National Secular Society.

On a Sunday, she ventured to the group's nerve centre, brushing past evangelists handing out Christian tracts outside the Golden Lane Mission, where gas jets above its door illuminated the words GOD IS LOVE.[33] At last, with 1,200 others who paid the two pence admission fee, she crossed the threshold of the Old Street Hall of Science to hear the secularist leader speak. What Annie Besant witnessed sounded like love at first sight.

'I remember well my sensations as I looked at Charles Bradlaugh for the first time,' she wrote. 'The grave, quiet, *strong* look, as he sat facing the crowd, impressed me strangely.' Annie also recalled his 'keen eyes, and magnificent breadth and height of forehead – was this the man I had heard described as a blatant agitator, an ignorant demagogue?' Never in her years of churchgoing had she felt such an orator's sway.

Bradlaugh had managed to cast his spell with a rather pedantic lecture pointing out the similarities of the Christ and Krishna myths. The social reformer Charles Booth noted that for London's poor, after securing the material basics, the next priority was to answer the question, 'How shall we be amused?' Lecture halls provided an affordable diversion, a chance to fraternise and temporarily escape from physically cramped or socially stuffy homes. It was also a time of trying hard, of taking notes and striving for self-improvement, no matter the subject. Some 3,700 Mancunians turned up to hear John Tyndall, discoverer of the greenhouse effect, deliver a lecture titled 'Crystalline and Metallic Forces'.[34]

No matter the topic, Charles Bradlaugh could hold a crowd rapt. 'The great audience,' Annie recorded, 'hung silent, breathing soft, as he went on, till the silence that followed a magnificent peroration broke the spell, and a hurricane of cheers relieved the tension.'[35]

Afterward, with National Secular Society enrolment certificates in hand (yet more Victorian paper), Bradlaugh spotted her in the crowd and asked, 'Mrs Besant?' She was stunned. How did he know? He just did. (Was it just a coincidence that she had first purchased his newspaper in a shop owned by a freethinker with the Cupid-ish surname 'Truelove'?) The pair fell into easy conversation. They continued talking the next day in Bradlaugh's study, 'a wee room overflowing with books,' she wrote, 'in which he looked singularly out of place'.

Zooming out for a moment, we can see that Charles Bradlaugh had chosen to live among his audience, London's working-class poor. He did not have much of a choice. Facing bankruptcy over legal judgments against his newspaper and activism, he had sent his wife, Susannah (slowly succumbing to what today would be diagnosed as alcoholism), and their two daughters to stay with her parents in the Sussex village of Cocking. Bradlaugh lived alone in two cheaply rented rooms that sat smack dab in London's impoverished but improving East End. A wide swath of its roiling narrow lanes had recently been cleared, Haussmann-style, to widen Commercial Street and the former Roman road now called Whitechapel High Street. The first block of charitable Peabody Trust 'model dwellings' for labourers opened nearby; Bradlaugh's Turner Street terrace faced the pioneering London Hospital – or *'orspital*, as locals pronounced it – which created special children's wards and pioneering care for the disabled. Its physicians included John Langdon Down, for whom Down's syndrome is named; among its patients was Joseph Merrick, called the Elephant Man, who would spend the last years of his life inside its walls.

Annie took to Bradlaugh a draft of an essay titled 'On the Nature and Existence of God'. Seated in his study, she read her words aloud. He listened. Since her departed father, had a man ever paid her this respect? Bradlaugh praised her work, and gently suggested edits. Her ears hummed. Their natural rapport echoed *Middlemarch*'s Will and Dorothea, 'looking at each other like two fond children who were talking confidentially of birds'.[36] He was 40, she was 26. Neither had received a formal education, but they had read and travelled widely for the time. Both had studied God's laws in the Church of England, and both had felt the cruel sting of antiquated civil statutes. Both were unhappily married, estranged from their spouses, and parents of two children. Theirs was a verbal consummation; the vicar's wife left the radical's room converted to atheism. Thus began a seemingly unbreakable partnership. 'I had won,' Annie wrote, 'the noblest friend that woman ever had.'[37]

At the start of the summer of 1874, after her mother's death, she had felt hopeless and adrift. By the season's end, Annie

Besant stood onstage in a two-piece suit before a full house at central London's Co-operative Hall, preparing to make her first public speech. The Co-op's secretary had invited her after attending a debate at the Liberal Social Union, where Annie, from the audience, had voiced her support for the abolishment of blue laws that shuttered libraries and museums on Sundays. The subject of her talk would be up to her. She chose 'The Political Status of Women'.

The knee-trembling nervousness – akin, she wrote, to the dread of visiting a dentist (practising smithy Victorian dentistry, no less) – vanished the moment she opened her mouth. 'As I heard my own voice ring out over the attentive listeners, I was conscious of power and of pleasure, not of fear.'[38]

Annie began by listing the common arguments against giving women the vote, including the notion that the 'weaker sex' was indifferent, domestically preoccupied, or genetically unfit. (Or, as one British biologist infamously put it: 'What was decided among the prehistoric Protozoa cannot be annulled by Act of Parliament.'[39]) But unlike other early suffragists, Besant broke new ground, and a Victorian taboo, by publicly indicting religion. 'As we have been told so often in Parliament,' she pointed out, 'women are commanded in the Bible to keep silence, and to be as generally unobtrusive as possible.'

From that moment forward, Annie Besant would do neither.

She prosecuted her case for granting women the right to vote as if speaking not to a friendly gathering of like-minded supporters, but to a jury. Miss Marryat had taught her well.

Rhetorically, Annie asked the men in the audience, 'Do you look on women as your natural enemies, and suppose they are on the look-out for every chance of running away from their homes and their children? It says very little for you if you hope only to keep women's hearts by chaining their minds, or limiting their range of action. What is it really worth, this compelled submission – this enforced devotion?'

A vote, she argued, was like money, valuable not for the paper it's printed on, but for what it represents. 'In a free country a vote means power.' The rows of men stuffed on the government's benches were afraid of what women would do if they gained it. Besant knew: they would at last abolish their coverture. 'We will win the right of representation in Parliament,' she promised, 'and when we have won that, these laws will be altered: There will no longer be a law that women, on marriage, become paupers. There will no longer be a law which gives to the father despotic authority over the fate of the child; which enables the father to take the child from the mother's arms and give it into the charge some other woman; which makes even the dead father able to withhold the child from the living mother.'

By rights, if Frank Besant died before Annie, the custody of Digby and Mabel would pass not to her, but to his parents or siblings. The law, Annie charged, was rooted in official contempt for women's ability to earn their own incomes and manage their own affairs. 'If this natural inferiority of woman be a fact, one cannot wonder how nature has managed to make so many mistakes. Mary Somerville [the Scottish scientist], Mrs. Lewis [better known as George Eliot], Frances Power Cobbe [the anti-vivisection activist], and Harriet Martineau [credited as the first female sociologist] were made, I suppose, when nature was asleep. They certainly show no signs of the properly-constituted feminine intellect.'

And since when, she added cheekily, was intelligence a prerequisite for voting? Witness Benjamin Disraeli's new government. (After his surprise return as prime minister earlier that year, Queen Victoria privately had exulted, 'The result of the election is astounding. What an important turn the elections have taken! It shows the country is not *Radical*. What a good sign this large Conservative majority is for the state of the country.'[40])

'The cream of womanhood is against you,' Annie warned the British Establishment in her first public lecture. 'We will educate women to reason and to think, and then the mass will only want a leader.'[41]

Standing in the audience, Charles Bradlaugh saw one, right there on stage. Her debut was, he said, 'marvellously successful', and 'the best speech by a woman' that he had ever heard.[42] That month, he added her to the staff of the *National Reformer* at a life-sustaining weekly salary of one guinea (£1 1s). The newspaper's office was tucked off Fleet Street, in a crumbling building opposite the home where Samuel Johnson wrote his dictionary.

Until he had felt bold enough to use his real name, Bradlaugh's articles had appeared under the byline Iconoclast. At first, Annie wrote as Ajax. She chose it after seeing a cast, at the Crystal Palace, of the statue *Ajax Crying for Light*. The name connoted strength, but also sacrifice. In *The Iliad*, the Greek warrior valorously fetches Achilles' body from the Trojans, only to see his friend's armour instead awarded to Odysseus. Betrayed by his leader, and then tricked by his god into an act of revenge, Ajax demands the truth. The chorus warns him of its consequences. Shouting into the empty darkness, Ajax pleads to see. 'If our fate be death, give light, and let us die!'[43] After the bloody cost of his mistaken vengeance is revealed, he takes responsibility, and falls upon his sword.

Annie was drawn to martyrdom, still. But what was the injustice that she could illuminate, and, no matter its consequences, also claim as her own?

4

THE FRUITS OF THEIR
PHILOSOPHY

––––––––

She spoke on morality, she spoke on civil liberty, she spoke
on marriage. She spoke before secularists, she spoke before
workers, she spoke before Unitarians. In a matter of weeks
in that autumn of 1874, a reprint of one of her lectures sold
7,000 copies. Leaving Mabel with a great-aunt, she spoke in
Durham, she spoke in Liverpool, she spoke in Glasgow.
Travelling alone, she slept in miners' cottages, frigid railcars,
and temperance hotels. Most audiences cheered; at times
they froze her out. In Aberdeen, she walked up the aisle
through a hostile hall, hearing only the sound of her boot
heels as she ascended the platform. 'In grim silence they listened,' she recalled. 'I could not move them; they were
granite-like in their own granite city, and I felt I would like to
take off my head and throw it at them, if only to break that
hard wall.' She was quick on her feet. When a heckler interrupted her, she 'made a quick retort, there was a burst of
cheering, and the granite vanished. Never after that did I have
to complain about the coldness of an Aberdeen audience.'[1]

After seeing her speak, one admirer wrote:

She still seems incomparably young and attractive, her face
alive with emotion and expression, her voice full and sonor-
ous, but musical and not unfeminine. She was perhaps too

uniformly earnest and indignant in her denunciation of bigotry, rarely indulging in wit. She was, or we thought she was, a martyr; she had won freedom from domestic and clerical oppression at the cost of social proscription . . . We young men, who had the passion of these things in our souls, responded readily to the passion with which she pleaded for them. We were carried away.[2]

He bought a copy of her portrait, on sale in the lobby. The National Secular Society produced two of these cabinet photographs. With her pinned-up chestnut locks, and her chin and gaze lifted towards heaven, Annie looked to be emulating the saint-depicting prayer cards she had collected as a girl. Her large portrait, 'fit for framing', cost two shillings; a small one, two pence. Yet Besant's first tours still lost money. After one eight-day circuit through the cold, coal-stained north, she returned home with 11 shillings less than when she started. However, Annie wrote, 'The labour had in it a joy that outpaid all, and the feeling that I found my work in the world gave a new happiness to life.'[3]

Her star rose as Charles Bradlaugh's seemed to stall. That autumn, his third attempt to represent Northampton in the House of Commons added only 100 votes to his previous total. His opponents had tarred him with the brush of abandoning his family; in truth, he remained tight-lipped about his estranged wife Susannah's descent into dipsomania. A Tory lawyer won the seat, instead. (That November, another Tory MP, Lord Randolph Churchill, who we will later see obstructing Bradlaugh's place in Parliament, toasted the arrival of his first child: a boy, born in Blenheim Palace, named Winston.)

Even as Victoria continued her cloistered vigil for Albert, dead for 13 years – 'Alone, alone, as it will ever be,' she wrote on her birthday (although her loyal servant John Brown carried her on his shoulders through wet grass, and had defended her against a seventh assassination attempt, this one by an Irish revolutionary who had scaled the fence of Buckingham Palace) – the platform of the new Conservative government was essentially Queen, Church and Empire.[4]

The prime minister, Benjamin Disraeli, attempted to rouse Victoria back into public life, with grand and legally questionable gestures that included orchestrating Britain's purchase of the Suez Canal. 'It is just settled,' he triumphantly wrote to his queen. 'You have it, Madam.'[5] Her Majesty was impressed, noting that Disraeli held 'very large ideas and very lofty views of the position the country should hold'.[6] After an Audience, the prime minister wrote to a friend, 'I really thought she was going to embrace me. She was wreathed with smiles, and, as she tattled, glided about the room like a bird.'[7] Soon Victoria would reign over a quarter of the globe.

Outside the palace, the acceptance that greeted the barefaced integrity of Annie Besant's speaking tours evinced the change, though slight, of British ideas towards the positions women could hold, and how they could be portrayed. In 1858, the year Annie turned 11, John Ruskin had felt compelled to destroy the scores of erotic nudes he discovered while cataloguing JMW Turner's work. In truth, he saved the art; it was a feint to protect Turner's reputation. The current generation of English painters would not be so chaste. In his Chelsea studio, Dante Gabriel Rossetti painted a series of sensual ripe-mouthed models that reached its apotheosis in 1874's *Proserpine*, depicting Jane Morris – then married to the textile designer and future Annie ally, William Morris – suggestively caressing a ripe pomegranate whose copious seeds she's ingested.

Rossetti and Morris seemed to be having a laugh over the

taboo of oral sex, one that even the erotic, anonymous Victorian memoir *My Secret Life* omitted from its otherwise exhaustive catalogue of crevice combinations. Anathema to the Church for being non-procreative and to secular moralists for its same-sex possibilities and portability outside the marriage bed – on shadowy street corners and fog-shrouded canal paths – Victorians associated fellatio with prostitution.[8]

Uniquely for her time, Annie Besant dared to speak publicly about the world's oldest profession, chiding those who paid for sex. 'When men of the world angrily object to women touching a subject,' she told an audience, 'they should remember that if they really respected the modesty and purity of women no such subject would be in existence.' She also attacked the Contagious Diseases Act of 1869, which permitted police officers to arrest women they suspected of being prostitutes, and subject them to a physical exam to check for venereal disease. Those who refused faced six months in prison. In an intimation of the battle over birth control to come, Besant asserted 'the sacredness of the individual liberty of women . . . [and] the inalienable rights of each over her own person'.

The law did not force the examination of men. 'A free woman,' Annie continued, 'is deprived by force of the custody of her own body – and for what? In order that men may more safely degrade her in the future, and may use her for their own amusement with less danger to themselves.'

Besant also empathetically challenged the prevailing wisdom that prostitutes turned to the trade because they were wicked sinners. 'Men are immoral for their amusement,' she stressed, 'women are immoral for bread. Ladies in the upper classes have no conception of the stress of agony that drives many a forlorn girl "on the streets".' The classified pages of *The*

Times may have been filled with ads seeking governesses skilled in music, French, German and drawing, but the earning opportunities for most Victorian women were limited to housekeeping, markets and textile factories. If the rich, Annie continued, 'would try what life is like when it consists of making shirts at three halfpence each (cotton not provided) and starving on the money earned, they would perhaps learn to speak more gently of "those horrid women"'.

Rather than clutching one's pearls at the prevalence of prostitution, Annie argued that women must be permitted to work the same jobs as men, at equal pay. 'Women will cease to sell their bodies,' she contended, 'when they are able to sell their labour.'

She concluded by attacking the inequity of societal scorn, which tarred only women as fallen. 'Her seducer passes unrebuked,' Annie noted, 'and in the families where she would not be admitted as a scullery-maid he is welcomed as fit husband for the daughter of the house. That which has ruined her and many others is only being "a little wild" in the circles where he moves . . . We ask for justice equal to both sexes.'[9]

The Contagious Diseases Acts would not be repealed until 1886. Here in 1874, a struggling Thomas Hardy at last broke through with the publication of his fourth novel, *Far from the Madding Crowd*. The tale of a bad betrothal and 'ruined' woman does not follow the well-trod path of previously popular Victorian novels like *Ruth* and *Adam Bede*. Instead of dying, or being transported to Australia, Hardy's wilfully independent (and childless) heroine Bathsheba gets a happy ending, of sorts, by marrying a man she likes, more than loves. Although first published anonymously for fear of censure, the book's success purchased for Hardy a handsome townhouse on fashionable Wandsworth Common.

On the shoddier side of London, Charles Bradlaugh

remained in his cramped rented Whitechapel rooms. His *National Reformer* did what newspapers do: bleed money. To raise funds, he set off on another American speaking tour. If he had noticed that in the time since his last visit, the US government had banned the advertisement or mention of contraception in print, he did not say. But soon that zealotry would spur Annie Besant into action.

The Comstock Act of 1873 – named for a New York City anti-obscenity crusader – was the first legislation of its kind in the Western world, and a harbinger of Britain's own restrictions.

Like the Contagious Diseases Acts, Comstockery brooked no dissent, or logic. An editorial cartoon from the time shows Anthony Comstock before a judge, shouting at a startled lady, 'Your Honor, this woman gave birth to a naked baby!' But the law was no laughing matter: a woman could be arrested as a prostitute if a man said she was one; a newspaper ad for 'womb veils' (diaphragms) could land the editor and vendor in jail. Comstock would later drive at least one indicted woman, Ida Craddock, to suicide.

As a young man, Anthony Comstock had wrestled against lust. In his journal he admitted losing. 'The Devil had full sway over me' was his passive explanation for masturbating. 'How sinful I am,' he wrote. 'I am the chief of sinners. Sin, that foe that is ever lurking.' [10] As New York's walrus-jowled answer to Inspector Javert, Comstock went on to create the Society for the Suppression of Vice. Its badge depicted him standing over a pile of burning books. One of Comstock's first acts was to brand obstetric medical texts obscene. Lucifer is cunning and takes unexpected forms.

Back in London, Annie Besant worked alongside the editor Charles Watts to keep the *National Reformer* afloat, all while caring for five-year-old Mabel. Mother and daughter moved to a rented flat on Westbourne Terrace, nearly adjacent to Paddington station, to shorten her commute to the office. She continued to lecture – one progressive reporter observed that coverage of her talks 'enlarge somewhat too much upon the personal appearance and attire of the lady. We do not want to know so much how a lecturer dresses, as how she speaks.'[11]

She had also begun to sing. To raise money for the NSS, Annie compiled and edited the one-shilling *Secular Song and Hymn Book* to sell at her talks. London was then the centre of piano manufacturing, and most middle-class homes had or aspired to own one.[12] (Victorians did not, as legend has it, cover the instrument's shapely legs out of modesty – only their own.)

For once, instead of being ahead of her time, Besant sounded very much of it. Ringing with promises of victory and glory, her hymns blended the spirituals she sang as a child with a trade unionist's oath to make heaven here on earth, as heard in the new left-wing anthem 'The Internationale'. This was an era when half of Britain's capital was owned by the wealthiest 0.01 per cent of the population (compared to about 10 per cent today).[13] One verse from Annie's anthems can stand for many:

> Freedom's voice no longer is dumb,
> To the sound of her trump we come;
> We are sworn to put tyranny down,
> We strike at the Throne and the Crown
> To arms! Republicans!
> Strike now for Liberty!
> March on: March on: Republicans!
> We march to victory.[14]

The lyrics made a sharp break with long-time popular Victorian sing-alongs that glorified patriotic domesticity, such as

'Home! Sweet Home!' whose chorus stridently proclaimed 'There's no place like home!'

Annie was spending less and less time in her own. In the spring of 1875, only six months after joining the National Secular Society, Besant – at Bradlaugh's urging – was elected by its members as one of two vice presidents, along with Charles Watts, who had loyally worked beside him since its founding nine years before. Her popularity, and looks that rivalled the celebrated London stage actress Lillie Langtry, rankled other passed-over old-timers.

Jealous colleagues called Annie the queen consort. They credited her rise to her closeness to Bradlaugh, just as Langtry's achievements had been diminished by rumours – later proven in court to be untrue – that her success resulted from an affair with William Gladstone. In matters of the heart and home, freethinkers could be just as traditional and censorious as the Establishment.

Charles Bradlaugh, whose temperament bent towards the law, did not dignify the tutting with a reply; Annie Besant, always pursuing justice, wrote one. Her printed output began its inexorable slide towards quantity over quality with her biography – her seventh pamphlet published in just six months – of the French philosopher Auguste Comte, a free-thinking friend of John Stuart Mill. The atheist Annie was drawn to the late Frenchman's theory of positivism, which favoured tangible evidence over airy metaphysics.

She more admired aspects of Comte's personal life, includ-ing his incompatible marriage. 'He appears to have been enthusiastic,' Besant wrote (without proof), 'with passionate and strong affections, and a most tender and faithful heart.' Like someone else her reader might know, he also had a 'grand and loving brow'.

Comte left his mismatched marriage to live with a Catholic

woman who could not divorce. Allegedly, this new relationship remained unconsummated. 'Those who are too base to believe,' Annie wrote, perhaps protesting too much, 'in a true and noble friendship between a man and woman will alone try to cast any slur on the frank and loyal love which bound those two great souls.' The new woman, Besant boasted, had been to Comte what Laura was to Petrarch, and Beatrice to Dante. Her 'friendship came as a revelation from heaven. It woke up all the music in his heart, silenced so long by care and toil and friendlessness . . . It revealed to him the beauty and grandeur of the human spirit.'

In case her envious critics missed her point, Annie underscored it by concluding, 'He loved her passionately, and yet most purely, with a deep, reverent, faithful love. She was to him the ideal of noble womanhood.'[15] Mrs Besant and Mr Bradlaugh formed a formidable pair.

In London, they admired musters of peacocks perched above sooty sheep in the royal parks, rode in hansoms that slowly navigated traffic currents like harnessed gondolas, and rambled along the Thames towpath to Kew Gardens for lunches of watercress sandwiches and tea. In the river's eddies, he taught her to fish for carp. At nearly one foot taller, his shadow would have cast further, and subsumed her own. But in conversation, as in life, Bradlaugh treated Besant as a peer. 'Where we differed,' she wrote, 'he never tried to override my judgement, nor force on me his views; we discussed all points of difference as equal friends.'

The twin Libras – with birthdays only five days apart – called each other A.B. and C.B. (Hear the shared second letter, a union of two b's in lieu of a marriage not to be.) 'All the brightness of my stormy life,' she recounted, 'came to me through him, from his tender thoughtfulness, his ever-ready sympathy, his generous love. He was the most unselfish man I ever knew, and as patient as he was strong.'[16] As she hated their smell, he abruptly gave up cigarettes.

That she could stand living in the Big Smoke evinces Besant's fortitude and forgiving love of her filthy hometown. Ash dusted the parks' plane and lime trees and stained hands that went ungloved. Within hours, white linen turned into the colour of dishwater; no wonder most Victorians favoured black clothing. (At the Duke of Wellington's funeral, the respectful lifting of so many hats made it appear that a large flock of crows had risen at once.[17]) After leaving Dorset's open heathlands, a young Thomas Hardy described for his sister how columns of smoke from kitchen chimneys gave London its peculiar smell, and turned 'everything visible the colour of brown paper or pea-soup'.[18] *Dickens's Dictionary* warned that 'Nothing could be more deleterious to the lungs and the air-passages than the wholesale inhalation of the foul air and floating carbon which, combined, form a London fog.'[19] The guidebook also listed 32 bathhouses, where for sixpence a Londoner could rinse this sooty film from their skin with hot water. A cold bath cost two.

Arriving together around this time, the French poets Arthur Rimbaud and Paul Verlaine discovered London to resemble a ruthless machine. Its pandemonium of carriages, cabs, omnibuses, trams and trains loudly rushed inhabitants through an eternal twilight of soot and steam. 'Imagine,' Rimbaud wrote, 'a setting sun seen through grey crêpe.'[20] (No wonder Claude Monet loved painting the city.) In April 1875 *The Times* began publishing the world's first daily weather map. Over London it printed the word DULL.

Annie Besant and Charles Bradlaugh enlivened auditoriums

in the capital and across Britain. In Brighton, town councillors called her a 'foul woman' and were incredulous that 'such an animal as Mrs. Besant' was allowed to speak at the town hall. An Essex newspaper called Bradlaugh a skunk, and excoriated 'that bestial man and woman who go about earning a livelihood by corrupting the young of England'.[21] Men swore and kicked at Besant in Hoyland, 'and the attempts to overturn the cab,' she recorded, 'were foiled by the driver, who put his horse at a gallop'. In Darwen, they were stoned with sharp flints.

In Congleton, they stayed with their fellow heretic Elizabeth Wolstenholme-Elmy, Britain's first full-time lobbyist for suffragism. Foreshadowing the shunning of Annie for her support of contraception, Christian suffragists excommunicated Wolstenholme-Elmy after she gave birth, at age 40, out of wedlock.

Wolstenholme-Elmy lived openly in Congleton with the father of her child, but to Besant the town proved less than welcoming. 'Mr. Bradlaugh,' she vividly related, 'lectured on the first evening to an accompaniment of broken windows.'

As Annie stood in the audience, a rock struck the back of her head. After the talk, 'we had a mile and a half to walk from the hall to the house, and were accompanied all the way by a stone-throwing crowd, who sang hymns at the tops of their voices, with interludes of curses and foul words'. The following night, as she lectured, the mob called for a brawny brawler to 'Put her out! Put her out! Put her out!'

Rising to his full height, Charles Bradlaugh bellowed 'Put me out!', threw the strongman to the floor, and frog-marched him out the door. Then he calmly looked up to Annie on the stage and urged her, 'Go on.' 'There was plenty more stone-throwing outside,' she recorded, 'and Mrs. Elmy received a cut on the temple, but no serious harm was done – except to Christianity.'[22]

The *York Herald* suggested that the speakers should raise ticket prices 'if the audience are to be entertained with a lecture and a battle on the same night'.[23]

The violence angered Annie less than the Christian heckler in Leicester, who charged her and Bradlaugh with writing *The Elements of Social Science*, the anonymously authored 'Bible of the brothel' supporting birth control and prostitution, first published in 1855, the year Annie turned eight. 'Personally,' she responded, 'I cordially dislike a large part of it, but none the less I feel sure that the writer is an honest, good, and right meaning man.'

Her critic was more upset by the book's call for the abolition of marriage. Annie assured her audience that on this point she and Bradlaugh were 'conservative rather than revolutionary', and not advocates for free love.[24] A wedding, however, did not protect a woman's rights, nor her body. That required advocating for changes to the law, by breaking the taboo of speaking publicly about the limits of life as a wife. Encounters with her misinformed accusers inspired her most passionate pamphlet, titled 'Marriage, As It Was, As It Is, and As It Should Be: A Plea for Reform'.

Queen Victoria may have once gushed in a letter, 'YOU CANNOT IMAGINE HOW DELIGHTFUL IT IS TO BE MARRIED. I COULD NOT HAVE DREAMED THAT ANYONE COULD BE SO HAPPY IN THIS WORLD AS I AM', but to Annie the institution had meant years of being taken advantage of sexually, and overlooked intellectually.[25] She did not want readers to shake their heads and say that the situation was unbelievable. What was unbelievable was that women such as herself still were not being believed. For the first time, she underlined each of her claims by citing the statutes that made wives subservient to their husbands.

'A married woman loses control of her own body,' Besant explained. 'It belongs to her owner, not to herself; no force, no violence, on the husband's part in conjugal relations is regarded as possible by the law; she may be suffering, ill, it matters not; force or constraint is recognised by the law as rape, in all cases save that of marriage; the law "holds it to be felony to force even a concubine or harlot," but no rape can be committed by a husband on a wife.'

She spoke from experience. 'The English marriage law sweeps away all the tenderness, all the grace, all the generosity of love, and transforms conjugal affection into hard and brutal right.'[26] It made marital sex an exercise of authority, instead of affection.

In this era's leading medical textbook, Dr William Acton assured his readers, 'I should say that the majority of women (happily for them) are not very much troubled with sexual feeling of any kind . . . love of home, children and domestic duties are the only passions they feel.' Doubling down, the doctor added, 'As a general rule, a modest woman seldom desires any sexual gratification for herself. She submits to her husband's embraces, but principally to gratify him; and, were it not for the desire of maternity, would far rather be relieved from his attentions.'[27]

Acton's views were typical of the time. What then was understood as male empowerment now reads like a terror of female sexuality and a woman's individual desires.

Annie Besant concluded her own printed appeal by hoping that future British couples could enjoy marriages built on a foundation of equality and respect, and the ability to remediate a mismatch, 'without injury to the character of either of those concerned in it'. Being allowed to remarry would also help to create 'worthy parents of the citizens of to-morrow'.[28]

In the summer of 1875, after the month-long visit stipulated by their separation agreement, her husband the Reverend Besant attempted to seize full custody of their daughter Mabel. The five-year-old had forgotten how to say her prayers; Annie had stopped enforcing that meal-and-bedtime ritual. In 1817, the poet Percy Bysshe Shelley had lost custody of his daughter due to his professed atheism. That same law remained on the books; if a court had once taken a child from a father over religion, then a mother stood little chance. Annie rushed by train to Sibsey, only to find that her husband had hidden their daughter in a home outside the vicarage. Lawyers were enjoined; Bradlaugh threatened brute force. Mabel was returned to her mother, for now. A humiliated Frank Besant hired a private detective to tail his recalcitrant wife.

※

Unbowed, Annie Besant and Charles Bradlaugh continued to court powerful enemies. Incensed by Victoria's squirrelling state funds from the Civil List to her private accounts, and Parliament's grant to the Prince of Wales of £142,000 (equivalent to £21 million today) for his trip to India, in the summer of 1875 Bradlaugh organised a demonstration in Hyde Park. The skies, for once, were surprisingly clear, and newsworthy. 'Though a large crowd assembled,' allowed *The Times*, 'the attendance was, for the day and weather, comparatively small.'

Bradlaugh declared that since the prince (the future King Edward VII) was not making a state visit, he should not be spending public funds. Instead, Prime Minister Disraeli, made Earl of Beaconsfield that month by Victoria, was allowing the queen's eldest son to indulge in the princely pastimes of 'lion and tiger hunting, pigsticking, and crocodile fishing'. Although, *The Times* reported, one audience member raised 'what he termed as a protest against the diabolical attempt of Mr. Bradlaugh to mislead the people of England,' his supporters howled the man down.[29]

In the winter of 1875, London's popular *Sporting Gazette* denounced 'Mrs. Besant, a clergyman's wife [and] new aspirant to popular favour' for her lecture against the monarchy. 'She wound up her attack . . . with the shriek of an inebriated Cassandra in these solemn and prophetic words: "The state of England at this moment is identical with that of the time of George II's death; the poor poorer, the rich richer, until the storm clouds which have been gathering so long will burst."' The correspondent concluded, 'It is clear that among the newly-asserted "rights of woman" must be numbered the right to spout blasphemous balderdash and seditious ribaldry.'[30]

Undaunted, Annie collected signatures for a petition against royal grants. 'The ever-lengthening roll lay in one corner of my sitting room,' she wrote, 'and assumed ever larger and larger proportions.' Eleven months later, in June 1876, Besant and Bradlaugh rolled 'the monster' on a mahogany pole, placed it in a carriage, and carried it to the House of Commons. Its first line proclaimed, 'The petition of the undersigned Charles Bradlaugh, Annie Besant, Charles Watts, and 102,934 others.' She claimed that the unrolled paper stretched nearly a mile long. *The Times* did not report the event. Annie recorded one nod from the *Newcastle Daily Chronicle*, appreciating her 'labour and enthusiasm'. But within the next year, the British press, including even the *Sporting Gazette*, would hang upon her every word.

※

By the summer of 1876, Annie had earned enough from lecturing and publishing to leave her cramped Bayswater rooms and return to her childhood neighbourhood of St John's Wood. On the border of Irish-settled Kilburn, she rented a handsome house in Mortimer Road (now Crescent), just west of Abbey Road. *Dickens's Dictionary of London* defined this quiet corner of London as 'much affected by the artist world'. *Winnie the Pooh* creator A.A. Milne will later live and attend school on Besant's quiet, leafy lane. After a Nazi air raid, George Orwell will dig the charred manuscript of *Animal Farm* out of the rubble of his own home, built where Annie's once stood, at number ten.[31]

She called her house Oatlands, perhaps after the Surrey palace built by Henry VIII for his fourth wife Anne of Cleves. (The queen had escaped the unconsummated marriage with an annulment, and generous settlement, comfortably outliving the king's other five wives.) The name carried another connotation, too. In the years before Annie had wed, the unhappy wife of the well-known poet George Meredith (whose confessional book of sonnets detailing the mutual pain of the dissolution of their ill-matched marriage, titled *Modern Love*, shocked Victorians upon its publication in 1862) chose to live independently in a cottage on the Oatlands grounds. After the separation, her husband forbade Mary Ellen Meredith from seeing their young son. She died of kidney failure, only 40 years old.[32]

Annie set about living the life denied to her as a wife at the vicarage. She hired a governess to care for Mabel and lined her study with books from floor to ceiling. She bought a piano, filled the conservatory with ferns and finches and rented her extra rooms to single and separated women who, like her not so long before, sought a foothold and a new life in the capital.

Charles Bradlaugh continued to teeter on the precipice of ruinous bankruptcy. In *David Copperfield*, the similarly compromised Mr Micawber believes, against all odds, that 'something will turn up'. Bradlaugh's fortunes also took a surprising turn: the rebellious brother of the author of the best-selling romance *Lorna Doone* left his secular hero a large bequest in his will. Henry Blackmore's family contested the gift, but the settlement still left Bradlaugh with what to him was the windfall of £2,500. 'We went straight from the Court to the office of his chief creditor,' Hypatia wrote. "That was only just in time, my daughter," he said, as we turned towards home.'[33]

The remaining funds allowed Bradlaugh to move up the property ladder, if only a few rungs. At 10 Portland Place he rented lodgings in a music shop that, rather inconveniently, granted him use of the top floor and basement, plus the lavatory on the first floor. (The new St John's Wood Library now occupies the site, at the renamed-and-numbered 20 Circus Road.)

Bradlaugh's 18-year-old daughter Hypatia moved in with him, but mostly only saw her father at breakfast. He had chosen the flat for its location. After breakfast, Charles usually picked up his books and legal papers and walked the mile to Oatlands. In the sunny study, A.B. and C.B. scribbled side by side, each alone in their writing, but never lonely.

It would be nice here to allow this pair an embrace, a kiss, more, but the existing evidence reveals no such intimacy. They moved in prescribed circumstances. Oatlands may have been large enough to shield prying eyes, but there were children, lodgers, visitors and a governess underfoot. Fashion also formed a formidable defence. In photos, Victorians – including the queen, buried under bolts of black bombazine – look more upholstered than clothed. A middle-class woman like Annie Besant often buttoned, hooked and laced herself into a dress, petticoat, camisole, corset, chemise and stockings with garters. Men also draped themselves in heavy fabrics: worsted wool and flannels, moleskin and gaberdine. The phrases *the burdens of the past* and *the weight of history* could also describe the mummifying Victorian wardrobe.

Thomas Paine may have coined the term 'double standard' to describe the stricter morals and laws that society applied to women, but it was the Victorians, starting with the anti-Contagious Diseases Acts campaigner Josephine Butler, who popularised its use.[34] Even if Annie Besant no longer feared eternal damnation, she was rightfully terrified of British law. If her husband's detective found evidence of adultery, Mabel would be taken from her forever.

The dead are not us; we may know how their stories end, but we cannot know all the details of how they got there. Annie will leave behind no commonplace book, or diary. She will burn her letters from Bradlaugh, just as her notes to him will be consigned to the flames by Hypatia, following the instructions in his will.

Their mutual affection, however, was no secret. In a rare surviving letter, Bradlaugh challenged a jealous colleague, 'Does it not occur to you that if you try to make my love for her a weapon against me you must expect some indignant rebukes? Never insinuate against us again – if you want to do your very worst say that I love her very dearly and esteem her very highly, and hope the day may yet come when I may have the right to share with her my home and give her the protection of my arm.'[35]

On another scrap of paper that remains, Annie let slip that 'Mr. Bradlaugh and myself are engaged to be married'. When word got back to Hypatia, she confronted Mrs Besant, who admitted that while it 'was not true now, she hoped it would be true!'[36]

Although Frank Besant's snooping detective never found the proof he was paid to find, Annie could not bury the evidence completely. She did feel romantic love, and was certainly no 'little prig', as she described her teenage self.[37] From the creamy, papery depths of Victorian archives we will later discover an ill-fated affair, followed by her amorous confessions to another married man. (He will, alas, go down with the *Titanic*.)

In her public life, Besant stayed circumspect about these doomed entanglements, and her tenderness for anyone – but one. Bradlaugh, she wrote, had 'the largest public following of any man since Gladstone,' who 'passionately supported him in politics; miners, cutlers, weavers, spinners, shoemakers, operatives of every trade, strong, sturdy, self-reliant men who loved him to the last'. She did not add herself to the list. She did not need to. Everyone knew.

It did not stop them from whispering. There is no gossip more believable than sexual gossip, because it always seems conceivable.[38] Wags called her a 'mollisher', a 'bobtail' and a 'brass flute' – Cockney rhyming slang for *prostitute*. In the *National Reformer*, Annie felt compelled to tell readers that she destroyed all anonymous letters unread, and considered 'advice from a stranger as a piece of impertinence'.

If people were going to put her name in their mouths, they at least ought to pronounce it correctly. Her estranged

husband's family stressed their surname's second syllable –
Be-SANT, sounding like *can't*. But Annie was ditching that
convention, and making the moniker her own.

'Accent on first syllable,' she now instructed her readers.
'Rhymes with *pleasant*.'[39]

The year 1876 delivered wider progressive change. In the
United States, the first trans-continental train completed the
three-day journey from New York City to San Francisco.
Alexander Graham Bell made the first call on his invention
the telephone, texting with his voice, 'Mr Watson, come here,
I want to see you.' Thomas Edison received a patent for his
mimeograph machine. In Pittsburgh, Henry J. Heinz produced his first bottle of ketchup, and began perfecting
the assembly line that would revolutionise production (and
fill British shelves with tins of baked beans). In Germany,
engineer Nicolaus Otto patented the four-stroke internal
combustion engine, soon to be ubiquitous under the hoods
of future automobiles, diesel trains and light aircraft. In the
United Kingdom, the Medical Act of 1876 for the first time
permitted British authorities to grant licences to all qualified
physicians, regardless of gender. Dr Elizabeth Garrett Anderson (Millicent Fawcett's sister) was one of three female
doctors – and the only ones listed in *Dickens's Dictionary* for
all of London – staffing Marylebone Road's New Hospital
for Women, which she founded to provide medical care for
indigent ladies.

Yet 1876 also marked a regression, though even Annie
Besant didn't see it at the time.

On 8 December, Bristol police arrested the bookseller
Henry Cook for selling the American birth control booklet

Fruits of Philosophy. The edition's title page bore the name of the *National Reformer* publisher Charles Watts, who had purchased the plates years before and printed it alongside dozens of National Secular Society pamphlets.

Unbeknownst to the London-based Watts, Henry Cook had previously served two years in prison for selling pornography from under his shop's counter. Between the pages of Knowlton's plain text, Cook had inserted images from his old trade that illustrated the doctor's explanations of human anatomy and recommendations for safely preventing pregnancy.

On 14 December, Annie Besant arrived at the *National Reformer*'s smart new Fleet Street office – located opposite one of Charles Dickens's favourite pubs, Ye Olde Cheshire Cheese – to find a nervous Charles Watts. Upon hearing of the Bristol arrest, he had telegraphed to Cook, 'Fear not, nothing can come of it.' But until now, Watts had never actually read the pages that he printed.[40]

Handing a copy of *Fruits of Philosophy* to Besant, he asked her opinion. She read it on the train en route to a lecture. The pamphlet advocated parental responsibility, and the restriction of family size within the means of its existence. While the 1830s American medical English lacked her narrative style, Annie concluded that she would have been proud to author such a work.

Unlike the Victorian Dr Acton – then instructing England that masturbation led to blindness – the American Dr Knowlton wrote about sex as a natural enterprise, and nothing to be ashamed of. Nor should it be limited to the purpose of procreation. 'A temperate gratification,' Knowlton wrote, 'promotes the secretions, and the appetite for food; calms the restless passions; induces pleasant sleep; awakens social feeling, and adds a zest to life which makes one conscious that life is worth preserving.'[41]

From the train station, Annie telegraphed Watts, 'Book defensible as medical work.'[42]

Charles Bradlaugh, on the other hand, felt it was indictable. He claimed that in the past he had urged Watts to pull the title from the press. Now that the horses had bolted, Bradlaugh instructed his long-serving co-worker to appear in Bristol and admit to the magistrates that he was the pamphlet's publisher. The hearing did not go well.

Charles Watts gave the court 13 copies of the book. Embarrassed when select passages were read aloud, he denounced the pamphlet's 'vile purpose', and withdrew his support for the arrested bookseller. After Boxing Day, Henry Cook would be sentenced to two years of hard labour.

Before returning to London, Watts promised a judge that he would cease to print *Fruits of Philosophy*. The matter seemed closed. The incident barely made a ripple in the great paper ocean of Victorian newspapers.

As the calendar turned to 1877, the biggest British story emanated from overseas. 'Often to-day,' *The Times* reported on 1 January, 'will England turn her eyes toward that far East with which her destinies have been so mysteriously associated. At the length of one continent she sees an [Ottoman] Empire writhing in what may be its last agony; near the length of another she sees the inauguration of a new Empire, and that her own.' On 2 January, readers learned that in the Raj, 'Queen Victoria was proclaimed Empress of India with all the pomp of Eastern state'. The occasion's official portrait shows her seated on the ivory throne, wearing, in a brooch, the 105-carat Koh-i-Noor diamond. The gem's name, Mountain of Light, belied the 56-year-old monarch's careworn appearance.

In her diary, the queen wrestled over the so-called Great Eastern Crisis threatening to draw Britain into a war with

Russia. The Liberal MP William Gladstone, who had been her least favourite PM, drummed up domestic outrage by writing a pamphlet detailing retributive Turkish killings of Christian Ottoman subjects. In the three months since its publication, *The Bulgarian Horrors and the Question of the East* had sold 200,000 copies. Prime Minister Benjamin Disraeli, who rightly feared that Russia would use the conflict as a pretence to reclaim territory lost to the Ottoman–UK alliance in the Crimean War, called Gladstone's pamphlet the work of an 'unprincipled maniac', and 'perhaps the greatest . . . of all the Bulgarian horrors'.[43]

In an intimation of the invective soon to be hurled at Annie Besant, one political insider warned that he saw the beginning of 'an outbreak of pseudo-Christian John Bullism . . . I know of no more contemptible or disgusting spectacle in the world than excited Britons, headed by idiotic Bishops, roaring.'[44]

The queen was not so sure. For the first time since Albert's 1861 death, she agreed to open Parliament, showing support for Disraeli's 'imperial policy' of threatening war, rather than waging it. Privately, however, she complained that it was 'a miserable thing to be a constitutional Queen, and to be unable to do what is right'.[45]

Meanwhile, news of the publisher Charles Watts's impunity made its way back to London. On 8 January 1877, police arrested him without warning in Fleet Street. He was arraigned at Guildhall for publishing an obscene book, released on bail and committed for a February trial at the Old Bailey.

Understandably, Watts panicked. Charles Bradlaugh promised to hire a skilled lawyer, with the aim of convincing a grand jury to return a 'no bill', or recommendation to drop the indictment. 'The case is looking rather serious,' Bradlaugh admitted to Watts, 'but we must face it. I would the prosecution had been against any other book, for this one places me in a very awkward position.'[46]

At Oatlands, Annie Besant argued with both men that the case absolutely must go to trial, as the publicity would shine a needed light on a woman's right to sex education and the power to make decisions about her own body and health. Knowlton's *Fruits* might be bruised, but it was all they had.[47] At length, both men finally agreed with her, even if they remained unenthused. 'I have the right and the duty,' Bradlaugh said, 'to refuse to associate my name with a submission which is utterly repugnant to my nature and inconsistent with my whole career.' However, 'The struggle for a free press has been one of the marks of the Freethought party throughout its history, and as long as the Party permits me to hold its flag, I will never voluntarily lower it.'[48]

Galvanised, Annie organised a defence fund, collecting over £8 at a talk that weekend in Plymouth. Concurrently, Charles Watts had a change of heart. He was switching his plea to Guilty, and planned to throw himself at the mercy of the Central Criminal Court.

Bradlaugh called him a coward, and, after 15 years of working and campaigning together, fired him from the *National Reformer.* The two would engage in an exchange of public recriminations that forced freethinkers to choose a side, threatening the National Secular Society's very existence. Many members, including Charles Watts's wife, Kate, cast Annie as the femme fatale behind it all. 'No sooner was Mrs. Besant assured of my father's loving friendship,' an angry Hypatia wrote, 'than she estranged him from his old friends, treating them carelessly and even contemptuously.'[49]

Annie learned of this turn of events, and faces, upon her return to London. She surprised even Charles Bradlaugh with her resolve. She had been prepared, she wrote, to stand by her colleague Watts in battle, 'but not in surrender'. She returned the donations to her Plymouth brethren, read *Fruits of Philosophy* once again, and planned on a course of action that no British woman had ever undertaken before.

Sharing the same roof as the notorious Newgate Prison, the stone blockhouse of the Old Bailey squatted stolidly in the centre of the City of London. (A fire would later occasion the rebuild into its current, taller – but no less imposing – form.) The courthouse was a five-minute walk from the *National Reformer* office, via Limeburner Lane. In the 5 February 1877 volume of its proceedings, under the heading Sexual Offences, a clerk's hand recorded:

CHARLES WATTS (41), PLEADED GUILTY to unlawfully printing and publishing thirteen indecent and obscene books – *To appear and receive judgment when called upon.*[50]

In the end, his admission brought the leniency he hoped for. No jail time, and a steep £25 fine, for costs. His reputation would take years to recover. In the court's permanent records, Watts's name appears alongside the bigamist Edward Longdon (Nine Months' Imprisonment), the horse thief Joseph Gibson (Twelve Months), the pickpocket Nathaniel Brown (Twelve Months and Twenty Lashes), the shilling counterfeiter Charles Town (Eighteen Months), the recidivist armed robber George Cavanagh (Six Years' Penal Servitude) and the murderer Frederick Treadaway (Hanging).

The view of London from the Old Bailey bench showed a city rife with larceny (of cigars, napkins and curtains), rackets on land and swindles at sea. A crook named Charles Baker managed to be convicted for fraudulently obtaining a book detailing one of the era's biggest frauds: the butcher-turned-confidence-man Arthur Orton's attempt to claim the Tichborne baronetcy and fortune. Baker went up for 12 months; Orton necked 14 years.

Victorian decorum did not stop a 15-year-old servant, Clara Parsons, from stealing earrings from her employer, or the labourer William Rose from pilfering an entire ship at the Victoria Docks. For his second offence, he was sentenced to 18 months. Frederick Clement got five years of hard labour for 'unlawfully conspiring, with other persons unknown, to obtain two sheep'.

The punishments for crimes against property were far more severe than the sentences of men who harmed women and children. 'Magistrates seem to have a specially soft corner in their hearts for wife beaters,' Annie observed in the *National Reformer*.

In the same court session, the ten-year-old son of the murdered Elizabeth Wren testified that he saw his father 'hit her on the side of her face with the palm of his hand, and she fell down against the door. I never saw her alive again.' Mr Wren almost got away with it, until the court realised he had previously been convicted of assaulting his wife. The judge sentenced him to two years in prison. That was five years fewer than the young man found guilty, for the second time, of pickpocketing a watch and its chain.

A man named Charles Clarke was tried for the abuse and rape of Ellen Annie Hayes. She was six years old. Clarke received the same sentence as a man convicted of kicking a dog and brawling with its owner: 18 months' imprisonment.

In the *National Reformer*, Annie recounted how a man who struck his wife in bed, chased her into the street and thrashed her unmercifully was released and told to keep the peace for 12 months. 'Yet people wonder why wife-beating is so common in England,' she wrote. 'One could almost wish that wife-beaters would transfer their attentions to the magistrates, and perhaps a little experience of their fists would ensure some kind of punishment being inflicted on them.'[51]

That February 1877, several women, all single and working as servants or maids, were charged with concealing their pregnancy. They were released without punishment with the warning to carry the child to term. Although in her diary Queen Victoria expressed empathy for abandoned pregnant women, and even spoke to her Lord Chancellor about 'changes in capital punishment, such as not sentencing unfortunate women to be hanged for infanticide, so often caused by despair', that law remained on the books.[52] A conviction, however, required proof that the newborn had been the victim of purposeful neglect, and not a mere casualty of Victorian poverty.

In the same session that Charles Watts pled guilty to publishing a birth control pamphlet, a lame boy named Charles Albert admitted to stealing a pair of boots 'out of necessity'. Sentence: 12 months. The 23-year-old Charlotte Silvester Wilsmore was tried for 'feloniously wounding her daughter with intent to murder'. A friend testified that after the unwed servant had given birth in the Lewisham workhouse, she said she would mail her illegitimate baby in a box to an adoptive family in Suffolk. Wilsmore's friend talked her out of that madness, but did not tell the police. Three months later, they were summoned when a surgeon extracted a sewing needle that had been fully inserted between the infant's ribs. The baby's convulsive screaming had forced the needle's eyehole above the skin, allowing the doctor to grasp it. After the child was returned to his surgery in distress two days later, he suspected its mother had attempted to overdose it with morphine. But he had no proof. Verdict: Not Guilty.

We cannot know if justice was served, only that mother and daughter never appear in the court record again. Perhaps they found assistance at the Pimlico home aiding 'servants fallen for the first time'. It was one of the nearly 900 charities listed in *Dickens's Dictionary of London*. Many cared for orphans and children with improvident parents.

Charles Dickens's portrayals of London's destitute children were grounded in fact. Like David Copperfield, as a 12-year-old with parents in debtor's prison he had worked in a boot polish factory beside the Thames. In adulthood he supported Britain's first children's charity, the Foundling Hospital, by renting a pew in its chapel to hear its orphan's choir sing on Sundays. While living a short walk away, on Bloomsbury's Doughty Street (today his museum), Dickens dreamed up *Oliver Twist*.

In the Docklands and East End, Annie Besant continually encountered real-life Olivers. Like Queen Victoria, she would not have disbelieved the desperate acts of cruelty that a forsaken woman could inflict upon her child. (In a questionable attempt to ameliorate punishment, the Infanticide Act of 1922 will declare all new mothers to be potentially insane.) Nor would Annie have been surprised at the Old Bailey testimony by a neighbour of labourers who worked 60 hours each week. The couple's four children 'were glad to get crumbs when other people shook their tablecloths out at their door'. Their one-year-old boy should have been 20 pounds. Upon his death, he had weighed only eight. For their wilful neglect, his parents were sentenced to only 12 months in prison, the same length as the perjurer convicted in the case heard before them. The court did not say who would care for the children they were leaving behind.

Like her queen, Annie Besant keenly felt the injustice of this state of affairs. But unlike her monarch, she decided to do something about it.

To Charles Bradlaugh she proposed that they form their own publishing company, taking the *National Reformer* and all the National Secular Society's pamphlet plates away from the pigeon-hearted printer Charles Watts. That they had no experience in business did not deter Annie, who held that 'all things are possible to those who are resolute'. The pair cobbled together funds to rent a dilapidated shop on Stonecutter Street, a passage linking Shoe Lane to Farringdon Street. The shop was even closer to the Old Bailey than their old one. If her scheme went as planned, she would have a shorter walk to her trial.

By the end of February the partners had opened the Freethought Publishing Company. As he sniped at and attempted to scoop Charles Watts's new rival publication, the *Secular Review*, she directed her partner to a more important fight: printing an updated edition of the prosecuted *Fruits of Philosophy* and challenging Britain's obscenity law.

With his eye on standing a fourth time for Parliament, Charles Bradlaugh did not share Annie Besant's enthusiasm for martyrdom. He did not even like the book. With the Church and Crown arrayed against them, he doubted they could win. His mentor John Stuart Mill had observed that their age was one 'in which real belief in any religious doctrine is feeble and precarious, but the opinion of its necessity for moral and social purposes almost universal'.[53] They could be sentenced to prison. Her arrest alone would likely mean surrendering custody of Mabel to her hated husband.

Mrs Besant said she would publish the pamphlet herself. Her willingness to take on the Victorian Establishment was not a lark. It was a plunge.

✹

As a younger man, the 43-year-old Bradlaugh's spirit had been grooved to run along the iron rails laid by radicals such as Carlile and Mill, who at the start of 1859's *On Liberty* defined his subject as 'the nature and limits of the power which can be legitimately exercised by society over the individual'. Mill presciently noted that this was 'a question seldom stated, and hardly ever discussed in general terms, but which . . . is likely soon to make itself recognized as the vital question of the future'.[54]

Annie Besant urged her friend to recognise that future was now.

As an idealistic teen, Bradlaugh had believed Emerson's promise that 'nothing can bring you peace but the triumph of principles'. Besant implored him to see Dr Knowlton's work as 'the symbol of a great principle, of the right to circulate physiological knowledge among the poor in pamphlets published at a price they could pay'.[55] The authorities had no right to stop its sale. If the country's best-known freethinkers refused to stand up to the government, who would? Dismissing the further erosion of civil liberties with a sigh and 'It might never happen, love' solved nothing. The time for self-reliance was at hand.

The apprentice had become the master. Readers of March's final edition of the *National Reformer* found the announcement, topping the page of advertisements for tailored trousers and Bordeaux burgundies, of a new edition of *Fruits of Philosophy*: 'The Pamphlet will be republished on

Saturday, March 24, with some additional Medical Notes by a London Doctor of Medicine. It will be on sale at 28 Stone-cutter Street after 4 p.m. until close of shop. Mr. Charles Bradlaugh and Mrs. Annie Besant will be in attendance from that hour, and will sell personally the first hundred copies.'[56]

On the day of the actual printing, Bradlaugh was in Scotland to give a talk. His daughter Hypatia described Annie's fear of a police raid and seizure of the stock before the sale. With her sister Alice's help, the women 'hid parcels of the pamphlet in every conceivable place. We buried some by night in [Annie's] garden, concealed some under the floor, and others behind the cistern. When my father came home again the process began of finding as quickly as possible these well-hidden treasures – some indeed so well hidden that they were not found till some time afterwards.'[57]

On the Saturday, Besant and Bradlaugh found a crowd waiting outside their printshop. In 20 minutes the first print run of 500 copies sold out. Despite her hand-delivery of the *National Reformer* to magistrates' post-boxes in Guildhall, the police never showed. Perhaps that weekend the men stood on the banks of the Thames between Putney and Mortlake. 'After one of the most gallantly contested struggles ever witnessed,' reported *The Times*, the Oxford and Cambridge Boat Race for the first time ended in a tie.[58]

The following day, a Sunday, Besant and Bradlaugh hand-sold 800 copies of Knowlton and mailed parcels of the pamphlet to fulfil orders across England and Scotland. Letters of support flowed in. The feminist journalist Florence Fenwick Miller admired Annie's noble stand against 'this attempt to keep the people in enforced ignorance upon the most important of subjects'. Miller included a donation for the defence fund she promised they would be needing. She wished she had 'fifty times as much to give'.[59]

A week passed, the Freethought press kept printing, and the *Fruits* kept spilling out the door. While Victoria fretted over telegrams about the Balkans ('So overwhelmed with work & interruptions of all kinds, that my head feels quite uncomfortable from it'), Annie Besant wondered why her own great game was not yet afoot.[60] Where were her pursuers? 'The Vice Society has plenty of spies and informers on its books,' she wrote. 'One wise sentence only will I recommend to that sapient body; it is from the cookery book of Mrs. Glasse, dealing with the cooking of hares—Men and brethren, "first, catch your hare." '[61]

Annie decided to help them. To the police she offered to be at Stonecutter Street daily from 10 to 11 a.m. At last, on April's first Thursday, she and Bradlaugh arrived to find 'three gentlemen regarding us affectionately'. They looked to her then 'as the unsubstantial shadow of a dream'.

The trio followed them into the shop. Detective Sergeant Robert Outram produced a search warrant. Bradlaugh said he could look around all he wanted; the last of the first print run of 5,000 copies had been sold the previous day. Outram nonetheless played his part as planned, placed the pair under arrest, and marched them down to Bridewell for booking.

If Annie Besant had any illusions that she would be treated differently than those arrested for street crimes, they were shattered when she was told to empty her pockets and hand over her purse, and was led by a matron into a cell to be searched.

'The woman was as civil as she could be,' she wrote, but 'it is extremely unpleasant to be handled, and on such a charge as that against myself a search was an absurdity.' Next, DS Outram put her and Bradlaugh in a hansom cab, to be arraigned at Guildhall.

Acting on pre-arranged instructions, Hypatia rushed home

taken on Oath this **fifth** *day of* **April** *in the year of our Lord* **One** *thousand Eight hundred and seventy-* **Seven** *at the Guildhall Justice-Room in the City of London, before the undersigned,* **One** *of the Aldermen of the City of London, sitting at the Guildhall Justice-Room aforesaid, being* **One** *of Her Majesty's Justices of the Peace in and for the said City and Liberties thereof, in the presence and hearing of* **Charles Bradlaugh and Annie Besant** *who* **are** *charged this day before* **me,** *for that* **they did on the 24th day of March last and on divers other days in the said City unlawfully sell & publish an obscene book — Against the peace &c**

Detective Sergeant Robert Outram's attestation of arrest

to fetch her father's volumes of William Russell's law text-book *A Treatise On Crimes and Misdemeanours*, and caught the next underground train back to the City. 'It was a warm morning,' she wrote.

> I was hot with running, and anxious, for I rather think that I had some sort of notion that "Russell" was a sort of golden key to unlock all legal difficulties. City men in the train, going to their ordinary business, looked at me rather curiously as I sat in the carriage closely hugging those three bulky red volumes (which would slip about on one another, for I had not stayed to tie them together) on criminal

procedure, of all things for a girl of nineteen to be carrying about with her on a sunny April morning.[62]

To Annie's surprise, she and Bradlaugh were led to the Guildhall basement. Descending those stairs today leads a visitor to a small museum displaying the ruins of the Roman amphitheatre. In 1877, stone-floored, whitewashed jail cells covered the artifact. In the dim gas light, Annie Besant had no idea that, as she added her own layer to London's long history, she was seated atop an ancient one.

For two and a half hours ('very dull,' she wrote, 'and very cold') she simmered as, in a neighbouring cell, 'Mr. Bradlaugh paced up and down his limited kingdom.' Together they listened to the names of prisoners being summoned, until theirs were the day's last names called to 'go up higher'.

Annie entered the dock, and measured up the magistrate. He appeared to her 'a nice, kindly old gentleman, robed in marvellous, but not uncomely garments of black velvet, purple, and dark fur'.[63] As the proceedings began, clerks handed her a succession of little tan envelopes holding telegrams from admirers, pledging their support.

A detective constable testified that on 24 March he had purchased a copy of *Fruits of Philosophy* from Annie Besant, who took his one shilling and returned sixpence change. 'Bradlaugh saw her take the money,' William Simmonds added matter-of-factly. (If he thought he had been a mere fragment of the day, with a role that was about to end, he miscalculated the watchful mind of the woman he had just identified.) 'I believe that a large amount of books,' the policeman concluded, 'are now kept upon those premises for the purpose of sale'.[64]

That suspicion was what compelled Detective Sergeant Robert Outram's visit to the shop on the day when the pamphlet's print run had already sold out. In the courtroom DS

Outram, too, had seemed kind, as she watched him find seats for Bradlaugh's daughters. Still, 'It amused me,' Annie wrote, 'to see the broad grin which ran round when the detective was asked whether he had executed the seizure warrant, and he answered sadly that there was "nothing to seize".' Bail was set for the next hearing, 'to which adjuration I only replied with a polite little bow'.

Walking into the waning spring sunlight, she was surprised to see a small crowd cheering. One voice called, 'Bravo! There's some of the old English spirit left yet!' The criminals had missed luncheon, and so set off to have a meal. Supporters straggled behind them like the tails of a soaring kite. Dining in the gathering dusk, Annie experienced the intoxicating thrill of reading about herself in the newspaper.

'The evening papers all contained reports of the proceedings,' she wrote with satisfaction, mentioning the *Daily Telegraph* and *Evening Standard*, 'as did also the papers of the following morning.'[65] They included, she especially noted, the hallowed *Times*, where her name – unlike the women in its birth announcements – appeared for the first time.

That night at the Royal Aquarium, Zazel would be shot from a cannon, but London's press had found a new celebrity. Victoria's favourite publication, the *Pall Mall Gazette*, placed news of Annie Besant's arrest – 'on a charge of publishing a book alleged to be immoral' – immediately after the lines detailing Her Majesty's daily engagements.[66] The queen's activities necessitated two lines of type. Annie's warranted 33.

No reporter anywhere, however, noticed that inside the courtroom the renowned orator had not uttered a single word. Like Zazel bravely climbing into the cannon's mouth, Annie may have been mute, but she knew what she was doing. The match had been struck and the fuse was fizzing brightly. She welcomed the coming explosion.

PART II

'THE QUEEN IS THE PROSECUTOR'

5

'OH, THEY ARE A STIFF-NECKED PEOPLE'

'At Guildhall,' *The Times* reported on 18 April, 'Charles Bradlaugh, publisher, and Mrs. Annie Besant, journalist, surrendered to their bail before Alderman Figgins, to answer the charge of publishing an obscene book . . . Long before the time arrived for commencing proceedings a crowd assembled in Guildhall-yard, and as many persons as the body of the court could hold were admitted. Among them were several ladies. Mr. Straight said he was instructed by the City Solicitor to put the case in such a form as would enable the Bench to send it to the Criminal Court.'

Douglas Straight, the 32-year-old prosecutor, was only three years older than Annie Besant. Although his dandyish dress and port-and-pheasant voice would suggest otherwise, the two were not entirely chalk and cheese. Neither acknowledged, or perhaps even knew, that they had both grown up in Harrow. Straight was all gown to Annie's town; his years attending the smart school overlapped with her brother's.

Like Besant, Straight was also an author who had published under a pseudonym, although the memoir of his schooldays celebrated, rather than criticised, the Establishment. To a modern reader, it sounds like a love letter to an abusive partner, pulsing with undercurrents of masochism, cruelty and suppressed sexuality. Harrow was a school of

Dandy Douglas Straight

hard words, and no end of violence. Two chapters are devoted to 'fagging', the system by which older boys commanded younger ones to do their bidding. 'By the time a boy is able to fag,' Straight wrote, 'he has had a fair drilling himself: he has learned the full value of kindness, consideration and courtesy in carrying it out.'[1] At Harrow he had also mastered the droll speaking style of the ruling class.

Straight put that skill to use first as a journalist, and then as a rather ineffective Conservative MP for Shrewsbury. As a Harrovian, he had been pushed down the school stairs by a 'cock' of the form. A master had seen the boy do it, and Straight 'had the pleasure of standing by and seeing him get one of the jolliest thrashings that ever fell to a bully's share . . . I need scarcely say that he did not trouble me with his attentions again.'[2] As an MP, Straight, who supported suffrage, introduced a bill that would have added whipping to sentences for brutal assaults on women or children. It died before reaching the floor.[3] The next year, he rose from the green leather banquette to defend the slew of social reform bills being introduced in the Commons, and backed one raising the age of consent from 12 to 14.[4] (It failed; not until 1875 would it be raised, to a compromise of 13.)

Douglas Straight's sharp mind and tongue better belonged in a courtroom, and as a lawyer he quickly became a bit of a London face. In 1870, he defended Thomas Boulton and Frederick Park, two young cross-dressers who had been arrested for attending the Strand Theatre, one sheathed in green satin and the other in a low-necked evening dress of white and crimson silk. After the pair had flirted with men and used the ladies' room, police charged them with the felony of 'the abominable crime of buggery'. Homosexuality was not then illegal; the crime was unprocreative sex.

One of the flaxen-wigged men, it turned out, lived as Lady Stella, 'wife' to a Tory MP who was the godson of then-Prime Minister Gladstone. In *The Queen v. Park* – or, as the London rags dubbed it, 'The Case of the Men in Petticoats' – the barrister Straight theatrically argued that while 'filthy imputations had been insinuated,' they could not be 'supported by one tittle of evidence'.[5]

In fact, the corroboration came in droves; Stella was a known sex worker, seen in theatres exposing herself, and unsubtly asking: 'Hello darling, do you fancy a blow job?'[6] As a sodomy conviction carried a maximum sentence of life with hard labour, the 25-year-old Straight cagily asked that the case be moved from the Old Bailey to a specially convened Court of Queen's Bench to be heard by the Lord Chief Justice, Alexander Cockburn. Opposing him was a rising Queen's Counsel named Hardinge Giffard.

Six short years later, these three men would face off against Annie Besant over birth control.

Back in 1871, Douglas Straight argued that no sodomite would brazenly walk down the Strand in a ballgown. Everyone knew that Victorian society concealed its sex. The special jury needed only 53 minutes to agree with him, delivering a verdict of Not Guilty, setting Boulton and Park free.

As a defender, Straight had played a leading role in gay and trans legal history. Now, in April 1877, he peacocked into the Guildhall courtroom in short wig, stiff collar, bands and black silks, game to prosecute the free press and the promotion of birth control. Besant – poorly depicted in a *Penny Illustrated Paper* drawing looking severe in a bonnet – found him charming. She paraphrased how, 'With extreme care and courtesy', Straight told the magistrate that he was not here to impart any acrimonious feeling into the prosecution. But, under the provisions of Lord Campbell's Act, as the Obscene Publications Act of 1857 was known, needs must.

Projecting his voice to the 'many hundreds [who] remained in the corridors of the Court of Common Pleas,' Douglas

'Mrs Besant' – 14 April 1877

Straight said the defendants' contention that they published and sold Charles Knowlton's pamphlet for the public good did not cleanse the work of its obscene character.[7] 'Mr. Straight said he would show that the book was indecent and unbecoming,' *The Times* reported. He cited pages 15, 16, 22, 24, 25, 26, 33, and the 'whole of chapters three and four'. He had flagged 19 of the booklet's 47 pages, comprising 40 per cent of its content.

Curious *Times* readers could follow along at home in their own copies of the pamphlet; the newspaper did not quote from the *Fruits*. Besant annotated her own copy as Straight told the court which pages were not fit for repetition in the presence of women. After Charles Bradlaugh refused to ask his two daughters to leave, the magistrate said he 'should not allow any extracts from the book to be read'.[8]

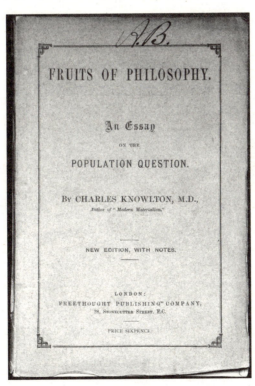

Annie Besant's annotated copy of the pamphlet she had published

Reporters in the courtroom from Birmingham and Belfast, Dundee and Derby, Gloucester and Glasgow, and Leicester, Leeds and Liverpool jotted furiously. Just as she had predicted, Annie Besant's insolence would saturate Great Britain. Joining the largest metropolitan dailies, small papers such as the *Ormskirk Advertiser* (Lancashire) and the *Todmorden & District News* (Yorkshire) ran the wire story, as did the *Y Gwyliedydd* (Wales), *North British Agriculturist* (Midlothian, Scotland) and *Northern Whig* (Antrim, Northern Ireland).

As its publisher, Annie Besant knew that the passages being branded obscene started after Dr Knowlton's description of the male and female anatomy. According to the Crown, explaining where babies came from was a prosecutable offence.

In the first batch of pages Douglas Straight deemed criminal, *Fruits of Philosophy* accurately described the process of menstruation and the properties of semen. Dr Knowlton also frankly discussed the female orgasm vis-à-vis conception, noting that 'Many females have conceived, if their unbiased testimony may be relied on, when they experienced no pleasure.'

The remaining sections that Straight called obscene correctly explained fertilisation. The prosecutor did not note that Charles Knowlton – and the Victorian physicians who updated his work – incorrectly maintained that a woman was most likely to become pregnant in the days bookending her period. Besant believed this mistake, too. Such was the state of women's medicine in a time when most of its practitioners were men.

Compared to what had come before, *Fruits of Philosophy* was a better book. But only just. In 1877 its science was already 45 years old, dating to an era that saw William IV on the throne, the Whigs in power and slavery still legal in most of the British Empire. Even the updated version still recommended, as a cure for impotence, swallowing 'one or two rising teaspoonfuls of cayenne'. That Elizabethan-sounding advice appeared in one of the two chapters that Douglas Straight found most offensive. Though, given London's prodigious boozing and profligate pollution, he may have also been shocked at Knowlton's suggestion to limit the intake of alcohol, and to increasingly 'exercise in the open air'.

Truly the doctor had no shame. He also sounded both progressive – recommending that the age of consent in women be raised to 17 or 18 – and lapsarian, cautioning men against masturbating, which 'not infrequently leads to insanity'.

Only three of the pamphlet's 47 pages taught the 'checking of conception'. Given the 100 million microscopic human cannonballs launched by male orgasm, Knowlton warned that relying only on the withdrawal method required 'sufficient care'. Condoms were then rare in western Massachusetts, where he practised, and so he recommended that women use a sponge.

For the first time in print, however, the doctor also suggested that after sex the woman could douche using a syringe filled with safe salts such as potassium carbonate, or a vegetable astringent made from white oak bark or red rose leaves. This spermicide 'destroys the fecundating property of the whole of it'.[9] To a Victorian male accustomed to primacy in society, home and bed, Knowlton's recommendation could read like a licence to murder his very masculinity.

For upper-crust Britain, however, the concept of checking pregnancy was not new. Physicians privately passed on information, and people swapped the secret. Had Queen Victoria (on this day at Osborne House, scribbling in her diary: 'Bad telegrams, – everything looking very warlike') been deposed as a witness for the defence, she might have been shown her

1858 letter to her eldest daughter. 'In a physical point of view,' she told the Princess Royal, 'and if you have hereafter (as I had constantly for the first 2 years of my marriage) – aches – and sufferings and miseries and plagues – which you must struggle against – and enjoyments etc. to give up – constant precautions to take, you will feel the yoke of a married woman!'

Whatever precautions Victoria and Albert had taken, they were not very effective. The queen conceived nine children. 'If one has a husband one worships,' she continued in her letter to her namesake,

> It is a foretaste of heaven. And if you have a husband who adores you, and is ready to meet every wish and desire of yours. I had 9 times for 8 months to bear with those above-named enemies and real misery (besides many duties) and I own it tried me sorely; one feels so pinned down – one's wings clipped – in fact, at the best (and few were or are better than I was) only half oneself – particularly the first and second time. This I call the 'shadow side' [of marriage] as much as being torn away from one's loved home, parents and brothers and sisters. And therefore – I think our sex a most unenviable one.[10]

Would owning a handbook such as Knowlton's not have helped Her Majesty, let alone her subjects? The doctor's recommended contraceptive method of douching cost next to nothing, required no sacrifice of pleasure, and was 'in the hands of the female'. It also helped prevent infection and disease. 'On the score of cleanliness and health alone,' he had advised his female patients, for whom the book was written, 'it is worth all the trouble.'

But the queen would, of course, never be summonsed to a courtroom. That week on the Isle of Wight, Victoria kept abreast of Russian sabre-rattling on the Continent via the daily anxious telegrams that kept arriving. In disgust, she exclaimed in her diary, 'What duplicity!'[11] Five days earlier, the United Kingdom, contravening its own treaty, had occupied Pretoria and annexed the South African Republic, a precursor of the First Boer War.

Swathed in layers of black and in this era looking, as one historian wrote, like 'a little old lady, potato-like in appearance', the 57-year-old queen took walks and counsel with the visiting Dean Stanley, of Westminster Abbey.[12] Likely unbeknownst to her, the priest had also been the favourite confidant of Annie Besant's mother. At the elderly woman's bedside, he had given Annie her last-ever Communion. That was less than three short years ago – but for Annie, a lifetime away.

Now she sat in the Guildhall courtroom, listening to learned Douglas Straight's convincing arguments against her. As he argued, she empathetically watched as Alderman Figgins 'devoted himself gallantly to the unwonted task of wading through physiological textbooks' – some 100, that Annie freely had purchased around London – 'the poor old gentleman's hair sometimes standing nearly on end'.

Charles Bradlaugh reminded the court that the test of obscenity was whether a work had been published exclusively with the intention of debauching and corrupting the minds of those who were open to such immoral influences. Such objective had not been proven, because it did not exist. 'If a razor were made use of to cut throats,' Bradlaugh argued, 'they would never think of prosecuting the cuttler for the crime of the murderer.' Did he know that Alderman Figgins's father had been a famous London printer (inventor of the fonts Arial and Helvetica), and so perhaps would be disinclined to prosecute a publisher? *The Times*, and Besant's notes, do not say.

If nothing else, the medical texts they stacked upon the bench exhausted the elderly judge. At four o'clock, he asked

Bradlaugh whether enough books had not been referred to. 'Mr. Bradlaugh,' one newspaper reported, 'said that would be the case if his Worship decided to dismiss the case.' The courtroom echoed with laughter.

'At the end of the day,' Annie Besant wrote, 'the effect made on him by the defence was shown by his letting us go free without bail.' The case was adjourned for two days, until Thursday. Ladies would not be permitted to attend. Alderman Figgins asked if Annie would like to withdraw her name from the proceedings by agreeing to his proposal to drop the charges against her. She refused. 'Mr. Bradlaugh,' a journalist recorded, 'said if committed for trial, Mrs. Besant would make her statement.'[13]

⁂

At Osborne House that same week, Victoria wrote in her diary that in her drawing room, 'a little theatrical performance took place'. There had been no attempt at scenery, just two chairs, a table, curtains and screens, plus footlights masked by flowers. Two actors played scenes from the comedies of manners *The Rivals* and *The School for Scandal*. A soloist also sang four songs, ending with one titled 'Women's Rights'.

It was not a rousing anthem, nor the sort of forbearing dirge that belonged in Annie Besant's hymnal. The tune was a farcical rejoinder to the suffrage movement, a cause that the queen did not support any more than she did birth control. One verse of 'Women's Rights' contended:

> 'Tis woman's right a home to have
> As perfect as can be,
> But not her right to make that home
> To every lover free.

The lyrics continued that it was a woman's right to rule the house, and petty troubles brave, but not her right to rule the head and treat him as her slave. The rhymes did not improve. It was a woman's right to claim respect from men of every grade, but not her right to walk around as master to each trade. The ditty climaxed with:

> 'Tis woman's right as wife to act
> Alone to Legislators,
> But not her right to mount the stand
> And speak as commentators.[14]

The world's most powerful woman, Queen of the United Kingdom of Great Britain and Ireland and Empress of India, very much enjoyed the performance. Victoria's diary entry that night concluded, 'How it brought back old times to mind!'[15]

At Guildhall on Thursday 19 April, 'There was a large number of spectators in court,' the *Manchester Evening News* reported, 'but to-day the ladies were conspicuous by their absence. There were no females present during the meeting.'

The journalist either did not attend the hearing, purposely omitted Annie, or considered her as something other than a woman. Moreover, Besant could not believe that the magistrate had told the Bradlaugh daughters to stay away. 'We know of no law which, in a Court of Justice, recognizes a difference of sex in the public admitted to the hearing of a case,' she wrote in the *National Reformer*. 'Ladies have the right and the duty to be present at a trial of this kind, where the discussion of which we are struggling is a question of vital importance to the female sex.'[16]

The session began with Alderman Figgins noting that many British newspapers had expressed the hope that his bench would send the defendants to prison with hard labour. Personally, he believed that *Fruits of Philosophy* was 'against the morals of the public', but whether it was obscene was a question that only a jury could answer. All he had to do was send the case for trial. Douglas Straight drew laughter from the men crowded into the gallery by interjecting that he was engaged the next week in another prosecution. 'It is a very long story,' he told the magistrate, 'but not so amusing as this.'[17]

For the defendants, this case was no laughing matter. Annie Besant rose from her seat. 'In a firm and clear voice,' *The Times* recorded, she read a prepared statement. 'While I may fairly ask from the court for its patient attention to the only remarks with which I shall have troubled the Bench during the hearing of this case,' she began, 'I am not without hopes that a grand jury may dismiss the indictment as containing a charge against us which it will be impossible to substantiate, and which, indeed, could never have been brought against us at all had the former publisher done his duty in defending the book he had issued.'

For 20 minutes she held the courtroom rapt, explaining why she had undertaken its publication, and invited arrest. 'There is, of course, much obscenity resting over the use of the word obscene,' she noted astutely. 'The plain, dry statement of physiological facts does not tend to produce lustful desires, and the perusal of a medical treatise does not throw a seductive charm over the sex opposite to that of the reader.'

Unlike other British newspapers, most of which omitted mention of Annie from their stories, *The Times* quoted her at length, and correctly. 'She took higher ground,' it reported, 'than any plea that cheapness of medical literature did not constitute obscenity. She urged that its price was an essential part of the value of the pamphlet in question. Medical knowledge, conveyed in long words, wrapped up in a foreign language, priced in gold, might be useful to members of the medical profession, but it was not useful to the people. Medical knowledge was wanted by the people, and ought to be put within their reach.'[18]

The Times did not, however, reproduce her rationale that followed. 'Lack of knowledge of simple facts concerning their own bodies,' Besant charged, sounding prosecutorial, 'throws many a young man and woman into the hands of quacks and charlatans, who live upon the ignorance of the poor.'

Annie likely did not know that 43 years earlier, Charles Knowlton himself had once tried the same defence, castigating 'Those who preach that a female's virtue is nothing but *fear*.' In court the doctor had also argued that if his jury would just 'read the whole book – and it is not a book to be read in part – and understood it . . . They must know that even in Massachusetts – at present as formerly witchcraft's best abiding place – it is no libel to publish the truth with a justifiable motive.'

In the end, Dr Knowlton had tried appealing to his jury's emotion. 'God knows that book was written with feelings of humanity – feelings that none but a physician could experience.'[19]

On the other side of the Atlantic, Annie enlarged her predecessor's perspective. 'There is another advantage in such publications as this,' she told her all-male courtroom, 'which, as a woman, I feel very strongly; most young and newly-married women would prefer learning such points, for instance, as the signs of pregnancy, from a book instead of from a male doctor, and thus one of the specially attacked portions of this books is one which is most valuable to women.'

Unique among Guildhall's plummy silks, whose impassive faces looked preserved in aspic, Annie had also seen first-hand in city slums and rural hovels 'how children are born but to die, and how women's health is sacrificed by constantly recurring child-bearing'. She was determined to spread know-ledge of an alternative, 'and for doing so stand committed for trial on a criminal charge'.[20]

'Mrs. Besant's statement,' wrote *The Times*, 'was followed by great applause, which could not be suppressed.'

Before releasing the defendants on bail, the judge com-mitted them for trial at the Old Bailey. 'However,' Annie wrote, 'we had not the smallest intention of going.'

❋

Forty-three years earlier, Dr Charles Knowlton had reflected on the aftermath of his own trials over *Fruits of Philosophy*. 'I may be very singular in my ideas of things,' he wrote in a pamphlet titled *A History of the Recent Excitement in Ashfield*, 'but I had thought that knowledge is better than ignorance; I had thought that a *physical truth*, in its general tendency, cannot be a *moral evil* . . . I had thought that the people of this coun-try were not under a priestly despotism – that the orthodox clergy had no right to become the *self-appointed censors of the American press!*'[21]

He had miscalculated. Twice, juries pronounced Knowl-ton guilty.

Up to this point in their own prosecution, the objectivity of the British press counted as surprisingly sympathetic to Annie Besant and her partner-in-crime, who already ranked as a rabble-rousing demon-figure.[22] Or were newspapers merely stuffing the pair up as strawmen to be tossed on an immolating bonfire of vilification?

Over 200 stories about the defendants ran across Britain that April. A few openly wished for their conviction. Annie wondered how many had read the charged book. In the *National Reformer* she told readers that the head of the *Halifax Times*, who had hoped for their strict sentencing, had written to her. 'This editor "presents his compliments," and "begs to be favoured with two copies of the work, for which fourteen stamps for books and postage are enclosed." Why does the editor want to possess a book he has characterized as deserving imprisonment?'

After she cheekily deposited the stamps into the Guildhall Poor Box, the man wrote again, demanding reimbursement. 'He says he does not ask "any favour" and he wants "the book in order to understand the case",' Annie reported. 'It seems a pity he did not try to understand it before he inserted so prominently so savage an attack upon its publishers.'[23]

Surprisingly, the national news had yet to chide their atheism. Reporters had not been present when the defendants asserted their right to affirm, rather than swear, an oath before submitting their affidavits. At one point Bradlaugh had to fetch a new law book from an adjoining office to prove the legality of a secular promise to tell the truth. Besant recounted in the *National Reformer* that 'To the ordinary question, "Do you believe in a God and creator of the universe," we both severally answered: "I do not," and the Commissioner, knowing Mr. Bradlaugh of old, was in his case therewith content; he did not seem quite happy about me. He looked at me doubtfully and solemnly, and at last said, "You do not believe in any God? Any God at all?" as though he fancied that I might have a little private deity of my own, somewhere out of sight, who might do to swear by. I gravely said, "None at all," though the funny way in which the question was put made me bite my lips to prevent a smile.'[24]

Only a handful of reports archly speculated about the defendants' relationship. Up the Cherwell, the *Banbury Advertiser* called her Bradlaugh's 'literary partner', and dismissed their post-arraignment Hall of Science debriefing as 'a large, though not what the reporters call an influential meeting'.[25] On the front page of *The Times*, however, a supporter placed a notice, headlined THE LIBERTY OF THE PRESS, saying that it had come to his attention that many readers desired to add to their defence fund.[26] Readers likely never suspected that the St John's Wood address to which they could send their sterling happened to correspond with Charles Bradlaugh's rented rooms.

A Belfast publication outed Annie as 'a sister-in-law of Mr. Walter Besant, the well-known litterateur, the joint author of *The Golden Butterfly*, and other popular works of fiction. Mrs. Besant is the wife of his brother, a respectable country clergyman, but they separated several years ago.'[27] The secular-minded Walter largely steered clear of Frank. Walter will appear later in these pages sucking up to Thomas Hardy, but for now, his degree of support for his relative can be deduced from two facts: in a future novel, *The Revolt of Man*, he will prophesise the toppling of a female insurgency and the restoration of male supremacy over England. On a future diary page in 1895, Queen Victoria will write that she breakfasted at Frogmore, and after luncheon knighted Mr Walter Besant.[28]

❧

Following his release from jail, Charles Knowlton had found his own reward working as a roaming country doctor in western Massachusetts. A third prosecution, brought by a reverend, fell apart, but only after two hung juries. He would never be bothered again. His medical practice thrived like never before. 'Well, it so happens,' he amusingly crowed in 1834, 'that most of the people in Ashfield, and many in the towns round about, are the strangest folks you ever *did* see. They will go to just what store they please; employ just what mechanic they have a mind to, and just what doctor – and all this, ever without consulting a *p-a-r-son*!! Oh, they are a stiff-necked people – a rebellious people; and after all they are not so much to blame for it; for they inherit this spirit from their forefathers – the veterans of the revolution!'[29]

The descendants of redcoats could be just as haughtily independent, and uncompromising.

Besant and Bradlaugh's defiant defence of a free press and the democratisation of sex education would unfold against the backdrop of one of the fiercest political arguments that had ever erupted in Britain: whether to once again go to war against Russia, 21 years after the Crimean War. Starting in April 1877, George III's granddaughter Victoria threatened to abdicate five times over the next ten months rather than see her country 'kiss the feet of the great barbarians'.

In the run-up to potential hostilities, Annie Besant had attended a London secularist conference advocating peace, and decried 'Mrs Jellybyism', named after the *Bleak House* character obsessed with saving far-away lands while neglecting her own neighbourhood. In a written response to Gladstone's *Belgian Horrors*, titled *Home Horrors*, one pacificist reformer observed that Britons' desires for social justice increased as the square of the distance from their homes.[30]

Queen Victoria, meanwhile, gleefully related to her eldest daughter how she had 'pitched into' the colonial secretary over Russia 'with a vehemence & indignation . . . oh! that

Englishmen were now what they were!! But we shall yet assert our rights – our position – & 'Britains [sic] never will be Slaves – will yet be our Motto.'[31] In another letter, she stressed that 'If *we* are to *maintain* our position as a *first-rate* Power – and of that no one can doubt, we must . . . be *prepared* for *attacks* and *wars*, *somewhere* or *other*, CONTINUALLY.[32] Over the course of the so-called Pax Britannica, the country would launch 72 separate military campaigns, or more than one for each year of Victoria's long reign.[33] Maintaining an empire meant eternal vigilance and a strong hand. That February, a major general named Charles Gordon was appointed Governor-General of the Sudan.

In hindsight, we see the mistakes and overreach; we know what awaits Gordon in Khartoum. Annie Besant envisioned that her prosecution would be the first in a series of reformist victories that would lead to a more open and equitable society for women. But as her trial unfolded in the spring of 1877, the country's gaze was largely fixed on settling a score far away.

At the junction of Pall Mall and Waterloo Place, the clopping current of London's horse-drawn traffic cleaved around the solemn Guards Crimean War Memorial, made from melted cannon seized at Sevastopol. The cost of that conflict, as memorialised in 'The Charge of the Light Brigade', Tennyson's elegiac ode to British cannon fodder ('Theirs not to make reply/Theirs not to reason why/Theirs but to do and die') now became subsumed by the din of rousing music hall ballads such as 'The Great MacDermott's War Song'. The piano sing-along coined a new word for extreme patriotism and aggressive foreign policy:

> We don't want to fight, but BY JINGO, if we do
> We've got the ships, we've got the men, we've got the
> money too.

We've fought the Bear before, and while we're Britons true
The Russians shall not have Constantinople.

On 18 April, one day before Besant stood up for herself at Guildhall, Victoria wrote of her intolerance of 'being subservient' to Russia and 'that we must be prepared "for a bold policy."'[34] (Amid this jingoism, a reader might never suspect that as a 20-year-old Victoria had swooned upon meeting the future czar, Alexander II, who had reciprocated.) By the weekend the queen worried that the Russian fleet might destroy Alexandria, Port Said, and her new bauble, the Suez Canal. 'War seems imminent & we are doing nothing to stop it.'[35] Finally, on 24 April, she hurriedly recorded: 'Bad accounts. Endless telegrams. The Russians without declaring war, have crossed over into Turkish territory ... Impossible for me to keep pace with or to note down everything.'[36]

On 27 April, the afternoon edition of the *Pall Mall Gazette* reported, 'Fifty thousand Russians are stated to have crossed the Asiatic frontier ... The Turks are advancing toward Alexandropol in three columns. A battle is expected shortly.' If she had turned the page of her chosen newspaper, Victoria would also have seen an update on the country's most-covered court case.

Earlier that day, before the Lord Chief Justice, Charles Bradlaugh had asked for their trial to be moved from the Old Bailey to the Court of Queen's Bench. Due to the 'great excitement' their Guildhall arraignment had caused in the press, he argued, an impartial jury could not be drawn from their peers. Moreover, their trial, Bradlaugh averred, was not to prove that the pamphlet had been printed and sold, but to weigh its propriety. Only a special jury at a special venue could fairly judge if a physician's pamphlet teaching the rudiments of conception and 'anticonception' counted as obscene.

It was a cagey move, one demonstrating the 43-year-old Bradlaugh's two decades of working in – and being prosecuted by – the legal system. First, the Court of Queen's Bench (or King's, when the monarch was male) was a branch of the High Court of Justice. As builders on the Strand constructed the Royal Courts – opened by Victoria five years hence – the Queen's Bench continued to sit in a courtroom adjoined to the northern end of Westminster Hall, shadowed by the clock tower and Big Ben. Relocating the proceedings here would bring their fight to the heart of the venerable Establishment.

Secondly, Bradlaugh knew that the legal test for obscenity had been established by an 1868 trial, *The Queen v. Hicklin*, over an anti-Catholic pamphlet that attacked the church's supposed iniquities. One section purported to reveal the lewd questions that priests put to female laity under the cloak of the confessional. The defence had (rather flimsily) argued that a few sexy bits of hearsay could not spoil the book as a whole. The presiding judge, the Lord Chief Justice, had disagreed. In ruling for the Crown against Hicklin, the judge determined that, regardless of context or intention, offensive sections – or even the blot of a single sentence – stained an entire work as obscene. (In decades to come, the list of books that will fail the 'Hicklin Test' will include Oscar Wilde's *The Picture of Dorian Gray*, James Joyce's *Ulysses* and D.H. Lawrence's *Lady Chatterley's Lover*.)

That same Lord Chief Justice, Sir Alexander Cockburn, now weighed the defendants' request to hear their case himself. Annie Besant had wanted to prove that a low-cost book frankly explaining sex and contraception was not obscene. Who better to decide this than the very judge whose ruling had set the precedent?

Sir Alexander seemed primed to take Charles Bradlaugh's

bait. The defendants' fate depended on 'the real and true nature of this work', he agreed. 'If upon looking at it we think that its object is the legitimate one of promoting know-ledge upon a matter of public interest, then we should be inclined to prevent the miscarriage of justice by allowing the case to be tried before a special jury.'[37] The Lord Chief Just-ice said he would need to read *Fruits of Philosophy* himself before deciding. Bradlaugh helpfully had a copy ready to hand up to the bench. The session adjourned.

Annie Besant did not keep a diary, or at least one that survives, and so we cannot know how she slept that weekend – whether, while snuggling with six-year-old Mabel at Oatlands, she felt the dread anxiety of having her fate held in a stranger's hands. If the hours held deep breaths of taut suspense, or could not pass quickly enough to exhaust her excitement, she left no record behind.

Through Victoria's writing we can picture the queen that weekend at Windsor Castle, picking cowslips, enjoying an organ recital and going for a drive in her carriage through Eton. Her words evoke scents and sounds, especially the rustle of paper as flocks of telegrams landed on her desk, detailing Russian advances. Prime Minister Disraeli said that 'the Faery', as he called her, telegraphed him for updates on the hour.[38] (Ever proper, even when on war footing, she also sent a telegram to Czar Alexander II, wishing him a happy birthday.) Sunday, the queen recorded, was very rainy. The days had turned cold and raw.

In her memoirs, Annie Besant never stoops to that level of mundanity, forsaking the clay that future biographers might animate on the page. Nor does she ever note that she is a lone woman endeavouring to shape a political, publish-ing and legal world controlled by the opposite sex. Both Annie and Victoria were surrounded by men, always. No wonder the queen's letters to her namesake daughter read like a frank confessional. She may have been supreme ruler, but she also felt her courtiers' casual misogyny – though to a lesser degree than the young orphan girls her political mentor, Lord Melbourne, brought into Windsor Castle as servants and sexually whipped to quench his flagellant thirst.

In her memoir Annie Besant often quotes the men around her at length, instead of her own thoughts and emotions. Her contemporaneous *National Reformer* columns better paint a scene. In late April, upon her and Bradlaugh's return to Westminster, Sir Alexander Cockburn 'had scarcely taken his seat' before announcing 'the case was one which might be fairly tried by a judge and special jury'. After reading *Fruits of Philosophy*, he said the defendants had raised the fair question as to whether it was what the indictment alleged it to be, an obscene publication. To him it did not seem 'calculated to arouse the passions'. The Lord Chief Justice agreed to hear the case at the Court of Queen's Bench.

'The decision is a great moral victory for us,' Annie reported. 'For our liberty we shall now have to plead, but sure am I that we shall have impartial justice shown us; and if we fail to win a verdict it will only prove that the present law is bad, and we shall have to set to work to change it.'

Annie took the release of the pair as a good sign. These discharges from the bench 'become as we go on,' she wrote, 'small by degrees and beautifully less. We began by an arrest on a warrant; from a warrant we passed to liberation on bail; and now we are free on Mr. Bradlaugh's sole recognizances.' Even as an accused criminal, the married Mrs Besant retained the same standing as a dependent child, and required Charles to sign for her, as the court did not recognise her promise to return.

That night she and Bradlaugh, along with his two

daughters, celebrated in the West End by attending a performance of *Richard III*. It was not their winter of discontent; they had started their glorious summer. The Lyceum Theatre was mere steps away from the hall where, only two and a half years earlier, Annie Besant had delivered her first public lecture, on the political status of women. Now, via the Westminster courtroom located at the heart of British power, she was about to step onto the empire's biggest stage.

6

TRIAL BY JURY

First, she needed to learn her lines. Richard III cried that he would give his kingdom for a horse; Annie Besant needed a law library. As the days dawned fine and bright (though, this being springtime London, punctuated with biting gusts and icy rain showers; rough winds really *do* shake the darling buds of May), Besant faced the fact that she had mere weeks to prepare for her defence before the United Kingdom's highest judge.

The Court of Queen's (or King's) Bench derived its name from the time when the monarch, in person, had sat and arbitrated cases wherever they were located. In the early thirteenth century, under Henry III, it moved beneath the magnificent hammer-beam roof of Westminster Hall. The 'courtroom' then was an alcove created by wood partitions and pew-like boxes in a corner of the eleventh-century structure, around which had grown the major institutions of the British state, including Parliament. The last king to sit on his nominal bench had been the short-reigning Richard III, who died in 1485.

Westminster Hall – today an empty, solemn antechamber used for special addresses and lyings-in-state – was formerly a bustling meeting place and market, with vendors selling stationary, sweetmeats, coffee and ale. In his *Dictionary of*

London, Charles Dickens, Jr. wrote that they 'plied their trade with as much zeal and noise as did the advocates higher up the Hall'.[1] At its entrance near Westminster Bridge lingered 'men of straw' – identifiable by the grain stalk stuck in their shoe – selling false evidence as witnesses. Shakespeare testified (legitimately) here; Guy Fawkes and his fellow conspirators were sentenced to be hanged, drawn and quartered; Sir Walter Raleigh was pronounced guilty of treason and beheaded in the adjoining Old Palace Yard. To begin the trial of Charles I, six trumpeters and the Serjeant-at-Arms carrying the mace rode into the hall on horseback. The king's refusal to recognise the court's authority did not spare his life. After the monarchy's restoration his killers were themselves killed, or dug up. For more than 20 years, Oliver Cromwell's exhumed head graced a pole at Westminster Hall.

At the turn into the eighteenth century, the czar Peter the Great watched the flock of white-wigged black silks striding around the hall and allegedly exclaimed, 'Lawyers! Why, I have but two in my whole dominions, and I believe I shall hang one of them the moment I get home to Russia.' In the nineteenth century, John Soane, lauded for drawing up the new Dulwich Picture Gallery, designed seven courtrooms attached to Westminster Hall's western wall, with high windows facing St Margaret's Street. Like the hall, they survived the 1834 blaze – London's largest since the Great Fire of 1666 – that destroyed the rest of Westminster Palace. The new Houses of Parliament, and clock tower, opened in stages across the 1850s. Annie Besant would not be standing in just any courtroom, but on hallowed historical ground, echoing with the leaden circles of Big Ben's hourly toll.

In an indication of the Conservative government's desire to conclude the case as swiftly as an executioner's blade, opposing Besant and Bradlaugh would be no less than the

Crown's Solicitor-General – second only in legal ranks to the Attorney-General – assisted by Douglas Straight, and another experienced criminal prosecutor.

The defendants elected to defend themselves, both because they could not afford a team of attorneys (let alone one) and because they wanted the platform. Reporters clamoured for passes to cover the proceedings. Though he had never passed the bar, Charles Bradlaugh felt as at home in a courtroom as Queen Victoria at the Great Spring Show, the flower exhibition then transpiring at Kensington Garden. ('It was my beloved Albert's last great interest,' she wrote in appreciation for its revival.)[2] Besant was but a bud in comparison. She would be the first woman to defend herself before this august court. She had also never studied the law.

Annie began a crash course in precedent, procedure and terminology. Inked in dense cursive on tissue-thin paper, the indictment sounded anything but light. She had to prepare her defence against the charge that she had

> Unlawfully wickedly knowing wilfully and designedly did print publish [and] sell a certain indecent lewd filthy bawdy and obscene book called *Fruits of Philosophy* thereby contaminating vitiating and corrupting the morals as well of youth as of other liege subjects of our said Lady the Queen and bringing the said liege subjects to a state of wickedness lewdness debauchery and immorality in contempt of our said Lady the Queen and her laws to the evil and pernicious example of all the others in the like case offending and against the peace of our said Lady the Queen her Crown and dignity.[3]

What language was this? What century was this? Before his beheading in 1649, the indictment of Charles I – treason; murder; unnatural, cruel and bloody wars – ran about the same length.

The official charge against her might be obscenity – fuelled by that witchy word *wickedness* – but the accusation also evinced the Establishment's fear of the disruptive potential of female sexuality. In her column, Annie might have 'chuckled inwardly' that the Secretary to the Society for the Suppression of Vice had written to her requesting a copy of the *Fruits*, because 'all his efforts to get copies otherwise have failed'.[4] Far less amusing was the critical line forming in a segment of the British press that educating women to take control of their reproductive health made them 'less of a mother, and more of a sort of safety-valve to sensual passions'. If they used the checks taught by the *Fruits of Philosophy*, one misogynistic commentator wrote, 'we know not whether we have not lost a spermatozoonal Milton or a foetal Cromwell'. The woman, in turn, would be reduced to 'a shameless and deflowered harlot who has responded to the desires of others; a social convenience, like a drinking fountain; a creature liable to be called into use anywhere, at any time, and by anybody, and who constantly carries a syringe in her muff'.[5]

Which publication was the more obscene?

As Annie crammed for her trial, letters and telegrams of support poured in from all corners of the United Kingdom. Over several issues, she reprinted the correspondence in the *National Reformer*. One representative note came from 'A poor man'.

'I married at the age of 22,' he wrote. 'My wife lived 12 [further] years. During that time she had 4 births, 2 deaths, and 9 miscarriages. I was in Dunfermline, working 14 hours a day for 8s. or 10s. a week. If I and my wife had been acquainted with the "Fruits of Philosophy" then, what a value it would have been to us!'[6]

One impoverished woman, expecting her fourteenth child

at age 32, promised to send a portion of her husband's wages to Annie's defence fund. An army officer said he and his wife had seven children, and could not afford another. Five pence 'per head per diem keeps life in us,' he wrote. 'The rest for education and raiment.' A physician applauded Annie's stand, as he daily saw the ruinous effects of the illegal and dangerous attempts to end pregnancies. 'Many clergymen wrote of their experience among the poor,' Besant noted, 'and their joy that some attempt was being made to teach them how to avoid over-large families, and letter after letter came to me from poor curates' wives, thanking me for daring to publish information of such vital importance.' A grandmother of 24 children – 'It is no giddy girl that writes to you' – sent her encouragement and her best wishes.

This outpouring, and, by early May, shilling-and-pence donations to the defence fund rising to £401, belied the real danger facing Annie Besant. It was all well and good that a sympathetic newspaper opined that attempting to deny the social realities that drove their work was 'about as hopeless a task as trying to upset the multiplication table', but Charles Bradlaugh recognised the times, and the immutability of their opponent.[7]

For two decades he had butted heads with the Establishment, and understood that he was at war with a continuum. Victory would never be absolute; even an unlikely win on this particular battlefield would come with casualties. Privately, he worried that he was leading Besant into prison, and permanently away from custody of Mabel. 'I have often faced hard toil,' he wrote of the preparation for their trial, 'but I have never had to encounter persistent, wearying, anxious labour greater than this.'[8]

Expecting to be convicted, Bradlaugh put his affairs in order, including transferring the *National Reformer* into safe hands. 'The course he then took proves in a startling way,' Hypatia recounted,

> how utterly alone he felt at that moment – old ties were broken, new ones were not yet tested; to whom could he turn to help him in this emergency? There was only his daughters – girls with no experience, and in many ways young for their years. But we might be ignorant, we might be stupid; still we loved him so well that we could not help being absolutely faithful to any trust he might confide to us . . . So I was the one whom my father selected to instruct in the possible editorial duties. I sat with him, note-book in hand, with fainting heart at the frightful prospect, and meekly took note of all his wishes. I was then taken into the bank, introduced to the manager, and recorded my signature, for I was to be the financial agent also!'[9]

She was 19; her sister, Alice, a steadfast presence behind the scenes, was 21.

Bradlaugh also issued subpoenas to famous faces whose appearance in the witness box might sway the jury in their favour. The radical Anglican priest Stewart Headlam – who preached to the poor of Bethnal Green – readily agreed, as did the popular publisher H.G. Bohn, whose low-priced, 766-volume series of general knowledge books, *Bohn's Libraries*, graced many a Victorian bookshelf. The Hackney MP Henry Fawcett, however, angrily replied that he would send his saintly suffragist wife, Millicent, abroad before allowing her career to be tarnished by appearing on the stand. 'Strange reverence for the High Court of Justice has this Member of Parliament!' Annie wrote in the *National Reformer*. On the final attempt to serve him a summons, 'Mr. Fawcett again refused to take the subpoena, and put his hands behind his back to prevent it being placed in them. Such conduct would be outrageous were it not so childish as to be simply ridiculous.'

'In startling contrast with Mr. Fawcett,' Besant continued, 'stands a far greater man, Charles Darwin.'[10] Earlier in his agitating career, Charles Bradlaugh had defended the naturalist's work. 'Between the cabbage and the man,' he had (somewhat quizzically) declared in support of the theory of evolution, 'I know no break.' Annie told her readers that Bradlaugh had sent a short note to the 68-year-old – ensconced at Down House in Kent, shunning public life – asking him to testify on their behalf.

Darwin replied immediately. 'I am much obliged for your courteous notice,' he wrote. 'I have been for many years much out of health & have been forced to give up all Society or public meetings, & it would be great suffering to me to be a witness in a court.' This was true: the gaunt and papery 'Man Who Killed God' had by this time lost all his teeth from bouts of retching stomach acid. He also suffered from whole-body eczema and bilious flatulence that drove his unhappy wife Emma to new levels of forbearance.

Besant and Bradlaugh did not expect what followed. 'I may add that I am not a medical man,' Darwin continued.

> I have not seen the book in question, but from notices in the newspapers, I suppose that it refers to means to prevent conception. If so I shd be forced to express in court a very decided opinion in opposition to you, & Mrs Besant; though from all that I have heard I do not doubt that both of you are acting solely in accordance to what you believe best for mankind. I have long held an opposite opinion, as you will see in the enclosed extract, & this I shd think it my duty to state in court.

Darwin copied a passage from his *Descent of Man* that argued that the survival of the fittest required the less fit to continually multiply. 'Hence our natural rate of increase, though leading to many and obvious evils, must not be greatly diminished by any means.'

That included checks on pregnancy. Darwin was a rank chauvinist who, in the same book published only six years before, wrote that men were superior to women in 'deep thought, reason, imagination, or merely the use of the sense and hands'.[11] (Later, in *A Room of One's Own*, Virginia Woolf will imagine Professor von X 'writing his monumental work entitled *The Mental, Moral and Physical Inferiority of the Female Sex*'. Charles Darwin beat him by a half-century.)

In his refusal to help Besant and Bradlaugh, Darwin reasoned that 'Besides the evil here alluded to I believe that any such practices would in time spread to unmarried women & wd destroy chastity, on which the family bond depends; & the weakening of this bond would be the greatest of all possible evils to mankind; In conclusion I shd likewise think it my duty to state in Court; so that my judgment, would be in the strongest opposition to yours.'[12]

Bradlaugh was disheartened. Besant, ever buoyant, sent their reply to Mr Darwin's 'most interesting letter', assuring him that due to his health 'we would not call him, but his gentle courtesy has remained a pleasant memory to me'. If Annie thought that Charles Darwin's dismissive demurral counted as chivalrous, then the gallantry that awaited her at the Court of Queen's Bench would come as quite a shock.

In mid-May, five weeks before the trial's start, a letter from Charles Bradlaugh appeared in *The Times*, below the Court Circular. He wished to notify readers that the General Post

Office had informed him that his mail was under surveillance. It claimed 'the right to open, read, and confiscate', anything that he posted. That weekend, the Royal Mail had seized copies of the Annie-authored *Freethinker's Text-book*, as well as *Fruits of Philosophy*.[13] In the version of his letter that ran in other London papers, Bradlaugh appealed 'through the Press and to Parliament against this monstrous course, and ask from your sense of justice publicity for my appeal'.[14]

At Windsor Castle, the queen 'Heard that the [Conservative] Govt had had a majority of 131 in the Hse of C. last night, which is a great thing'. She and her youngest child, 20-year-old Princess Beatrice, walked to Frogmore and then drove along the Thames in a single-pony carriage. 'So lovely,' Victoria wrote in her diary, '& all looking so green, & the lilacs coming out, one of the prettiest times of the year, I always think.'[15]

In the House of Commons, the radical Peter Alfred Taylor – a former MP and old ally of John Stuart Mill – presented a petition from Besant and Bradlaugh 'praying for an inquiry' into the censorship being extrajudicially established at the Post Office.[16] The response from the floor was that the seizure was legal. There was no debate. The next week, Annie Besant told a London newspaper that her mail also was being opened.[17] Along with the birth control tract, the Royal Mail refused to deliver a copy of her first lecture, *The Political Status of Women*.

This free publicity only drove up interest in Dr Knowlton's pamphlet. In *The Times'* crime column (more stolen watches, more abused women, more pedestrians killed by horse cabs), readers learned that a Scotland Yard detective arrested a hawker for 'selling in the public streets an indecent book termed *The Fruits of Philosophy*'. The title was being flogged on corners across London, 'and steps were being taken to suppress the traffic'.[18] The next day's paper reported that an army officer had asked a bobby to arrest the barrow boy who had sold him the work. Had he been disappointed by its content? No saucy governesses or cockish priests here. Compared to the unlaced corsets of Victorian pornography, Dr Knowlton's book was like that day's *Times* weather forecast for London: temperate and dull. Still, there was nothing else like it.

Later that week, a 'beetle-crusher' (as police were called, for their thick shoes) with the Dickensian name of Detective Butcher collared a lad selling the book on Villiers Street, drawing a brisk trade from the swells entering Victoria Embankment Gardens. Before her arrest, Annie Besant estimated that Knowlton's pamphlet quietly sold about 700 copies a year. In the two months since her arraignment, sales had surpassed 133,000.

'The crusade against the vendors of obscene literature proceeds,' grumbled a London columnist, 'and the question is becoming extremely complicated. Mr. Bradlaugh and Mrs. Besant are on trial for publishing and selling *The Fruits of Philosophy* intentionally and on high moral grounds, and, meanwhile, scampish hawkers are reaping a harvest by selling the pamphlet in the streets and thrusting it under the noses of visitors to the Academy.'[19]

The patrons of Piccadilly's Royal Academy of Arts did not whistle for the police. But three days later, on 23 May, the pamphlet again made headlines when detectives arrested Edward Truelove for selling it at his High Holborn shop. The bookseller had been the lamplighter of Annie Besant's path to Freethought; here she had purchased her first copy of Bradlaugh's *National Reformer*. (Today the site is a Little Waitrose supermarket.) Truelove, age 67 and sporting a long, woolly beard, was no newt on this voyage. In the 1850s he had published that anonymous 'Bible of the brothel', *The Elements of Social Science*, which, to avoid the evils of onanism and the 'legalized prostitution of marriage', advocated a *ménage à trois* of premarital sex, free love, and contraception. Happily married, with one child, a daughter, Truelove's reform-minded friends included Florence Nightingale.

With the men arrested for drunkenness and assault, and the cab driver who had run over a 14-year-old boy with his horse (Victorian pavements bore no painted yellow warnings to 'Look Right'), Edward Truelove stood in the dock at Guildhall. A witness testified that he had been ordered to Truelove's bookstore by that *Fruits*-sniffing secretary of London's Society for the Suppression of Vice, a puritanical organisation founded by Royal Proclamation a century earlier and led by the solicitor Charles Hastings Collette.

His middle name was proof of nominative determinism; the man was a battlefield personified. In his spare time, Britain's answer to Anthony Comstock had authored a handbook for artillery drill instruction. Now he trained his fire on books.

After quickly flipping through *Fruits of Philosophy*, the Guildhall magistrate agreed with C.H. Collette that the pamphlet was 'filthy and disgusting', and found its birth control teachings 'demoralizing and most prejudicial to the national welfare'.[20] He refused to fine Truelove, but rather committed him to criminal trial. Charles Bradlaugh posted his colleague's bail. The war against contraception had widened to a second front.

※

As May sped to its end, Queen Victoria laboured to separate fiction from fact. The Russians had crossed the Danube (*false*); the British expedition to Gallipoli was not to be

pressed at present (*true*). On a pouring wet morning, the com-
poser Richard Wagner called at Windsor Castle. In her diary
Victoria recorded, 'He has grown old & stout & has a clever,
but not pleasing countenance.'[21] On 24 May, Her Majesty
turned 58. 'My poor old birthday,' she wrote. 'Alas! the difficulties just now, indeed since a year, are very great, but I trust
we shall weather them all & do what is right! May God spare
me yet a time to be of use to those I love, to my Country &
to the world at large!'[22]

Three days later, at showery Balmoral – where her mood
had been lightened by news that the owner of the castle's
neighbouring Ballochbuie Forest would at last sell to her –
Queen Victoria heard 'a most beautiful & practical sermon
on selfishness, how it was impossible to be really happy
unless one was unselfish & did not merely act for reward
hereafter. That true happiness came chiefly, if not entirely
from the state of mind one was in oneself. The text was from
St. Luke x. v. 25 "What shall I do to inherit eternal life." '[23]

That day, Charles Bradlaugh's estranged wife, Susannah,
died in her Sussex cottage. In a letter sent earlier that week to
her daughters, who now lived with their father in London,
the 45-year-old invalid wrote, 'My chest is bad. I really feel ill
altogether . . . Do not neglect writing me, my darlings, for my
heart is very sad.' The official cause of death was coronary
artery disease engendered by alcoholism. A more accurate
diagnosis may have been a broken heart. Susannah ended her
final letter by sending her 'great love to dear Papa, and also
to your own dear selves'.

As he prepared for his trial, Bradlaugh simultaneously
planned his wife's funeral. *The Times* did not print a death
notice. (Only the *Times* of Yorkshire's tiny Driffield did.) If
Annie felt one step closer to marrying her best friend – the
mere remaining hurdle was Reverend Frank Besant's

mortality – she let Susannah's departure pass without mention in print. In her own autobiography, Hypatia reprinted her mother's last message and remained tight-lipped. 'I shall perhaps be pardoned – in my capacity as daughter, if not in that of biographer – for leaving the matter here, and not going into it more fully. It is a painful subject for one who loved her parents equally.'[24]

As the undertaker dressed Susannah's coffin, Charles Bradlaugh appeared at Guildhall again in support of Edward Truelove, whom C.H. Collette had accused of continuing to sell *Fruits of Philosophy*. Bradlaugh argued that as a jury had yet to declare the book obscene, his friend had broken no English law. The magistrate disagreed, ordering police to raid Truelove's shop and seize any remaining copies. With a lemon peel grin, Collette warned Bradlaugh that next he would turn the police on his and Annie's printshop. Bradlaugh thanked him for the publicity.

On the day of his wife's Brookwood burial, a solicitor argued on his behalf before another magistrate against a man accused of assaulting Bradlaugh at his lecture in London's Fitzrovia. The defence argued that because the night's topic had been *Fruits of Philosophy*, the attempt to start a riot had been warranted. The court agreed, dismissing Bradlaugh's complaint.

His week from hell ended the morning following the funeral, inside a judge's chambers. On 11 May, Charles Bradlaugh stood before Justice Lush (an ironic surname, given Susannah's affliction), asking to know who had initiated proceedings against him and Annie Besant. 'I come to your lordship to help me,' he implored. By rights, the accused should know the name of their accuser.

With wigged gravitas, Justice Lush intoned, 'The Queen is the prosecutor.'[25]

In a return visit to the judge's courtroom two weeks later, Bradlaugh asked for their trial date to be set, hoping it could begin soon. The prosecution also wanted to start post-haste, as *Fruits* was 'being sold in the streets by thousands at sixpence a copy'.[26] The Lord Chief Justice agreed to start on 18 June, only 19 days away.

Britain's highest-ranking judge was a bit of a wild card for prosecution and defence alike. Short, with pouchy hazel eyes, a sharp beakish nose, and a Napoleonic hairline and jowls, Sir Alexander Cockburn drew renown for both his dissolute lifestyle – often pouring himself onto his bench minutes before court commenced – and the elaborate and eloquent judgments he had made on some of the Victorian era's most sensational trials.

Lord Chief Justice Sir Alexander Cockburn

The character of the Learned Judge in Gilbert and Sullivan's 1875 hit comic opera *Trial by Jury* bears an uncanny resemblance to Cockburn. In 'The Judge's Song', he sings:

> When I, good friends, was called to the bar,
> I'd an appetite fresh and hearty.
> But I was, as many young barristers are,
> An impecunious party.
> I'd a swallow-tail coat of a beautiful blue –
> And a brief which I bought of a booby –
> A couple of shirts, and a collar or two,
> And a ring that looked like a ruby!

Starting as a young advocate four decades earlier, Cockburn – like a magpie to a shiny sovereign – had found his way to the trials that generated the most publicity. As an advocate, he rejected a posting to India with his eye on something better. He quickly climbed the legal ranks: as a barrister, Cockburn successfully defended the high-ranking Church of England's Dean of York from charges of selling indulgences. As a Queen's Counsel, he had won acquittal for the winning party in the United Kingdom's last honour duel with pistols at paces. After being appointed Attorney-General, he had pioneered the use of forensic science in the courtroom by proving the guilt of William Palmer, who to gain an estate had murdered a man with strychnine. Cockburn won further renown after freeing an admitted assassin by pleading that when he had pulled the trigger, the man had not been sound of mind. Alexander Cockburn had invented the insanity defence.

> The briefs came trooping gaily,
> And every day my voice was heard
> At the Sessions or Ancient Bailey.
> All the thieves who could my fees afford

Relied on my orations.
And many a burglar I've restored
To his friends and his relations.

As Lord Chief Justice, Cockburn had overseen the trial of
the cross-dressing Boulton and Park (acquitted); the sensational case of a schoolmaster whose corporal punishment
had killed a student (guilty); and what was then the longest-
running trial in British history, of a conman butcher's claim
to the Tichborne baronetcy (guilty). Cockburn's ruling in the
Hicklin case had also set the legal standard for obscenity,
which the legal amateur Annie Besant now studied to disprove before him.

For now I'm a Judge!
Chorus: And a good Judge, too!
For now I'm a Judge!
Chorus: And a good Judge, too!
Though all my law be fudge,
Yet I'll never, never budge
But I'll live and die a Judge!
Chorus: And a good Judge, too!

One of the Lord Chief Justice's most infamous rulings
may explain why Annie Besant did not keep a diary, or preserve
her correspondence. Because of Sir Alexander Cockburn, it
could all be used as evidence against her.

In 1858, one year after the Crown had loosened its restrictions on divorce, a London civil engineer named Henry Oliver
Robinson filed to separate from his wife, Isabella, on grounds
of adultery. As his only evidence, he submitted her journal.
'Here I lived in a world of my own,' wrote a shocked Isabella,
'one that scarcely any one ever entered. I felt that in my study,
at least, I was a ruler; & that all I wrote was *my own*.'[27]

Not according to British law. Her diary, like every quire, sheaf, page and scrap of a married woman's papers, was legally owned by her husband. Months before the trial, passage of the Obscene Publications Act had forbidden the British translation of Gustave Flaubert's *Madame Bovary*, but in *The Times* and other newspapers, Britons could read a real-life version of the novel. Across the torrid, Thames-stinking summer, Mrs Isabella Robinson's private words were read aloud in the courtroom and reprinted in the press. Every instance, she later reflected, felt like a sexual assault.

In her private journal, the bored and lonely Isabella – a housewife whose life, like Emma Bovary's, had grown 'cold as a garret whose dormer window looks on the north' – recorded her sensual longings and stolen moments with other men.[28] The trial recalled Britain's previous most scandalous divorce, when Victoria's mentor Lord Melbourne proved that Lady Caroline Lamb had cuckolded him with Lord Byron, ruining her reputation, but resulting in her best-selling roman à clef, *Glenarvon*. Isabella's alleged affairs brought no such satisfaction, or revenge. She had made them all up. None of the men she fantasised about had ever returned her affections. Proof of actual adultery might have been less humiliating.

Although three judges heard the Robinson case, Sir Alexander Cockburn had taken the lead. Sweating under his horsehair and ermine in the Westminster Hall courtroom, he had rejected her defence of insanity. Isabella's secrecy evinced a sound mind. As did her faithful recording, bracketing confessions of her sexual frustration with details such as the day's weather conditions. Furthermore, Cockburn argued, if expressing imagination on the page was proof of madness, then British asylums would be brimming with novelists.

The evidence and intricacies of the case still required three months of deliberations. Cockburn believed, from reading the unreleased portions of Isabella's diary, that her accusing husband himself was a rapacious philanderer. The Lord Chief Justice empathised with her passages expressing 'so many instances, complaints of imperfect pleasure or of painful disappointment'.[29] Of the 302 divorce cases brought since the passage of the new law, Mr Robinson's was one of only six to be rejected. In the end, Sir Alexander Cockburn had ruled in favour of the unhappy wife.

And a good Judge, too!

Isabella Robinson won, but she also lost. Victorian paper had made a Victorian jail. Her diary left her trapped in a loveless marriage. She had walked out of Westminster Hall a disgraced woman, whose frank talk about sexual desire had graced newspapers across Britain. Nineteen years later, in the same august building, under the name of the same queen, and before the same fur-mantled judge, Annie Besant faced the same fate.

But this time, for the first time, the accused would defend herself.

In court, the odds were completely against her. While Annie Besant left no record of her feelings as she closed her Hansard, tied her bootlaces, kissed Mabel goodbye, and rode in a cab — perhaps it would be her tumbril — to at last meet her accusers, we can only assert that she was about to argue before the one British judge who was most likely to be sympathetic to her rebellion.

Fusty old Sir Alexander Cockburn may have become an operatic caricature, but he was also a man of secrets. At this moment, one is unknown even to himself. As the 74-year-old pulled up his black stockings and donned his full-bottom wig and heavy scarlet robe, the judge was unaware that sediments of fatty plaque were silently bricking up the entrances to his heart. Three years from now, Cockburn will end his day in a Westminster courtroom, walk home to his Mayfair town-house and adjourn for good. The heart attack, his third, will kill him instantly.

His long *Times* obituary – occupying half a page of the broadsheet's rarefied real estate – will hint at another secret, one that Annie Besant, like most of the world, does not yet know. Sir Alexander, the death notice will reveal, 'had the opportunity of taking a seat in the House of Lords, but declined the offer'.[30]

This was only half the story. The fuller version was that for decades, the Lord Chief Justice had dodged the displeasure of the very Crown he served. In one of the rare mentions of his name in her diary, Victoria once condemned Cockburn's conduct on the bench as 'far too violent & personal'.[31] In another entry, she recorded that she had knighted him, per protocol, after he became the Solicitor-General in 1850. Later that year, Cockburn defended in court an ex-cavalryman who attacked the queen in Mayfair with a walking stick, crushing her bonnet and inflicting a black eye. Although Her Majesty was so little injured that she was able to show herself at the opera that evening, Cockburn's arguments could not sway the jury. The man was sentenced to seven years transportation beyond the seas.

Cockburn nevertheless ascended the judicial preferments – Attorney-General came next, and then Chief Justice, and finally Lord Chief Justice. He had dodged whispers of being 'mixed blood', as a Jamaican newspaper once wrote, claiming him for the West Indies, since his mother had lived in pre-revolutionary Haiti as the child of a French nobleman.[32] As with Annie's Irish-English parents, and Victoria's English-German ones, Cockburn's mix was likely cultural. Even then, England was half-English, and he was half-English, too.

With his queen, Cockburn shared a childhood fluency in German; like Victoria's mother, he had been born in Germany, where his father served as British Consul. They also shared an affinity for yachting, although Her Majesty's 360-foot steamer was nine times larger than his own boat. They both loved music, the theatre and books. His wide social circle included Charles Dickens. The queen liked the writer's comedy; Cockburn admired his criticism of Victorian society, especially the courts. Cockburn had also inherited his father's baronetcy, an honorific rank bestowed for loyalty to the Crown. But he and Victoria were not friends, nor even mutual admirers.

In 1856, she ignored Prime Minister Palmerston's letter reporting that Sir Alexander 'is not desirous of being immediately placed in the House of Lords, but he would be glad to be allowed to look forward to such a favour from your Majesty at some future time. Viscount Palmerston begs to submit for your Majesty's gracious approval that such a prospect might be held out to Sir Alexander Cockburn ... Of course any expectation would for the present be a confidential and private communication to himself.'[33]

No such letter would ever come. Behind the scenes, the queen had dented Cockburn's escutcheon. Her Majesty 'more than once previously refused' to elevate him to the Lords 'upon the ground of the notoriously bad moral character of the Chief Justice'.[34] In 1865, a perturbed Victoria finally wrote to her prime minister, 'As it appears that a promise was made to Sir A. Cockburn, though unauthorized by her, the Queen will sanction his Peerage.' She retained her opinion, however, of the 'absolute duty of requiring that

Peerages shall not be conferred upon any persons who do not in addition to other qualifications possess a good moral character'.[35] (Imagine her reaction today.)

Lord Palmerston dropped his request. In 1868, his successor William Gladstone at last formally offered Cockburn a place in the House of Lords. The Lord Chief Justice turned it down.

Sir Alexander's legal fame, and self-pride, reached across the Atlantic, and upon his death the *New York Times* will help to explain the queen's dislike of him. 'The private life of the Lord Chief Justice was far from being blameless,' the paper's obituary will report, 'and not the least of the scandals with which his name has been associated was his introduction into London society of a daughter, one of many illegitimate children.'[36]

This was partly true; Cockburn, who never married, fathered with his lover Amelia Godfrey a daughter, Louisa, and a son, Alexander. The Cockburn crest featured a cock, and a Latin motto meaning 'Vigilant and Bold'. Because his heir had been born out of wedlock, the baronetcy will follow the Lord Chief Justice into the grave. Refusing the royal preserve of Westminster Abbey, per his wishes Cockburn will be buried at Kensal Green, whose sun-favoured grounds feature a Dissenters' Chapel and the Reformers' Memorial. He had been a lifelong Liberal.

Annie Besant knew none of these secrets on the bright, warm summer morning of 18 June 1877 as she wended from St John's Wood down through bustling Marylebone and around the horse-clogged Piccadilly Circus to Haymarket. Nor did she, like the rest of the country, suspect that as a young man in the late Regency period, Alexander Cockburn had written a Gothic romance. The unpublished novel — featuring dungeons, nuns, ghosts, a lusty monarch, heaving bosoms and mistaken identities – was the type that Jane Austen mocked in *Northanger Abbey*.

'I know not for whose perusal I write these lines,' begins one of Cockburn's passionate chapters, 'but a secret impulse excited me to trace them with my blood, my blood which flows slow and thick from my arm.' The manuscript's boxed pages – crisp Victorian stationary, sleeping on a shelf in London's Middle Temple Library – are crammed with a young Cockburn's neatly inked cursive lines. Even after the passage of 200 years, a reader can clearly understand his script, if not his plot. 'Yes children,' one harridan tells the book's star-crossed lovers, 'I have reason to suppose that you are brother and sister, and on that account your improper intercourse has escaped the censure which it otherwise merited; the voice of nature has united you.'

It's a terrible lie; the wicked stepmother is conniving to split the couple so they will marry the partners that society expects. 'It was as if,' our hero observes, 'the storm had blasted the opening blossoms of our love.' What is true is that our heroes do not use, or know how to use, contraception. In the novel's happy ending, the couple expose the stepmother's nefarious plot. The child is born, and is loved, by his unmarried parents. Cockburn wrote this in his fledgling twenties, before he had been called to the bar, and before the birth of his own illegitimate children. Like Queen Victoria in her diary and letters, his private writing reveals a deeper, flawed and more interesting human being than the waxy visage put on public display.

To Annie Besant, slowly passing Trafalgar Square and coming down crowded Whitehall, Sir Alexander Cockburn was a preening publicity-hungry judge with only a professional interest in her prosecution by the Crown. Nothing more. As her quickening heel-falls echoed off Westminster

Hall's Yorkstone floor like the hooves of the war-horse in the Book of Job – *neck clothed in thunder, rejoicing in his strength, He saith among the trumpets, Ha ha; and smelleth the battle* – she had no reason to suspect that for her, the Lord Chief Justice might be more than a good judge, but the best judge, too.

'I feel a kind of pride in being tried at Westminster,' Annie admitted, 'with its grand architecture and splendid surroundings; well as I know that the sentence will fall none the less heavy if we are convicted, there is yet a satisfaction in tilting in such a field. To be tried at Westminster, before the Lord Chief Justice of England, is the justification of our attitude.'[37]

But this was a criminal trial. Annie Besant's freedom would not be decided by one man, but 12.

7

DAY ONE

It was more a jury of peerages rather than her peers. From across the courtroom the special jurors looked alike in the egg carton of the wooden jury box: two rows of six seated men dressed in white shirts and black waistcoats, sashed by gold watch chains that sparkled when kissed by the sunbeams shining through the high ceiling's windows.

Before their abolishment in 1949, the use of special juries dated back to medieval England. In cases of exceptional importance to the kingdom, such as ones involving seditious libel and high treason, an ad hoc panel of trusted knights replaced the 12 'next Neighbours', or commoners, who might not deliver the desired verdict. Over the centuries, the practice evolved to include experts, such as a dozen fishmongers empanelled to hear a business dispute over the freshness of seafood. In his 1722 novel *Moll Flanders*, Daniel Defoe correctly described the special juries of matrons summoned to determine if a condemned prisoner was pregnant, which would spare her from the noose.[1] By the nineteenth century, service on special juries became limited to citizens of high social and economic standing. The Juries Act 1870 restricted selection to persons (read: men) legally entitled to be called esquire, merchant or banker. Those who qualified to be included on the roll also had to live in a home taxed at the highest rate.[2]

The gentlemen waiting for *The Queen v. Charles Bradlaugh and Annie Besant* to begin had that morning departed addresses fronting the locked gardens that oxygenated the posh London society terrariums of South Kensington and Belgravia. These were not the sort who shouldered their way into a packed community hall to hear a speaker castigate the wasteful monarchy and a pernicious Church. These were the aristocrats who kept box seats at the Royal Opera House, and on Sundays frequented pews. At Eton (with false modesty simply called 'school') they had sat in the same 'divs' under the same 'beaks', and then played cricket at Oxford or rugger at Cambridge. One juror captained a cavalry regiment; another managed a bank. Three weeks from now, when the All England Croquet and Lawn Tennis Club (as it was then styled) will stage a fundraiser for a new pony roller to maintain its grass, these are the types of toffs who will pull up in their horse-drawn broughams to politely applaud the white-flannelled men swinging racquets at the first Wimbledon Championship.

Although special jurors were usually selected by ballot, followed by a process of striking those deemed unacceptable by either side, this trial's lot had been chosen opaquely, by the court. The foreman was Arthur Walter, son-in-law of an Anglican priest, who would soon replace his father as the owner and chief editor of *The Times*. The elder Walter had planted his progeny in the jury box.

If Arthur, as he waited for the proceedings to begin, had unfolded that day's edition, he would have seen a front page announcing many births to unnamed wives, the Crystal Palace's Handel festival programme, an announcement of Alexandra Palace fireworks to honour the visiting former

American president Ulysses S. Grant, and a notice of Madame Tussaud's new 'War Group' display of the waxen Ottoman sultan and Russian czar. The Royal Aquarium was displaying H.R.H. the Prince of Wales' collection of Indian fish, fresh from his expensive excursion to the colonial adventure playground of the Raj. At 5.30 and again at 10.30pm, the young aerialist Zazel would become a human cannonball. The advertisement promoting her derring-do borrowed from Shakespeare's *As You Like It* speech that begins, 'All the world's a stage'. Zazel would be 'Seeking the bubble reputation even at the cannon's mouth'.

Inside the Court of Queen's Bench, the costumed men took their places. The special jury, sitting cheek by jowl, mutely faced forward, like an audience waiting for the curtain to lift. Their box seats put their backs to the wall that ran alongside Westminster Hall. The court really did resemble a balconied theatre, illuminated by natural light pouring through the ceiling's raised circular cut, and a row of first-storey arched windows facing west, towards today's Parliament Square Garden. The slanting sunrays burnished the ruby-coloured carpet. Annie Besant had never set foot inside such a beautiful room.

At Balmoral, Queen Victoria began her diary for Monday 18 June 1877 with the reminder that today was 'The anniversary of our greatest triumph at Waterloo', 62 years before. She celebrated by taking a break from reading the bellicose telegrams invading her despatch box and instead went riding through Glen Gelder's empty serene heathland. 'It was most heavenly & such pure delicious air,' she wrote. 'Seated ourselves at the back of the little Shiel, looking towards the northern hills, & took tea & sketched, whilst Janie [Spencer, Baroness Churchill] read to me out of the papers.'[3]

Her Lady of the Bedchamber might have narrated from a

Pall Mall Gazette front page that reported – under the news of Turks and Russians exchanging fire on the Danube, and Her Majesty's return to Windsor later that week – from Westminster Hall: 'The trial excited great interest,' the paper's correspondent related, 'the court being crowded at an early hour, and its approaches densely thronged. There was a large attendance of the members of the bar.'[4]

Unable to secure a seat on the ground floor, a budding, penniless playwright fresh from Dublin elbowed into a standing spot upstairs. George Bernard Shaw's future held its own charges of obscenity – plus a Nobel Prize and an Academy Award – but at this moment the rail-thin 20-year-old's life was wholly focused on catching a glimpse of the defendant whose hazel 'faithful eyes' had smitten him from a photograph.[5] Seeing only the back of Besant's tight chestnut curls, young Shaw fell silent with the rest of the courtroom at the sound of three knocks.

After emerging from behind an arras at precisely 10.30, the Lord Chief Justice – with 'eyes severe' and 'in fair round belly and good capon lined' just as Shakespeare described the judge in *As You Like It* – sat in his tippet, robe and girdle, thickening the upholstery of a high-backed chair. Upon his stage, on this would-be throne, he was literally elevated, the high priest of the law.

The defendants and prosecutors bowed to the bench. The custom was not directed at Sir Alexander Cockburn, but the Royal Court of Arms, hanging on the wall behind him. The ritual was a reminder that the judge was merely a representative of the Crown. Officially, British justice was the sovereign's prerogative. Common law was not codified, but a sort of story whose telling had begun nearly a millennium before. The term 'court' derived from Edward the Confessor's eleventh-century Royal Court. That itself was the name of a London theatre, at Sloane Square.

This production's cast sat costumed on a long bench before the Lord Chief Justice at the level of an orchestra pit. On one end, Annie Besant and Charles Bradlaugh wore civilian clothes. 'The table before them,' noted the *Pall Mall Gazette*, 'was loaded with law books and legal documents.' On the other end roosted two of the great silks of the London bar. Douglas Straight and another barrister were assisting the Solicitor-General, Hardinge Giffard, a jurist so august, he would go on to literally write the book on English law. After becoming Lord Halsbury (making an exception to the rule that no criminal lawyer could ever receive a peerage), Giffard will compile the comprehensive 31-volume encyclopaedia *Halsbury's Laws of England*. (Like a yew tree it has grown across generations, to 103 volumes; the latest edition appeared in 2023.) After this trial, as a Conservative MP, Sir Hardinge will continue to tangle with Bradlaugh on other stages; as the nation's Lord Chancellor, he will serve under three Tory prime ministers for 17 years, and clash with Annie Besant over trade unions.

Like Douglas Straight – and their quarry seated beside them – Sir Hardinge Giffard was a native Londoner, growing up near the Regent's Canal in Pentonville, then a modest neighbourhood where the likes of the *Bleak House* law clerk Mr Guppy could afford to live. Like Annie Besant, Giffard's parents were Irish and English; after migrating, his Dubliner father founded the capital's *Evening Standard*. Giffard had worked as a journalist at the popular newspaper. In photos and portraits, where the angle of his tight-lipped mouth matches his slumped shoulder, he radiates contemptuous supremacy, looking like a man who would not relish mingling with and reporting on London's unwashed masses. Studying law at the

Inner Temple, founded by the crusading Knights of Templar, proved a better fit. After only two years of reading below the framed periwigged gaze of his predecessors, Hardinge Giffard was called to the bar.

For all his professional accomplishments, the 53-year-old still managed to look both combative and miserable, like a man perpetually trooping towards an internal Holy Land. A caricature of him sketched around the time of Annie Besant's prosecution imagined Giffard's face as a steaming tea kettle, ready to blow.

Sir Hardinge at full boil

'As a criminal lawyer,' Charles Bradlaugh wrote in the *National Reformer* on the eve of the trial, 'the Solicitor-General is probably without his equal at the bar, and if a conviction can be obtained, his legal skill will certainly obtain it.'[6]

❋

The opening of a trial is like the start of a play. Seeing a king's ghost on Danish ramparts sets a different tone than watching teens duel in a square in Verona. This curtain rose to a display of shocked self-regard. 'The Solicitor-General made a bitter and violent speech,' Annie Besant wrote of Giffard's opening argument, 'full of party hate and malice, endeavouring to prejudice the jury against the work by picking out bits of medical detail and making profuse apologies for reading them, and shuddering and casting up his eyes with all the skills of a finished actor.'

He really was quite good. We were gathered, Sir Hardinge declaimed to the packed courtroom, to stop the publication of a book. 'Probably, gentlemen,' he said, turning to the special jury, 'you never heard of it, and happily, I think, I may say, the world had never heard of it' until recently. 'And the result is that the question which, in truth, has to be decided by this indictment, is, whether or not the defendants were entitled to sell for sixpence this book, which I hold in my hand, to every person to whom it may occur that it is interesting, or amusing, or exciting to the morbid appetite, to purchase a book of this description.'

Giffard milked the pregnant pause. *Fruits of Philosophy*, he continued, subjected readers to 'a minute description of physical means whereby the population may be checked'. It instructed how the 'commerce of the sexes may be permitted to continue, and the consequent birth of children may be averted'.[7]

The court transcript does not note if the room hissed or

167

gasped, or even understood that Sir Hardinge was talking about birth control. In a British courtroom, a barrister's job is to sway a jury to believe a story; a judge's role, like a narrator's, is to tell them what's happening. Here the Lord Chief Justice interrupted to ask how the pamphlet's content made it obscene.

In reply, Hardinge Giffard quoted the judge's own definition of obscenity, from his landmark ruling in *The Queen v. Hicklin*. *Fruits of Philosophy* did indeed 'deprave and corrupt those whose minds are open to such immoral influences'. Sir Alexander Cockburn parried back that Charles Knowlton had made clear in the book's introduction that his intended readers were married couples wishing to limit their family size. Giffard contended that the American doctor had daubed the word 'marriage' on a few pages to favourably colour the pamphlet's complexion. It may be true, he continued, that a medical text 'treating on obstetric matters should be published; but who would say it would be right to publish such things indiscriminately throughout England? We have here, in the work before us, a chapter on restriction published, not written in any learned language, but in plain English – in a facile form, and sold in the public streets at sixpence.'[8]

Annie Besant sat perched at the other end of the bench, taking notes on sheets of foolscap, waiting her turn.

The Lord Chief Justice again challenged his wigged counterpart to explain what exactly in the text the Crown believed to be criminally indictable.

With a flutter of black silk sleeves, Sir Hardinge Giffard lifted his copy of *Fruits of Philosophy* and read Annie Besant's preface aloud at the speed of the stenographer's dip-pen. Every courtroom utterance had to be preserved in ink on yet more Victorian paper. After he finished, Sir Alexander Cockburn remained unconvinced, saying that he had not heard anything indecent. Charles Bradlaugh interjected that the prosecution was required to point out the specific offending passages. The defendants were prepared to quote similar, unprosecuted, content from the mountain of medical texts stacked before them.

The Solicitor-General retorted that chapter three, titled 'Of Promoting and Checking Conception', would suffice. In his recommendations to cure sterility, Charles Knowlton referred 'to the use of cayenne; and gentlemen, I do not desire to read it. I would rather refer you to the chapter, and you will perceive for yourself what it purports to be.'

Annie Besant watched Sir Hardinge squirm. It was a fine, clear day, already 24 degrees Celsius outside, and rising. Wearing court dress in a sunny, stuffy room could not have been comfortable. 'I am afraid for our defence,' Bradlaugh told the court, 'I shall have to require the prosecution to read the work to the jury, unless we are allowed to know the exact words relied upon by the learned gentleman.'

'Yes, I think that is fair,' the judge replied.

Sir Hardinge Giffard protested that it would be unfair to the defendants to select only a part of the book. 'I thought we needed only to give the jury that which it seemed to me was the key to the whole publication. If not, the whole book must be read.'

'I quite agree,' the Lord Chief Justice replied, 'but still I was supposing that if there was anything independent of the whole scope of the work that you could put your finger on and say it tended to obscenity, it is right that the defendants should know it. It is well known that sterility is a source of great discomfort to women who wish to be blessed with children, and any man who can suggest a mode for its removal would be a benefactor to humanity; but, as you say, that may be used as a disguise to instil bad notions into the mind. That is a question for the jury to decide, and for that purpose they must have the subject before them.'

Sir Hardinge demurred. 'I shall have to read the whole of that chapter; but I did not wish to give the jury the pain and trouble to hear it.'

'Very well, read it,' answered Cockburn. 'The book must be read, sooner or later, either by you, Mr Solicitor, or the officer of the court.'

'I thought it was unfair to read a part.'

'Whether you read it,' the judge admonished, 'or whether it is read by the officer of the court, or the defendants, matters little; the jury must hear it.'

The assembled reporters readied their pencils.

'I will point out one of the passages,' Giffard told the special jurors, 'which, I think, evidently not only shows the object of the writer but illustrates the mischief and evil that the work is liable to produce. It is really extremely painful to me *(hesitating)*, very painful, to have to read this.'

The Solicitor-General announced that the Crown would put its prosecution on chapter three, which explained safe methods of contraception. Reading aloud its seven-plus pages filled the masculine recesses of Westminster Hall with words its painted portraits of kings, stone white harts and carved wooden angels likely had never heard here before. *Vagina. Menstruation. Withdrawal immediately before emission. Syringing. Vagina. Dislodging and destroying the fecundating property of the semen. It is in the hands of the female. Vagina.*

'Gentlemen,' Sir Hardinge Giffard at last exhaled. 'I have read the whole of that, and I assure you that it has been with extreme pain and regret that I have found myself compelled to read it.'

Annie Besant stifled a smile. 'For a man accustomed to Old Bailey practice,' she wrote, 'he was really marvellously easily shocked; a simple physiological fact brought him to the verge of tears, while the statement that people often had too large families covered him with such modest confusion that he found it hard to continue his address.'

Sir Hardinge regained his composure. 'You may tell me about American doctors,' he sneered, 'but it is not to be permitted that doctors in England shall have a right to circulate such filth!'

The jury's duty, he concluded, was to decide whether the fast-selling *Fruits of Philosophy* did not suggest to the unmarried as well as to the married, 'the boy of 17 and the girl of the same age, that they might gratify their passions without the mischief and inconvenience and the destruction of character which would be involved if they gratified them and conception followed'. (Victorians may have fretted about teen sex, but not enough, then, to raise the age of consent above 13.)

But the true obscenity, the Calvary upon which the Crown's prosecution now stood, was that teaching women contraception would liberate them from the marriage bed. Sir Hardinge accused the low-priced pamphlet of the crime of announcing to the world: 'Here are the means by which the unmarried female may gratify her passions.'

For this special jury of all-married men, and to this room cleared of all daughters, wives, widows and indeed all women save for Annie Besant, the Solicitor-General at last exposed the defendants' cardinal sin. Their pamphlet freed women from societal strictures. The never-wed Lord Chief Justice, whose unmarried lover, Amelia Godfrey, was the mother of his two children, remained judiciously silent.

'The truth,' Sir Hardinge continued, 'is those who publish this book must have known perfectly well that an unlimited publication of this sort, put into the hands of everybody, whatever their age, whatever their condition in life, whatever their modes of life, whatever their means, put into the hands of any person who may think proper to pay sixpence for it – the thesis is this: if you do not desire to have children, and wish to gratify your sensual passions, and not undergo the responsibility of marriage; if you are desirous of doing that, I show you by a philosophical treatise, forsooth, how you may effect that object satisfactorily and safely, after a long experience, collected from a great number of scientific persons; the expedient I recommend has never been known to fail.'[9]

In its account of the day's proceedings, *The Times* reported, dryly, that 'The Lord Chief Justice observed that the Solicitor-General objected to the whole of the book from the beginning to the end of it.'

'The Christian religion is happily still a part of the law of this country,' Sir Hardinge Giffard evangelised to the court. 'Don't talk to me about doctors! I care not if every physician in England had written a book of this character – although God forbid that I suggest any physician could do so!' *Fruits of Philosophy*, he bellowed before taking his seat, was 'calculated to deprave the minds of those into whose hands it may fall'.

Next, Douglas Straight called William Simonds to the stand. The detective constable repeated the droll facts from his sworn deposition, explaining how Annie Besant had sold him the book. 'She supplied me with a copy. I gave her a shilling, and she gave me sixpence change.'

Speaking for the first time that morning, Annie interrupted to ask a question that the jury might have thought immaterial, or proof of why women were not allowed to practice law. She was, however, sowing a seed to harvest later. Annie did not ask the sworn Simonds if, since coming into contact with *Fruits of Philosophy*, he had noticed signs of low morals or mental depravity. Instead, she surprisingly inquired, 'What wages do you get?'

'Thirty-one shillings and six pence' weekly, the policeman replied.

'Has it been raised at all?'

'Yes; I get an extra portion for my clothes.'

'You did not get much in the beginning?'

'No; about 28 shillings, or 29.'

No further questions. Douglas Straight said that his side had proved that the defendants had sold the book in question, and so would rest. 'This was the case for the prosecution,' reported *The Times*.

'It fell to my lot to open the defence,' wrote Annie Besant.

⁂

What did the jury see when the woman, standing just over five-foot-two in boots, turned to address them? A runaway vicar's wife turned blasphemous pornographer, or an archetype of blessed British contrarianism, and successor to John Stuart Mill? A trial is a drama, but also a tug-of-war. The crime of obscenity was a greased rope; unlike other crimes, evidence would not decide the outcome, only the private feelings and standards of 12 upper-crust men. For two hours, the prosecution had pulled them towards its version of the truth, and now, at 12.30, it was the defence's turn. Rather than flexing the strong oratory for which she was known, Annie Besant opened with humility.

'My lord, and gentlemen of the jury,' she began, 'It will not seem strange to any of you if, in defending myself here today, I find myself slightly over-weighted by the amount of legal ability which the prosecution has thought it well to

Annie Besant, as she appeared around the time of her trial

bring against me. I know that names such as those who stand as advocates against me must carry – and must rightly carry – a certain amount of weight with those to whom I have to appeal. When you find the learned Solicitor-General engaged in the case, and when his great legal knowledge is not enough to conduct it without the assistance of two other counsel learned in the law, you must come to the conclusion that you have two great criminals before you, because, if it were not so, the prosecution would not go into the very large expense entailed in this case.'

Did she pause to punctuate the gentle joke with her signature look? As an infant 29 years earlier, Annie, already curious to explore her world, had pulled herself up in her cradle and cut her forehead on its canopy, paralysing a muscle above her eye. 'To this accident,' her niece remembered, she 'attributes the curious trick she had of raising one eyebrow above the other. It had a queer effect, and she made great play with it when she was lecturing. She had an indescribable way of dropping her head a trifle onto one shoulder, with a whimsical sort of smile, a most engaging trick. No one could imitate her, though people often tried, for it really was very effective.'[10]

After seeing England's greatest actor playing the titular Richard III, Annie told her column's readers, 'The first soliloquy has too much eyebrow movement.' She had still enjoyed Henry Irving's skill. 'The pretence of virtue with underlying scoff and mockery throughout is a masterpiece.'[11] Addressing the special jury, as well as her supporters thronging the courtroom balcony, Annie echoed the actor's performance.

'I might feel less hopeful of success,' she continued, 'did I pretend to rival the learned Solicitor-General in legal knowledge, in force of tongue, or in skill of dialectic. But, gentlemen, I do not rely on these: I rely on a far mightier power; I trust to the goodness of my cause, and I am sure that, when you have heard the evidence which I shall lay before you, you will feel that to give a verdict of guilty would be to give a verdict against the weight of the evidence, and would have a most unfortunate effect upon the public outside.

'I have spent the few weeks I have had between my arrest and the present time in studying the case I have to set before you. I have done my best during these few weeks which have intervened to make myself acquainted with those trials of the past which bear upon this subject, and those state trials from which I could gather some ideas by which I might move you, or some words which I could use when appealing to you. It is not as defendant that I plead to you today – not simply as defending myself do I stand here – but I speak as counsel for hundreds of the poor, and it is they for whom I defend this case.'

Rather than raise the taboo of sex, Besant (whose tongue, like her jurors, was tattooed with an educated London accent) invoked the safer ground of class. Who among the queen's subjects could deny its existence? Certainly not her pet prime minister. As a young MP, Benjamin Disraeli's best-selling novel *Sybil* described the same widening economic chasm as Friedrich Engels's *The Condition of the Working Class in England*, also published in 1845. The impoverished titular character of Disraeli's story holds the impossible dream of becoming a barrister; she's rescued from a future in a convent by marrying an aristocrat. The improbable plot is less remembered than its famous passage in which a character asserts, 'Our Queen reigns over the greatest nation that ever existed.' Another replies, 'Which nation . . . for she reigns over two . . . Two nations; between whom there is no intercourse and no sympathy; who are as ignorant of each other's habits, thoughts, and feelings, as if they were dwellers in different zones, or inhabitants of different planets; who are formed by a different breeding, are fed by a different food, are ordered by different manners, and are not governed by the same laws.' Disraeli named these nations 'the RICH and the POOR'.[12]

'My clients,' Annie Besant continued in the crowded courtroom, 'are scattered up and down through the length and breadth of the land; I find them amongst the poor, amongst whom I have been so much; I find my clients amongst the fathers, who see their wage ever reducing, and prices ever rising; I find my clients amongst the mothers worn out with over-frequent child-bearing, and with two or three little ones around too young to guard themselves, while they have no time to guard them. It is enough for a woman at home to have the care, the clothing, the training of a large family of young children to look to; but it is a harder task when often-times the mother, who should be at home with her little ones, has to go out and work in the fields for wages to feed them when her presence is needed in the house.

'I find my clients among the little children. Gentlemen, do you know the fate of so many of these children? . . . These poor are my clients, and if I weary you by length of speech, as I fear I may, I do so because I must think of them more even than I think of your time or trouble. You must remember that those for whom I speak are watching throughout England, Scotland, and Ireland, for the verdict you will give. Do you wonder I call them my clients, these poor for whom I plead? They cannot bring the fee of gold such as is received by the learned gentlemen who are briefed against me here; but they bring what is better than gold – they send up a few pence week by week out of their scanty wage for as long as the trial lasts; they send up kindly thoughts and words of cheer and of encouragement; mothers who beg me to persist in the course on which I have entered – and at any hazard to myself, at any cost and any risk – they plead to me to save their daughters from the misery they have themselves passed through during the course of their married lives.'[13]

Her motive for teaching birth control was to improve their lot, not her own. 'Gentlemen,' she went on, 'I may perhaps say one word for myself before I go right into my case. The learned Solicitor-General has had the kindness to say that he does not impute bad intent to us in publishing this work. What bad intent could there be? I had nothing to gain in publishing this work – I had much to lose. It is no light thing for a woman, whose ambition is bound up in the name which she hopes to make, to have the imputation thrown upon her of publishing indecent books and of disseminating obscenity amongst the young. I risk my name, I risk my liberty; and it is not without deep and earnest thought that I have entered into this struggle.'

The Crown, not her own promotion, Annie pointed out, had fuelled the pamphlet's skyrocketing sales. 'People buy it now simply because it is prosecuted.'

She said that a poor woman with only sixpence to spare should be allowed to purchase 'the knowledge which richer women can obtain' for six shillings – 12 times more – in medical textbooks. 'The learned Solicitor-General spoke most disdainfully of a book that should be sold for sixpence; but when people have to live on thirteen shillings a week, sixpence is quite as much as they can afford to pay for a book containing useful and necessary sanitary information.'

Annie told the court that although she did not pretend 'to the extreme delicacy displayed by the learned Solicitor-General', she would allow her co-defendant Charles Bradlaugh to read aloud from *Fruits of Philosophy*. 'I do this, not as admitting that these details are obscene or indecent in any respect, but simply because I think that such a course will be pleasanter to all concerned.' Her testimony instead would explain their logical and compassionate motive for publishing.

'The malice of the prosecution has overreached itself,' Annie argued. 'The very way the indictment has been framed makes it fatal to the prosecution. But you have got more to do than to find the whole of the book obscene.' According to its florid wording, the Crown would have to prove that her object in publishing was to corrupt Britain's youth and every other liege subject of the queen. She reminded the special jury that the consequences would fall heaviest upon the only woman present in the courtroom.

'You must affirm every allegation in the indictment to be true,' Annie insisted. 'Gentlemen, I will ask you to remember that, when you go away to consider your verdict . . . and if I press this specially upon you, gentlemen, it is because I feel that in this matter I have so much to lose if your verdict should go against me, and I will ask you, therefore, if at any time during the trial (which may, in some parts, perchance, become wearisome to you), if, at any moment, you think you are kept here to your own annoyance and inconvenience, I ask you to put that momentary annoyance of, at the utmost, but a few days' detention in a crowded court, against the penalty which lies on me, unless I can succeed in obtaining a verdict of not guilty – a penalty which does not mean confinement for a few days, or for any length of time which the judge can sentence, but which means, practically, almost the extinction of my future life until I can wipe off the stain which your verdict, if guilty, will put upon me. Do not mistake me by thinking that I should think myself guilty; I should not do so. I have done this thing with full thought and with full knowledge of the responsibility I incurred. Knowing it all, I should proceed to do it again, with the experience I have had since my arrest. I should bring in myself not guilty, whatever your verdict might be'.

As this was a criminal trial, she stressed, 'You must get at the intent. Take the case of two men, one of whom has a pistol, and the second man, who has not a pistol, is found shot. It does not follow that the first man, even if found with the pistol in his hand, has been guilty of murder. If that man were set before you on the charge of murder, you would find out what the intent was which might have governed his actions. You would ask if there had been malice between them, or quarrels between them, in the time that had gone. You would ask what intention perhaps was in the mind of the man who shot, before you would bring him in guilty of the murder of his fellow man. I put it to you that much more, in dealing with a medical book, you must show the intent to be malicious, before you can, by any possibility, bring in a verdict of guilty against me here.'[14]

Showing off her homework, Besant quoted from Erskine, from a trial for seditious libel: 'When a man accused of libel is brought before a jury, they are to consider only the mind and intention with which the matter was written.' Next she cited a case where a book was found to be libellous against the king, but no sentence was passed. 'Erskine says: If you give the defendants the credit of honest feelings and upright intentions, on my part any farther defence is unnecessary; we are already in possession of your verdict; you have already pronounced them not guilty; for you will not condemn the conduct when you have acquitted the heart.'[15]

Knowledge, Annie asserted, could not be made felonious by a criminal mind. 'Every book, however good the book may be – any of your old classics, any of your standard English works, may be read for the vilest purposes, if the impure mind is to be permitted to characterise them and put upon them the shame that only comes from its own obscene impurity.' Here she opened a copy of *Tristram Shandy*.

'I am very reluctant to interfere, my lord,' interrupted Sir Hardinge Giffard, 'but I think I must take your judgment whether or not such passages ought to be read.'

Charles Bradlaugh objected that precedent allowed the right to refer to other publications.

'Have you got the authority?' the judge asked.

'It is the case of the *King v. Carlile*,' Besant quickly retorted.[16]

The Lord Chief Justice ignored her, perhaps thinking of his waiting roast chop and glass of sherry, and called an adjournment for lunch. The cast retreated to the wings, the audience turned to the exits, and the scribblers sprinted to make their deadline for their papers' afternoon editions. Outside the day shone brightly. The stock market held steady, with prices trending upward. The wickets fell rapidly at Lord's, where in pleasant sporting weather, the home-side Marylebone Cricket Club took to the emerald field against Cambridge.

The London *Echo* ran their trial dispatch in that day's fifth edition, only two hours after its reporter had witnessed Annie argue that, as the paper put it, 'The whole right of the discussion of the population question was bound up in the verdict they would give on a sixpenny pamphlet, which the Solicitor-General despised on account of its price.'[17] *The Echo* cost a halfpenny. In the story running beside the trial's, readers could sop up the gory details of the Islington man who that morning had murdered his two-year-old daughter. The girl's mother discovered her child with a throat slashed ear to ear. Found drunk in a pub, the killer said he did not know what made him do it. That evening, London theatre-goers could choose from light comedies whose plots spun on money, sex, and dread: *Lend Me Five Shillings*, *The Conjugal Lesson*, and *A Fearful Fog*. The great London gyre churned on.

Sir Alexander Cockburn began the day's second act by agreeing with the defendant that she could read aloud from all the texts she wished.

'I do not propose to read any quotations from *Tristram Shandy*,' Annie replied. 'It would be an utter waste of the time of the Court.' It would also have required her to mime. Laurence Sterne's eighteenth-century novel relied on the reader to fill-in its 'dirty' blanks. One asterisked passage can stand for many: ''Tis enough, said'st thou, coming close up to me, as I stood with my garters in my hand, reflecting upon what had *not* pass'd – 'Tis enough, Tristram, and I am satisfied,

said'st thou, whispering these words in my ear, **** ** ****
*** ******; _ **** ** **** – any other man would have sunk
down to the centre.'[18]

And most readers would pause, guessing which four-letter
word (did it begin with *f*?) thou had whispered before the
two-letter one (was it *me*?). Over 100 years later, publishers
continued this chaste charade. Straight talk about sex and
reproduction could not blot the Victorian page. Working-
class people, especially, were left to fill in the blanks. Silence
and misinformation reigned.

A study of over 600 working-class diaries from this era
reveals the shock and fear teenaged girls felt at their first
period. One teen thought she had 'burst a blood vessel and
was doomed to death'. Another felt 'I must have done something wicked and was being punished'. A mother taught her
daughter her only lesson in 'anatomy': 'You'll have this every
month until you're fifty and keep away from the boys.'

The boys were kept just as ignorant. A man remembered
asking his mother where he had come from. Her reply was 'a
terrific smack on the side of the head which sent me reeling
away'. His generation had 'inherited the vast reticence of our
parents'. New pregnancies were often a surprise to children
at home. Sometimes even the word was avoided: one girl
remembered her mother describing her condition as 'heavy
footed'. Many correspondents wrote that babies were not
spoken of until they appeared, via the stork or a physician's
black bag, like a present delivered by the magical Father
Christmas. 'How could baby fit into such a small bag?' one
diarist wondered.

Women became pregnant without knowing how. Their
embarrassed mothers changed the subject. Some feared that
their child would emerge from their navel, others that a
doctor would cut them 'up the front'. None of this trove of

A Victorian postcard – 'And the villain still pursues her'

662 autobiographies mentioned pleasurable marital sex, only unending seasons of pregnancy and childbirth. The only form of contraception women practised seemed to be avoidance.

One woman who did not want any more children stayed up late mending. 'My husband would be asleep when I come to bed.' More common was the mother of seven, whose husband told her, 'You can't go against nature', and impregnated her twice more. In her diary, she wrote that if she had a choice, she would have had 'two or three [children] at the most'.[19]

Inside the Court of Queen's Bench, Annie Besant flattered the special jury with her gratitude for its education, since 'to hand up to an ignorant jury a passage from *Tristram Shandy* would be utterly condemnatory of the whole book . . . I feel I have nothing to fear from a miscarriage of justice, such as I might fear from a jury less cultivated.'

In the works of every great English dramatist, she continued, you could find 'passages, which, if taken by themselves, might be said to have a tendency to vitiate and corrupt. I take

Shakespeare as an example, whom no one would desire to see blotted out of our literature and imagine that some spy of some society – we will say of the Society for the Suppression of Vice – took one of Shakespeare's poems and founded a prosecution on it.'[20]

(In a London courtroom 83 years later, before another ermined judge, a barrister seeking to end the ban on *Lady Chatterley's Lover* will echo Annie's words, arguing that *Antony and Cleopatra* is more than a play about adultery. As in Besant's trial, witnesses will be asked if Lawrence's novel was a book they would like their wife or servant to read. The defence will be sorry to upset the prosecution by suggesting that many Britons did not have servants. 'It is the attitude,' the defence will say of the prosecution, 'that it is all right to publish a special edition at five or ten guineas, but quite wrong to let people who are less well-off read what those other people read. Is not everyone, whether their income is ten pounds or twenty pounds a week, equally interested in the society in which we live? In the problems of our relationships, including sexual relationships? . . . If it is right that the book should be read, it should be available to the man working in a factory as it is to the teacher working in a school.' In England, the barrister will continue in 1960, we have banned books by Hardy, Ibsen, Wilde, Joyce and Shaw. When will it end?)[21]

Watching on his feet from the courtroom's terrace in 1877, the callow George Bernard Shaw sided with Annie Besant's own defence. With blue eyes twinkling, he will later recount to her niece, 'She held them all in the hollow of her hand, did Annie! She was a GODDESS! A GODDESS!'[22] He did not say which one. To the men and women who packed her Freethought lectures, she may have been Athena, purveyor of knowledge and justice. But to the jury, she could well have been Discordia, bringer of chaos and strife.

It must have felt incredible, holding the crammed court-room's attention with her voice. (Shaw, beguiled in the balcony, also found her slim figure and good looks irresist-ible.) Your common sense, she told the 12 men, knew that no man or woman would purchase a medical book with the aim of arousing sexual passion. She paused after noticing her audience squinting. 'My lord, I don't know whether I am going out of my case,' Annie addressed the judge, 'but I think if the light could be preventing from falling on the jury box, it would be an improvement. It is a great point to me to keep the jury in good temper, my lord.' Laughter filled the room.

'I must do you the justice to say,' Sir Alexander Cockburn replied, 'that up to this time you have said nothing that could produce any other result.' He directed the net curtains to be drawn.

Theia, the goddess of sight. 'They just worshipped her,' Shaw will later remember. 'Why, if Annie got up on the plat-form, and said that a rose was a violet, well, a rose <u>was</u> a violet, and they all believed it!'[23]

Apate, the goddess of deception. The court transcript did not record how the prosecution was faring as she spoke. Sit-ting cross-armed and confidently unbothered? Or outwardly stoic but feeling the creeping realisation that they had under-estimated their opponent?

'The Solicitor-General,' Besant continued to the more comfortable jury, 'made one remark which I had the pleasure of agreeing with, and I did not agree with much that fell from my antagonist's lips. He said that you are the guardians of public morals.' Even the Lord Chief Justice's opinion was not binding; only they could 'do justice between the Queen and ourselves', or join the ignominious juries who had 'returned verdicts of repression, verdicts afterward to be reversed, as all such verdicts are, on appeal to the higher court of posterity.'

The special jury would agree, would it not, that the right to discuss theology had been won, as had the right to publicly argue politics. Why should sex and contraception remain taboo? 'Difference of opinion is not to be taken as proof of obscenity,' she contended, 'and the more you may differ in opinion from Knowlton so much the more jealously should you guard his right of discussion.'

She was fighting for the freedom of booksellers to operate without fear of detective police spies and self-appointed secret agents of the Society for the Suppression of Vice. 'This pamphlet,' Annie continued, 'is valuable to us just as is the piece of silk to the soldier who wins the battle for his country; it is the flag which represents the cause we have at stake . . . I fight that I may make here the right of open and free discussion on a great and important social subject.'[24]

Besant might well have been enjoying herself at this point, mellifluously quoting from memory passages of John Stuart Mill's *On Liberty* and citing previous verdicts. Next she circled back to her first utterance in court, earlier that day. 'I asked Detective Simonds what his weekly wage was, and how long he had been in the detective force. Probably, when I asked him those questions, you may have thought that I was asking useless ones without an object . . . I asked them with no idle intention. I asked them for this reason: It is one of the principles of English justice, that those accused shall be placed face to face with their accusers, and shall understand who brings them to answer before the bar of justice. Our difficulty in knowing the aim of the prosecution is, that we don't know at the present moment who is prosecuting us.'

Annie recounted how, upon their arrest, they had been told at Guildhall that the City of London was filing the charges. In preparation for this trial, Charles Bradlaugh had received a letter. 'Imagine our astonishment when we were told that "the Corporation of the City of London has nothing and never had anything to do with the prosecution against you and Mrs. Besant." This came to us as a greater surprise because Mr. Douglas Straight, instructed by the City Solicitor, said in open court that he appeared on behalf of the Corporation. You may imagine that we found it difficult to discover what private malice had been brought to bear in the institution of the prosecution against us.'

The City police commissioner also denied involvement. 'We wrote to detective William Simonds asking if he were the man responsible. We received in return merely an answer expressing his pleasure at receiving our letter. Now Mr. William Simonds has been in the force for 13 years. He commenced at 28 shillings a week, and has risen to 31 shillings and sixpence, and he has some clothes in addition. I will ask you to use your common sense whether Mr. William Simonds on 28 shillings a week, rising to 31 shillings and sixpence, has made such large economies that he has been able to save sufficient money out of his salary to find the fees and engage the services of the Solicitor-General and Mr. Douglas Straight to prosecute us? If it be possible to live upon so small a sum of money and also put by sufficient means to fight one's difficulties with the aid of a powerful retinue of legal advisers such as the learned counsel engaged in this case, there can be no necessity for appealing to Dr. Knowlton's work with any desire to keep down one's family on the ground of want of means.'

Again the courtroom exploded in laughter.

'Why, when Dr. Knowlton's work was commenced to be published in England – that was forty-two years ago,' Annie continued, 'Mr. William Simonds must have been a little boy.

He must have made this prosecution the far-off ideal of his life, and undoubtedly he must have commenced to have saved the sixpence or nine pence a week, which he should have spent in sugar-plums or toffee, to have then commanded means sufficient to have retained the services of the Solicitor-General and these other gentlemen. Now, see the position in which we stand with regard to this prosecution, which is a disgrace to English justice.'

If they won, she explained, the whole of their court costs – including the guinea (£1 1s.) paid to each special juror – would fall on William Simonds. 'We know that the Queen is nominally our prosecutor, but there is no public fund out of which the costs of our prosecution can be paid.' (Who else was thinking of poor William Simonds? Eleos, goddess of compassion and mercy.)

'Or,' Annie asked, 'are there people hidden behind the coat of the city detective, of whom we have a right to hear?' She gestured to the courtroom's silent crowd. 'Its representatives are here today, brought here lest the failure of the Solicitor-General and the two learned counsel whom he leads should need the fostering care of these hidden abettors.'

This really was turning Shakespearean. *Friends, Britons, countrymen, lend me your ears. Collette is an honourable man.*

'Forty or fifty years ago,' Annie explained, 'there was a society called the Society of Vice, but better known as the Bridge Street gang; in this Society, under cover of a few respectable names, a herd of spies and informers carried on their despicable work, and hunted down honest booksellers, whose works are now found on the shelves of every thinker. This society sank out of sight under a weight of shame and disgust, but it has again arisen, and is once more at its foul work. It is today worthily represented by its secretary, Mr. C. H. Collette, solicitor, and he boasts, openly, that he "prompts" the Solicitor-General against us. That he is starting all these prosecutions is very suggestive, and I ask you whether you will countenance a society like that, sheltering itself under a police detective in order to prosecute a man and a woman who are spending their lives in trying to do good to their fellow creatures?'

Perhaps Annie here spoke too quickly for reporters to correctly transcribe her words. More likely, the Establishment protected their own. Rather than fingering Charles Hastings Collette, London newspapers, including the Giffard family's *Evening Standard*, left his name out of their stories. Instead, the press outed Detective Simonds as the spy and informer for the Society for the Prevention of Vice. We cannot know if he was just a patsy; after stepping off this stage, Simonds will sink back into anonymity.

As the sun slanted lower in the courtroom's west-facing windows, Annie recounted the origin of *Fruits of Philosophy*. The special jury had no way of knowing that many of her facts were wrong. She chided the Solicitor-General's 'curious – if not a pretended – ignorance' when he spoke of a 'Mr Knowlton'. In Besant's telling, he was 'an M.D. in good practice in Boston, which city is said to be considered by the Americans as the "hub of the universe" – the "hub" meaning the acme of culture, of education, of scientific thought and ability'.

Charles Knowlton in fact had been born and raised on a Massachusetts farm, where he suffered nervous anxiety from a teenage diagnosis of *gonorrhea dormientium*, as nocturnal emissions were medically called. Shock therapy did not cure him, although his condition miraculously dried up after falling in love with his doctor's daughter. After they married, Knowlton pursued an education in medicine.

He started in a graveyard, digging up a corpse for dissection.

Unable to afford the tuition to Dartmouth medical school, Knowlton unearthed more bodies to raise funds. After one corpse deteriorated in the heat on the back of his horse cart, he planned to sell its bones. A professor of anatomy paid him 20 dollars for the putrid mess. Knowlton would go on to write his M.D. dissertation on the role of dissection in medical education. And then, shortly after graduation, it was part of the evidence that got him sentenced to two months in prison, for grave robbing and illegal dissection.

Charles Knowlton, looking nothing like a
man convicted of body snatching

'I think it important to you to know,' Annie innocently told the Court of Queen's Bench, 'that Dr. Charles Knowlton was not only looked up to and respected throughout his native town but throughout the whole of the United States.' In the tone that could convince listeners that a rose was a violet, Besant said he had lived a blameless life, omitting his convictions for publishing *Fruits of Philosophy*. The Solicitor-General, she contended, had gone too far, even in a criminal prosecution, 'to cast unfair slurs on the name of a dead man'.

Annie found surer ground when recounting the history of Knowlton's pamphlet in England, leading to the arrest of the Bristol bookseller and guilty plea from Charles Watts, 'bringing us into the disgrace of his yielding'. She had never been a printer or publisher before, but in her understanding, when someone produced an obscene work, they did not attach their real name to it. There had been no such concealment here. 'However much we may disagree with Dr. Knowlton,' Annie admitted, 'we are responsible for every syllable that he has written. I hold that everyone who prints and publishes a book ought to be held to the fullest extent responsible for that which he issues to the public. I hold that nothing is so cowardly, nothing is so mean or so disgraceful, as for a publisher to issue a book, or for an editor to issue a journal, and then, when challenged by the law, to shrink back and say I did not know what I was doing.'[25]

That singular statement from one of the few – and certainly the bravest – female publishers in all of England, went unreported in the newspapers. As did her defiant rebuttal – to this jury, bench and room full of men – to Sir Hardinge Giffard's objection, after he had rustled into his reserves of strength to read it aloud, that the pamphlet's recommended contraceptive methods could be used 'without even a partial sacrifice of the pleasure which attends the gratification of the productive instinct'.

'I put it to you,' Annie Besant challenged her courtroom audience, 'that there is nothing wrong in a natural desire rightly and properly gratified. There is no harm in feeling thirsty because people get drunk; there is no harm in feeling hungry because people over-eat themselves, and there is no harm in gratifying the sexual instinct if it can be gratified without injury to anyone else, and without harm to the morals of society, and with due regard to the health of those whom nature has given us the power of summoning into the world.'

Did the special jurors blush or lower their heads in high dudgeon? Annie Besant did not halt. She was having her day in court.

'I put it to you gravely,' she continued, 'that it is only a false and spurious kind of modesty, which sees harm in the gratification of one of the highest instincts of human nature.' The Church of England, Annie pointed out, taught that to ensure reproduction, God had made sex pleasurable. (Although, she could have added, He did not say for whom.) 'The notion that pleasure qua pleasure is wrong is an ascetic notion, which is at the base of a large amount of the profligacy of the present day.'

Next she told the court a potted version of the law of population, as laid down by the Reverend Thomas Malthus. This oration devolved into maths, and for the first time she was losing the room. Charles Bradlaugh waited until Annie had finished yet another geometrical sentence ending on 'millions', before saying to the Lord Chief Justice, 'I do not know how long your lordship will sit. At this stage Mrs. Besant is about half-way through.'

'We must go on, I think,' Sir Alexander Cockburn replied, 'for another half-hour, unless Mrs. Besant feels exhausted.'

'Oh no,' she answered. 'I can go on.'

No laughs appeared in the transcript here. 'Mrs. Besant intimated (though she had spoken several hours),' *The Times* reported, 'that she had not yet nearly finished her address.' Although she had stolen the show, the paper would headline its story THE QUEEN V. BRADLAUGH AND ANOTHER. Annie Besant was not a goddess. In eliding her name, the paper was nothing if not consistent. She was a married, common Victorian woman.

As the trial's first day wound down, she admitted that contraception was, as her critics charged, a subversion of nature's immutable laws. However: 'It is the natural way, as the Solicitor-General put it (although not delicately, perhaps), for a man to go about naked; though that is not respectable, that is the natural way of doing things. We, however, prefer the artificial fashion, which has the decency of clothing, instead of that which the Solicitor-General put, and I plead for what is called the artificial check – the preventive check' on unwanted pregnancy.

'Mrs. Besant had not concluded her speech when the court rose,' a wire service reporter telegraphed to newsrooms nationwide, delivering Annie's impassioned defence to morning papers set beside egg cups and tea on tables from Devon to Dublin and Belfast to Aberdeen. 'The defendants,' the story related, 'were cheered by a large crowd as they left Westminster Hall.'[26]

8

'FOR US WOMEN'

———————

The actors reappeared in their appointed positions on the bright Tuesday morning of 19 June and again bowed at 10.30 as the Lord Chief Justice took his seat. Reading aloud a letter from an audience member complaining for want of ventilation in the stifling courtroom, Sir Alexander Cockburn apologised that there were no more windows to open. Outside, the mercury climbed to 26 degrees.

A trial lacks dramatic unity; the second day began not with an alteration of action or change of players, but with Annie Besant resuming where she had left off. Thus far this novice had impressed the court, and her critics. Even *The Times* admitted her 'remarkable ability' as well as her 'earnestness and evident sincerity'.[1]

This day's testimony would fill 75 printed pages. Even when set in tiny, narrow type, Annie's voice sounded anything but timid, and her cause too catholic to ignore.

She began by telling the special jury that she had been pleased that morning to receive a letter from the esteemed Scottish professor Alexander Bain, author of Britain's authoritative textbook on psychology. Twice-married, Bain also had not fathered any children. This close friend of John Stuart Mill had sent his support in what he deemed 'one of the most critical trials in the history of our liberties'.

Next Annie reiterated Malthus's warning of the effects of over-population. The recent famine in Ireland lived in the jurors' memory, and in 1877 colonial India was in the middle of a two-year famine that would kill 8 million British subjects. (Annie, like most Victorians, did not then understand that multiple factors, beyond population, collide to produce food shortages.) China may have been the world's most populous country, but its 405 million people, she pointed out, were spread across land 40 times larger than the British Isles, whose population was already 40 times as dense. (She might more convincingly have told the court that by forbidding the discussion of sex and reproductive choice, Victorians were binding women's minds the way some Chinese were binding women's feet.)

Annie's inimitable speaking strength lay in her knowledge that pain observed was not the same as pain shared. So while she dutifully quoted from clergymen's accounts of east London overcrowding – families of nine, eleven and fourteen living in 'a state of squalid misery that a horse kept in the worst possible stable was better provided for' – Besant sounded, as ever, most compelling when she related the truths she herself had observed, and could never unsee.

'I have myself seen four generations of human beings crowded together into one small room,' Annie recounted, 'and I will ask you if, after such an experience as that, you wonder that I risk even prison.'[2] In the poor parish of Bethnal Green, children under five comprised more than half the total number of deaths; in wealthy Hanover Square the (still alarming) figure was less than one-third.

In its daily trial summary, *The Times* opined that Mrs Besant seemed to protest too much. *Fruits of Philosophy* was not being charged as obscene for its uncontroversial stance against unsupported and unhygienic childbirth. In an unsigned story that may have been written by the special jury's foreman (the publisher's son) the newspaper questioned Annie's decision to wield a shield of long quotations from unprosecuted books and speeches by the likes of Charles Darwin and Millicent Fawcett, neither of whom supported birth control. If *The Times* knew that both authors had refused to testify on the defendants' behalf, it didn't say. That day's dispatch would end with a letter from a London publisher who wanted to make clear that, despite what Annie Besant had told the court, in past decades he had merely stocked Charles Knowlton's pamphlet in his printshop. The blame for printing it rested on his partner, who (conveniently assuring the publisher's innocence) had recently died.

This popinjay's call grated on Alice and Hypatia Bradlaugh, who miserably paced outside the courtroom in the expanse of Westminster Hall, 'watching for anyone to come out with any news of how the case was going on. Melancholy figures we must have looked, nearly always alone, dressed in black gowns – for our mother had died suddenly in the midst of all this – and very frightened at heart at what might happen.' In this same space Anne Boleyn had been feted at her coronation banquet; *Utopia* author Sir Thomas More had been condemned to death.

The only effect of the turncoat publisher inoculating himself from the trial's contagion, Hypatia wrote, 'could be to injure the defendants. It may be imagined that my father did not take it as a very kindly act. Indeed, Mrs. Besant put it that the letter was one carefully calculated to prejudice the jury against us, and sent to the very paper with which one of our jurymen was connected.' As for the years the publisher had remained quietly anonymous, 'silent while he sold it, silent while he profited by the sale, would it have been too great an exercise of self-control,' she asked, 'if he had maintained his silence for two days longer?'[3]

Charles Darwin may have done Annie a service by not accepting her invitation to the witness box. His absence allowed her to refute his contention, in *The Descent of Man*, that suffering was a necessary condition of progress. The government, she argued, apparently agreed with her, as it had passed the Sanitary Act of 1866 and the Vaccination Act of 1867 to 'unnaturally' check disease that would otherwise cull society's less fit members.

Annie rejected, too, Darwin's idea that the objective of any population check should be to create a 'higher race'. Some future contraceptive campaigners, bearing the standard of Darwin's cousin Francis Galton – progenitor, in 1883, of eugenics – would aim to end the 'reckless breeding' (as will say Marie Stopes, born in 1880) in impoverished, immigrant and minority communities, 'assisting the race' (as will say Margaret Sanger, born in 1879) 'toward the elimination of the unfit'.

Annie Besant far predated these discredited doctrines. She did not advocate 'social engineering' (a term then still uncoined) in favour of a few, but for the right to teach sex education and access contraception for all. To the special jury she quoted John Stuart Mill: 'The idea, in this country, never sems to enter any one's mind that having or not having a family, or the number of which it shall consist, is amenable to their own control. One would imagine that children were rained down upon married people, direct from heaven, without their having art or part in the matter; that it was really, as the common phrases have it, God's will, and not their own, which decided the numbers of their offspring.'

Annie also acted to protect women's health. 'For to me,' she continued in the courtroom, 'that is a very vital point in dealing with this book. We have seen the effect on society of over-population; we have not seen the effect on the women themselves, for the premature deaths which keep down the population do not save the health of the mother, who is exhausted by the over-rapid child-bearing. It may save some of the social effects of over-population; it does not save the unfortunate mothers whose health is ruined, and you will find that put very plainly in Dr. Knowlton's work . . . Here is one point I shall want to prove to you, more from the evidence of witnesses than from a book. There is no question that amongst the women of the poorer classes there is a vast amount of suffering caused by over-rapid child-bearing.'

In fact, this affliction did not discriminate by class. Unbeknownst to Annie, less than a mile away from the Court of Queen's Bench, behind the walls of Buckingham Palace, Britain's wealthiest woman had borne the same burden.

'I was in for it at once,' Victoria wrote to her eldest daughter, '& furious I was.' The queen had married Albert in February 1840; by April, 'it was known & understood' by the household that she was 'in an interesting condition'.[4]

'It is spoiling my happiness,' Victoria admitted to her grandmother. 'I have always hated the idea and I prayed God night and day for me to be left free for at least six months, but my prayers have not been answered and I am really most unhappy. I cannot understand how one can wish for such a thing, especially at the beginning of a marriage.' If she delivered a 'nasty girl', Her Majesty swore she would drown it.

The queen's accoucheur, Sir Charles Locock, addressed her using words as indelicate as the names of his tools, which included the Long Scissors and the Blunt Hook. Victoria, like Annie Besant, was small-boned and short. Dr Locock, who disliked her, cattily said that in pregnancy she would grow 'ugly & enormously fat', and look 'more like a barrel than anything else'.[5]

The doctor dissuaded Victoria from taking anaesthesia during labour, although she would later overrule him and demand chloroform. The queen delivered her first child in a room full of squabbling doctors, bishops and footmen, only to hear the bad news: 'Oh Madam, it is a Princess.'[6] Albert consoled her by covering her face in kisses.

Although she adored the Princess Royal, Victoria was not enamoured of infants. To her they seemed 'mere little plants for the first 6 months'.[7] (She infamously called babies frog-like, although anyone who has changed a nappy has seen the resemblance when the Moro reflex splays their limbs.)

Victoria's high libido and love for Albert sped along the race to produce a male heir, albeit at the cost of her mental and physical health. Three months after delivering her first child, the queen was pregnant again. 'Men never think, or at least seldom think, what a hard task it is for us women to go through this *very often*,' she confessed. 'It is indeed too hard and dreadful what we have to go through, and men ought to have an adoration for one, and indeed to do every thing to make up, for what after all they alone are the cause of!'[8]

Her second birth, of Edward, broke something within. 'My poor nerves were so battered . . . I suffered *a whole year* from it.' Her 'nasty doctors', as she came to call the lot of them, prescribed draughts for headaches and pain. Postpartum depression would not be understood until the next century. In her own era, living in palaces and surrounded by servants, Victoria suffered alone.

The queen saw visions that included coffins floating before her, and 'spots on people's faces, which turned into worms'. She began to fear she had inherited the madness of her grandfather, George III. A physician arrived at the bedchamber to find Her Majesty 'lying Down, and the tears were flowing fast over her cheek as she addressed me – overwhelmed with shame at the necessity of confessing her weakness and compelled by the very burden of her mind & her sorrows to seek relief'.

She said she could not bear further pregnancies. 'If she had another Child,' the doctor transcribed, 'she would sink under it.'[9] In 17 years Victoria would deliver nine children.

Of course she ached in secret. So when Annie Besant, explaining the damaging effects of excessive childbearing, told the special jury that 'You get one special class of disease, that every doctor would tell you about, and called, in common parlance, among themselves, "falling of the womb"', she had no way of knowing that her nominal prosecutor suffered from it, too.

Not until after the queen's death was it revealed that Victoria had suffered from a painful ventral hernia – a bulge of the intestine through her abdominal wall – and a prolapsed uterus. No doctor had treated her; unable to exercise or – as she so loved – to dance, the queen gained weight and cloaked herself in ever-expanding layers of clothing. Only the ladies who dressed her knew of her discomfort, and the tonics, nostrums and opiates that compounded Victorian medicine (aspirin would not be discovered until 1897) provided little relief.

'Doctors tell you,' Annie continued, 'that you will very rarely find women among the poor who are mothers of large families, who do not suffer from a weakness of this kind.' The loyal subjects assembled inside the Court of Queen's Bench had no idea that Britain's wealthiest woman endured it, too. This knowledge gives a new gloss on Her Majesty's seemingly indolent diary entries, such as the one written on this Tuesday, 19 June: at Balmoral, Victoria 'Walked a little near the river & then sat out writing'. But what other physical activities could the queen comfortably do?

'That which is necessary to the health of the man,' Annie Besant emphasised to the jury, 'is fatal to the health of the woman.'

To the 12 male faces looking down upon her, Annie explained the dangers of over-lactation resulting from the belief that a nursing mother could not conceive, as well as the horrid chemical mixtures some women had imbibed to end their 'condition'. A supporter had mailed to her a widely available medical dictionary that explained a two-pence 'cure': ingesting ergot of rye. The plant's fungal disease poisoned humans with symptoms ranging from headache and vomiting to gangrene. Ignorance and quackery were too dangerous to be protected by law, stressed Annie Besant. She had wilfully courted arrest, and was 'so anxious to gain a verdict' in order to prove that the government could not forbid the protection of women's health.

The Lord Chief Justice praised her presentation of ideas as 'perfectly honest and perfectly pure'. At that, the court adjourned for lunch.

Outside in sunny London, the Marylebone Cricket Club triumphed over Cambridge by six wickets. Professor Bell lectured on his telephone, but, one newspaper argued, the probability of this new system of telegraphing superseding the old did not appear to be very great. On the south bank of the Thames, a chandelier's stopcock silently leaked in a Battersea home. Artificial odour would not be added to gas for another 60 years, far too late to save Mr. W.G. Adams, then stepping into his parlour with an unlit pipe in his mouth and about to strike a match. The explosion could be felt for blocks around Bridge Road. In the running of the Manor Stakes at Royal Windsor Racecourse, the heavy favourite, a seasoned horse named Modesty, was bested by a newcomer, named Gadfly.

Back inside the courtroom, 'The anxiety to hear the pleadings is so great that even the lawyers have had to submit to regulations,' one correspondent reported. 'There is not a vacant space on the floor of the Court. Even reporters have been shut out.'[10]

Annie Besant resumed by raising in her hand the Tory government's Official Directory of the School of Science and Art, a South Kensington technical training institute located on Exhibition Road. The booklet, she pointed out, was produced by the queen's printers, the very same firm that published Acts of Parliament. 'You will find,' she told the jurors, 'that they issue a list of books in which they examine the young boys and young girls who present themselves for examination in the sciences.' Next Annie read excerpts from lessons in anatomy and reproduction, asking rhetorically if any of these texts aroused passion in the 13, 14 and 15-year-old girls assigned to read them 'at the express sanction of the Government, of which the Solicitor-General is an officer'.[11] If Dr Knowlton's pamphlet were obscene, then these texts were immeasurably filthier, as they included illustrations of the reproductive system.

Annie admitted that she was happy to see these medical texts circulated to young people, and wished them to be made available beyond the select school's walls. 'I say deliberately to you, as mother of a daughter whom I love, that I believe it will tend to her happiness in her future, as well as to her health, that she shall not have made to her that kind of mystery about sexual functions that every man and woman must know sooner or later.' The government was doing a service, she averred, when it taught teens the facts of life that she endeavoured to teach adults. 'It is only because former Governments have not thought it their duty to circulate physiological knowledge that we are condemned for doing it.'

Better to learn it in a classroom than the streets. 'When this teaching has had its full course for a generation,' she promised, 'this work of Knowlton's will not be wanted any longer.'

This prediction would prove more prescient than her argument that Britain would never restrict gun ownership because a deranged person used the weapon for murder instead of hunting game. 'You are asked,' Annie told the jury, 'to prevent the circulation of this book because women may abuse the knowledge there given . . . If I may judge from my own personal experience [it] is valued by poor men and women in all parts of the country, and I can't help remembering that the editor of *The Times* newspaper said that he judged the feeling of the country by the state of his letter bag in the morning.'

It was a deft nod to the man's heir apparent, listening in the jury box. Based on the correspondence in that day's *Times*, Britain's mood was one of donating shillings upon pounds to the Anglo-Turkish Ambulance Fund, and debating over the unstable design of a new ironclad battleship, whose name unintentionally expressed the Tory administration's way of governing. It was called the HMS *Inflexible*.

'Fear,' Annie continued, 'as you know too well, does not keep women chaste. Do not think you can stop the knowledge by stopping this book.'[12]

Next she shared the contents of letters sent to her by

women from all classes and corners of the country, imploring her to save their daughters. Although Besant had no way of knowing it, that protective sentiment had been felt by no less a mother than Queen Victoria, who had written to her eldest daughter, recently married in Germany:

> It is an awful moment to have to give one's innocent child up to a man – and to think of all that she must go through! . . . And that last night when we took you to your room, and you cried so much, I said to Papa as we came back "after all, it is like taking a poor lamb to be sacrificed." I know that God has willed it so and that these are the trials which we poor women must go through; no father, no man could feel this! Papa never would enter into it all! As in fact he seldom can in my very violent feelings.[13]

Her Majesty could have given the Princess Royal the book Annie Besant told the court she had received before her own nuptials. The text was still sold at railway bookstalls. The title of Dr Pye Henry Chavasse's *Wife and Mother, or Information for Every Woman* made plain the limited role its reader was intended to play. But nowhere in its 575 pages could she learn about sex. The chapter titled 'Menstruation' was immediately followed by one named 'Pregnancy'. The book's one reference to 'marital relations' appeared all the way back on page 522, and then only to warn that they 'should be suspended in cases of acute inflammation of the uterus'.

In contrast, argued Annie Besant, *Fruits of Philosophy*'s frankness was 'simply invaluable to a woman'.

Before yielding the floor to her co-defendant, she reminded the special jury that Sir Hardinge Giffard (who, as the freshly elected Conservative MP for Launceston, had momentarily taken leave to attend business in the adjoining House of Commons) had put it to the jury that reading Dr Knowlton's

words aloud had *pained him*. But he had given no consideration to the sanctioned ignorance wounding his opposite sex
and lower class. What followed must have delighted the
apprentice playwright George Bernard Shaw, watching the
scene unfold from the balcony.

> **The Lord Chief Justice**: The learned Solicitor-General is
> not here, and I think you must be just to him. He was
> rather challenged to read them.

> **Mrs Besant**: Do you think that I ought to be gentle with
> him, my lord, as he is absent?

Guffaws rippled across the courtroom.

> **The Lord Chief Justice**: What I said was, that you must be
> just to him.

> **Mrs Besant**: That is quite fair; but I thought, if he felt so
> very much pain, he might have avoided the special anguish
> of mind he seems to have had in dealing with these pas-
> sages. I will not press the point any further, however, as
> the learned counsel is not here. I do feel the position is
> especially painful for him, because, if he does not get a
> verdict against a woman, it does make the position of a
> learned counsel very painful.

Laughter resounded off the wainscoted walls.

> **The Lord Chief Justice**: You have gone through this long –
> and, I must say, very able – address up to the present
> without saying anything that could be regarded as painful
> or offensive to anyone.

> **Mrs Besant**: And I will try to do so to the end. My feelings
> towards the Solicitor shall be more charitable than his
> were to me, for he accused me of some of the vilest

things a woman could do. But I will not press the matter further, and perhaps, by not too roughly defending myself against him, I shall make my case the stronger.[14]

Less than four years ago, she had been an unknown housewife in an unheard-of vicarage in an unvisited town. Before three strikes of Big Ben signalled the hour, the eyebrow-cocking activist finished her two-day run of standing alone in the courtroom's spotlight.

'The great question we are fighting,' Annie Besant proclaimed, 'is one of liberty of publication, and we ask you by your verdict to say that there is a right to sell all honest thought honestly expressed. That is the point I put to you. I do not, however, pretend to say or think that if we fail today – although I think that an impossible result – that then the circulation will cease; because I think the feeling in this country on the subject is so strong, that if we are convicted and punished, you would find it necessary to institute innumerable prosecutions against persons who entertain our views on this subject.'

'Aunt Annie,' her niece would recall, 'never let anyone have the last word if she still had anything left <u>she</u> wanted to say.'[15] But here Besant glided to a gentle end. She thanked the jury for its extreme patience in listening to her throughout what she knew had been a very long address. 'I ask you,' she concluded, 'as an English woman, for that justice which it is not impossible to expect at the hands of Englishmen – I ask you to give me a verdict of "Not Guilty", and to send me home unstained.'

'The conclusion of the address was received with applause,' the stenographer recorded, 'which the officers of the court suppressed.'[16]

The next day's edition of Queen Victoria's preferred paper, the upper-register *Pall Mall Gazette*, ran a summary of the trial on its front page. Annie Besant's words appeared directly below this one-line bit of news: 'To-day is the fortieth anniversary of Her Majesty's accession to the throne.'[17]

'It seems hardly possible!' Victoria wrote in her diary. 'God has been very gracious & merciful to me!' She passed the day reading war telegrams, eating luncheon, taking tea, planting a tree in honour of the day, and going for a carriage drive. 'Janie', her Lady of the Bedchamber, read to Victoria a novel that the queen found 'very interesting'. Its title was *Too Much Alone*.[18]

Inside the mobbed Queen's Bench courtroom, Annie Besant chatted with Charles Bradlaugh as the proceedings began their third day. She was a hard act to follow. And Bradlaugh fell at the first hurdle, when the Lord Chief Justice corrected his interpretation of the court case that had set the precedent for obscenity. Sir Alexander Cockburn gently reminded jurors that he himself had written it. A short time later, he interrupted Bradlaugh to prompt him to address the 12 men in their box, and not the bench.

The soil atop his wife's grave was still fresh; just outside the courtroom his waiting daughters treaded fretful laps. Only one passer-by, en route to the House of Commons, stopped to offer his sympathy to the mournful pair. The County Cavan MP Joseph Biggar was the wrench in the gears of Parliament, known for filibustering until winning concessions towards his hoped-for free Irish state. He was a bruiser of a man with broad shoulders, but to Hypatia Bradlaugh he was a compassionate gentleman. 'My sister and I never afterwards heard Mr Biggar's name mentioned,' she wrote, 'without recalling how he thus kindly went out of his way to say a pleasant word to a couple of girls miserably walking up and down outside those Law Courts at Westminster.'[19]

The reporters listening to her father's argument were not as benevolent. Bradlaugh had started by asking the Lord Chief Justice if it were an offence itself to advocate for contraception. 'If it corrupts the public morals with relation to birth it is,' Sir Alexander Cockburn replied, unhelpfully. 'That is a matter for the jury.'

'Then comes the difficulty,' Bradlaugh continued, 'indicted as we are under the common law, into which I am placed, that there has never yet been a similar book submitted for judicial decision.'

The Lord Chief Justice patiently restated that the question, being decided for the first time by a jury, was whether the teaching of birth control depraved and corrupted public morals.

Compared to Annie Besant, Charles Bradlaugh came off as too glib, and too clever by half. He chose to begin by repeating Sir Hardinge Giffard's jibe that British doctors would never write filth like their American cousins. From a stack of 40 London-published medical texts, Bradlaugh proceeded to read one passage after another whose anatomical explanations matched those he cross-referenced in Knowlton.

'At this point,' *The Times* wrote, 'after this had gone on for several hours, the Lord Chief Justice interposed, and observed that he did not think that Mr. Bradlaugh quite grappled with the case against him.' Tenting his fingers for emphasis, he said that surely the defendant was testing the jury's patience. The prosecution's argument, Cockburn reminded Bradlaugh, 'is that this is *not* a medical book'.

It was a sixpence pamphlet that taught readers, among other methods, how to douche with spermicide to kill ejaculated semen. But no man present, least of all the one facing imprisonment for publishing this fact, dared to say such a phrase aloud. In the Victorian courtroom, survival of the fittest required polite caginess. Before the court adjourned for lunch, all that the mighty Charles Bradlaugh could muster was the milquetoast murmuring that 'as the advocates for the checks on over-population', the defence contended that 'moral or immoral as the book may be thought by others, the pamphlet states neither more nor less than is necessary or legitimate for the purpose'.[20]

His script badly needed a rewrite, and fast. Fortunately for the defence, after lunchtime Annie Besant was due to return to the stage to examine their trio of star witnesses – the only people in England brave, or foolish, enough to appear on their behalf.

The weather remained unseasonably hot. In its *Times* advertisements, the Royal Aquarium billed itself as 'the coolest and largest place of entertainment in London'. Twice each night, Zazel took explosive flight. In a fortuitous bit of timing, as the press continued to debate the seaworthiness of the HMS *Inflexible*, a West End play was premiering named *The Scuttled Ship*. There seemed to be no end to the information squeezed into newsprint, an empire's breadth condensed onto a tissue-thin page that raindrops would torpedo into ruin. The Royal Mail steamship *Balmoral Castle* sailed from London to Britain's new African colony of the Transvaal. The cargo vessel *Duke of Sutherland* chugged from London for Columbo, calling at Port Said. The white wakes of passenger ships unzipped the Thames as they headed for Gibraltar, Bombay, Calcutta, and Singapore. In the morning's trading, Anglo-American Telegraph shares had risen from 59¼ to 59¾. It all seemed so important at the time.

❦

Like that year's Football Association Cup winners Wanderers F.C., Bradlaugh came out after the break with a change in tactics. Annie Besant had spoken genuinely to the jury on behalf of Britain's silent half, voicing the obvious fact that she, uniquely in the courtroom, was a woman. What differentiated Charles Bradlaugh from the assembled, including his co-defendant, was his class. After huddling with Besant during the break, he decided to speak from his heart. At a time when a person concealed, not advertised, a hardscrabble youth (Dickens's readers then had no idea that his depiction of David Copperfield's child labour was largely memoir), it could not have come naturally for Charles Bradlaugh to face the 12 men who were his social betters and admit that he hailed from Britain's other nation.

'I know the poor,' he told the special jury. 'I belong to them. I was born amongst them. Among them are the earliest associations of my life. Such little ability as I possess today has come to me in the hard struggle of life. I have had no university to polish my tongue; no alma mater to give me any eloquence by which to move you. I plead here simply for the class to which I belong.[21]

'My co-defendant referred,' Bradlaugh continued, 'in earnest language, to the letters which she had received from women, and clergymen, and others, throughout the country. I, too, have received many warm words of sympathy from those who think that I am right . . . If we are branded with the offence of circulating an obscene book, many of these poor people will still think "No".'

A guilty verdict for promoting 'birth-restriction checks' would fall upon the millions of Britain's poor, he concluded. The courtroom echoed with applause.

For once, the usually hostile *Times* reprinted his words nearly verbatim. Given that the newspaper had an inside man, a hint of how the jury was leaning came in an editorial sentence asserting that Bradlaugh and Besant should not be coupled with the pornographers of Holywell Street. Readers presumably remembered this twisting alley off the Strand, where, before the 1857 passage of the Obscene Publications Act, overhanging shopfronts had flogged the asterisk-free adventures of Lady Bumtickler, *The Fanciful Extremes of Fucksters*, and even fan fiction that salaciously depicted the royal bedchamber antics of Albert and Victoria.

'Having thus concluded his defence,' *The Times* continued, 'a defence delivered, as was that of Mrs. Besant, with great earnestness and apparent sincerity, Mr. Bradlaugh proposed to adduce additional evidence, although he said he hardly knew what would be admissible.'[22]

Sir Alexander Cockburn told him that as it was impossible to guess what the evidence would be, he could call his three witnesses. Annie Besant stood to question the first, Alice Vickery, an accomplished 33-year-old as singular to British medicine as the last remaining quagga had been inside the London Zoo. Two women holding the floor in a courtroom like this was also without parallel.

Mrs Besant: I presume, my lord, I can put any question until some objection is raised. Your name is Alice Vickery?

The witness: It is.

— And you reside at number 333, Albany Road?
— Yes.

– Are you a chemist by examination of the Pharmaceutical
  Society of Great Britain?

– I am.

– And the first lady, I believe, who passed the regular examination of that Society?

– Yes.

– Did you study midwifery and diseases of women at any
  London hospital?

– Yes: at the Women's Medical College.

– For how long?

– I have studied medicine for six years.

– Are you at present a fourth-year student of l'Ecole de
  Médecine at Paris?

– I am.

(Here Annie Besant, who, for a rookie, already sounded
comfortable in court, could have noted for the jury that the
witness had moved to France because no British medical
school would then admit women. Three years from now,
Alice Vickery will be among the first to matriculate from the
London School of Medicine for Women, the college then
being founded by Elizabeth Garrett Anderson and Sophia
Jex-Blake. In the first draft of history, when she debuted in
print with her testimony, many British newspapers will mis-
spell her name as 'Vicary'.)

Mrs Besant: Have you attended practical midwifery at the
City of London Lying-in Hospital?

The witness: I have.

– Have you received a certificate for this?

– I have.

– Have you also the certificate for midwifery of the Obstet-
  rical Society of London?

Alice Vickery's 1870s carte-de-viste

– I have.

– Do you produce it?

– I can do so.

(The witness rustled through her sheaf of Victorian papers and produced the proof that she should be heard.)

– Have you attended hospital practice for several years in London and Paris?

– I have.

– And attended the practice of Surgery, I believe, under the famous Professor Verneuil of Paris?

– Yes.

– And you have devoted some six years of your life, you say, to these studies?

– I have studied at least six years.

– Have you read the pamphlet which is the subject of the present charge?

– I have.

– With the means of judging derived from the experience of which you have told us, do you consider this pamphlet to have been written by one well-acquainted with medical science at the date of its publication?

– Most decidedly I should say it had been written by one well acquainted with medical science nearly 40 years ago.

– You consider that it is a work written by a competent medical man for general circulation?

– I think it a most important work.

Here, at last, on the trial's third day, came an expert's medical opinion, uncoloured by cant. Next Annie moved to establish why *Fruits of Philosophy* should not be considered obscene.

Mrs Besant: In your hospital experience have you any knowledge of the effects of large families?

The witness: I have seen a good deal of them.

– You are speaking from the experience of which you have told us, when you say that?

– I am speaking from my own experience and knowledge. I am not dealing with books, but with facts. I am speaking of my knowledge of families and of the mothers who bear them. A great deal of suffering is caused by over child-bearing to the mothers themselves; to the children, because of the insufficient nutrient which they are able to give them and to the children before birth from the condition of the mothers.

– Have you found, in your experience, any bad result to the health of the mother from over-lactation of children amongst the poor?

– Most certainly. There are many evils resulting from over-lactation. One thing is a falling of the uterus, and another the permanent weakening of the mother's health.

– The next question I have to ask you is a most important one. It is: Is it within your own knowledge and experience that poor married women often desire to check the increase of their families, and that they very frequently seriously injure themselves, by adopting detrimental means, such as deleterious drugs, from complete ignorance of those means which might be adopted without any injury to their health?

The Lord Chief Justice: That is a very complicated question, and if it is competent to put it at all, I think it should, if possible, be simplified.

Mrs Besant: I am afraid, my lord, it is rather complicated, but I think I could, if you would allow me to do so, divide it. *(To witness:)* You have told us that, in your opinion, the health of married women is sometimes injured by over-childbearing. Are you aware whether they ever adopt any means to check the increase of their families?

– Most certainly.

Alice Vickery told the court that across the Channel, she had also seen women who, like their British counterparts, continued suckling for 'even longer than two years', as they erroneously believed they could not become pregnant again while nursing.

Mrs Besant: That is the direct result, in your opinion, of trying to check an over-increase of family without the physiological knowledge of how to do so?

The witness: Certainly.

The Lord Chief Justice: You must draw the conclusion in your summing up.

Mrs Besant: *(To witness:)* You are aware, I suppose, from what experience you have had, that there are in Paris married women whose husbands consent to the use of mechanical means for the restriction of their families?

The witness: My patients have told me more than once that their husbands have suggested means for preventing conception.

– They told you that it was so?

– I have heard it in several cases.

– I am going to ask you a rather curious question, but I mean no discourtesy. Is it your experience among your fellow-students that knowledge of physiological details tends to deprave and corrupt?

– Most certainly not.

– Have you found that women possessing such knowledge are less pure-minded than the ignorant?

– Oh, no.

The Lord Chief Justice: But those would be strong-minded ladies, Mrs. Besant.

Mrs Besant: I hope, my lord, that all women are strong-minded enough not to use knowledge for an improper purpose.[23]

The Times printed much of this exchange, leading the starchier *London Daily News* to complain that the *Fruits*, 'whether they be the nourishing and refreshing growth of a sound tree or simply Dead Sea apples, have been commended to thousands and tens of thousands of lips . . . The reserve which we have thought it right to practice has been nearly peculiar to ourselves.'[24]

Unlike the *Daily News*, *The Times* also reproduced much of the next witness's most damning statements to the prosecution's case. Like Alice Vickery, Dr Charles Robert Drysdale was willing to stake his reputation on behalf of the defence. The 48-year-old belonged to both the Royal College of Physicians and Royal College of Surgeons, was the senior physician at Hackney's Metropolitan Free Hospital, and a consultant to the Farringdon lying-in hospital whose board was chaired by Alderman Figgins, the elderly City magistrate who had arraigned Besant and Bradlaugh at Guildhall.

The doctor was also – unbeknownst to the courtroom – the younger brother of George Drysdale, the unnamed author of that 'Bible of the brothel', *The Elements of Social Science*, the 1855 treatise championing free love and declaring marriage to be legalised prostitution. Dr Charles Drysdale shared his other secret with the woman who had warmed the seat of the witness box before him: for the past eight years, he and Alice Vickery had lived – in a free union – as husband and wife. The couple would go on to have two children, spend their lives promoting contraception, and be laid to rest under a shared Brookwood tombstone identifying them as physicians, feminists and co-pioneers. For opening one of London's first family planning clinics (45 years later, in 1921), their son, Charles Vickery Drysdale (a eugenics adherent), will earn a Blue Plaque, hanging today outside his former office in Walworth, south London.[25]

Charles Bradlaugh examined this witness, whose high collar looked as starched as the black strands of hair plastered across his balding head. A pair of downy sideburns softened Dr Charles Drysdale's otherwise diagnostic mien.

To the question of whether he considered Knowlton's book to be accurate, he replied, 'I have always considered it an excellent treatise . . . It is certainly written by a physician, and an excellent man. Considering that it was written forty years ago, when it is thought that people did not know so much as we do – although I do not believe that we are so very far in advance of the men of those days.'

The Lord Chief Justice asked if its pages contained anything calculated to excite sensual or libidinous feelings. 'Certainly not,' Drysdale retorted. 'On me it had the contrary effect.'

Laughter cascaded from the courtroom's balcony.

As he explained his medical experience – 'I have seen nothing but poverty since I came to this great metropolis' – Dr Drysdale glanced at the papers in his hand.

Prosecutor Douglas Straight rustled to life in his black silks. 'What are you looking at?' he demanded.

'I am only referring to some notes. May I not look at them?'

'I am afraid you must put them away, and trust to your memory.'

'I am much obliged to you,' Drysdale replied. 'But I do not know who you are.' Again laughter galloped around the room. 'I would rather be guided by my lord than by you.'

After waiting for the chortling to subside, Sir Alexander Cockburn allowed the doctor to consult anything that he had just jotted down as a memory aid.

'One fact I will mention,' Drysdale said, 'to draw the attention of yourself and jury to the very important point of infant mortality. That is a very interesting point indeed. With all our advances in science we have not been able to decrease the general death-rate in London. Twenty years ago it was 22.2 per thousand persons living. In 1876 it was almost exactly the same, being, in fact, 22.3. Instead of dying more slowly than we did 20 years ago, we die a little faster. That fact might seem to be a great disgrace to the medical profession, and to those who had to advise as to the public health. Indeed, it has been asked, what is the use of public health officers at all.

'The real reason of this increase in the death-rate is, that the children of the poor die three times as fast as the children of the rich. If all the parents of the children were as well off as, say the gentlemen of the bar – (*laughter*) – or of the special jury, the consequence would be that the number of children that would die would be very small indeed. Mr. Hanson has pointed out that to every 100,000 children amongst the richer classes – which would, of course, include the barristers – (*laughter*)'.

The Lord Chief Justice: And solicitors, too, I should think – (*laughter*).

Dr Drysdale: And solicitors, too, my lord, no doubt – in 100,000 children of the richer classes, it was found that there were only 8,000 who died during the first year of life; whereas looking at the Registrar-General's returns we find that 15,000 out of every 100,000 of the general population die in their first year. If you take the children of the poor in the towns you will find the death-rate three times as large as among the rich – instead of 8,000 there would be 24,000 among the children of the poor. So that you see, the children of the poor are simply brought into the world to be murdered.

Nobody laughed.

Mr Bradlaugh: Do you happen to know, from your own experience, whether checks to population of the character referred to in this book are adopted by the peasant families in France?

Dr Drysdale: I should like to know if I am allowed to say what I like? *(Laughter.)* Will it be safe? *(Loud laughter.)*

Mr Straight: If it will re-assure the witness, I may say that it will be quite safe so far as I am concerned.

Dr Drysdale: I do not know, I am sure. *(Laughter.)*

The Lord Chief Justice: You can only state what are the facts.

Dr Drysdale: I mean is there any privilege in a witness from being prosecuted? *(Loud laughter.)* I should like to know I shall not be prosecuted by the Government.

Mr Straight: If it is any satisfaction to Dr. Drysdale, I will not prosecute him. *(Laughter.)*

The Lord Chief Justice: But we do not know who your clients are, Mr. Straight.

Mr Straight: I think there is not much doubt about it.

Mr Bradlaugh: I have much doubt. *(Laughter.)*[26]

Douglas Straight did not reply. The proceedings were veering into Gilbert and Sullivan territory. A plague of *Oh-those-Froggies* guffaws erupted when Charles Robert Drysdale rather innocently answered that in France, most families that he had examined at hospital attested to practising the withdrawal method. Nearly every couple he met there had at most two children.

After the gallery's giggles died down, the audience drowned out Dr Drysdale's voice with vaudevillian howls as he told Annie Besant that in rural England he had treated worn-out women who in their lives had given birth 21, 23, and even 25 times. (*It is indeed too hard and dreadful what we have to go through.*) Over the laughter, Drysdale loudly declared this chattelisation of women to be 'one of the greatest social crimes a man could commit'.

Besant silenced the courtroom by saying a word that polite Victorian society did not speak aloud: 'abortion'. Did the doctor know of the lengths poor women went to procure one?

'It is not alone among the poor,' Drysdale replied. 'I have known it, time after time, amongst educated ladies, who have taken most drastic medicines to try and get rid of the effects of conception.'

The doctor considered the practice 'almost as bad as murder. But I do not see any crime in preventing conception, otherwise those who remain unmarried should all be prosecuted.' He joined in the loud laughter that met this remark. For her final question, Annie Besant called back to her opening remarks, two days before. 'Have you, in your own experience, seen many cases of over-crowding?'

'Near to my dispensary in Holborn,' Drysdale testified, 'I have seen too much of it. In the neighbourhood of Gray's Inn, where these gentlemen of the bar abound *(laughter)* – and these gentlemen of the bar might see for themselves if they would *(laughter)* – I must confess to have been ashamed to find such an amount of misery existing there from over-crowding. I wish that two or three gentlemen would only take the trouble to go into the little courts and alleys off Chancery Lane and Gray's Inn Lane and see the frightful misery and crowding there as I have seen there. I have seen six children in one room all huddled up together, and all down with typhus fever, the same room being used by three adults; I have seen such things repeatedly, over and over again.'[27]

'The associations of over-crowding corrupt the young mind, I suppose, and loss of modesty is followed by prostitution?'

'They do not know what modesty is.'

Annie's nimble, if circular, turn of logic suggested to jurors that her allegedly immodest promotion of contraception in fact maintained Victorian propriety.

After Dr Drysdale stepped down – as with Alice Vickery, the prosecution declined to cross-examine – the day's final witness took the box. The well-known publisher H.G. Bohn told the court that before his retirement, for 40 years he had printed physiological textbooks. He had volunteered his testimony because he 'felt very strongly on the subject, because many years ago one of my publications had been attacked by what I understood to be the action of the Society for the Suppression of Vice'. Upstanding Anglicans did not have a monopoly on outrage; the legal action, it turned out, had been made at the instigation of Roman Catholic priests. The complaint had been withdrawn, but as a result H.G. Bohn had temporarily withheld editions of Rabelais, and of Boccaccio's *Decameron*. Fear, like self-preservation, was contagious. Bohn told the court he had never considered the need to suppress printing medical texts. Listening to Annie Besant, he told the special jury, made him wish he had halved his physiology books' price, in order to double their circulation.

And with that, Annie concluded the defence. The next morning, she would make a short summing-up. Douglas Straight said the Crown's reply would likewise be brief. 'Then we shall finish tomorrow,' the Lord Chief Justice pronounced. The record shows that the Court then rose, and Mrs Besant and Mr Bradlaugh were again cheered loudly as they left the hall.

9

SENTENCE FIRST – VERDICT AFTERWARDS

Annie Besant must have pulsed with a wonderful sensation that final morning, retaking her seat in the plush Queen's Bench courtroom. She had struck the ball squarely and firmly; all that remained was the roar of the crowd. She was going to leave Westminster Hall not as a martyr, but a winner.

Sir Hardinge Giffard likely felt the same about his chances. Yes, the defendants had spoken ardently about the purity of their motives and Dr Knowlton's ideas. But the Crown contended that *Fruits of Philosophy* was obscene. Had the Solicitor-General really proved it? He didn't need to. The prosecution rested on the authoritative sentence that book-banners brandished everywhere: *We are offended.* Would the aristocratic special jury dare to disagree with Her Majesty's government?

Outside the courtroom's ceremonial trappings of black silks and horsehair wigs, the summer solstice morning of Thursday, 21 June dawned cooler and – per *The Times* – 'very dull', but promising fine weather for the start of the Henley Royal Regatta up the Thames. (That afternoon, the rowers and picnickers will be surprised by an ambush of drenching rains, spoiling the luncheons in the meadows.) In Maida Vale, the wife of A. Walford Werdon delivered a daughter. The wife of J.G. Caswell gave birth to a girl in Kensington Gardens.

Shares of Anglo-American Telegraph slipped to 59½. The queen, departing Balmoral for Windsor, noted in her diary that the lilacs and broom were in bloom. The haymaking had begun, and looked so cheerful.

Inside the Court of Queen's Bench, Annie Besant the underdog opened the closing arguments. Standing and smoothing her buttoned suitcoat, she said that the jury had to decide if *Fruits of Philosophy* was a medical work, or an utterly obscene book, written with intent to deprave. If the latter, then why would she have openly appended her name to it, and courted arrest? The book was written in plain English, not medical Latin. They lived in enlightened times, Annie reminded the court, not the sixteenth-century Papal States, where a cosmologist had been burned at the stake for supporting Copernicus. (His name was Giordano Bruno; despite her conversion to atheism, she could still retrieve the names of Christian martyrs with the ease of a judge citing case law. On this point, at least, Miss Marryat would have been proud.)

The great Italian unifier General Garibaldi, she added, had donated to her defence fund. But would this name-drop impress 12 patriotic Englishmen?

('The Solicitor-General is quite enamoured of Mrs. Besant,' teased a waggish London newspaper. 'Her facile flow of language has conquered his constitutional heart. By the way, Harrow men will recollect her as the daughter of one of the dames of the houses.'[1])

Annie assured the jurors she did not want to waste their time by calling further witnesses, 'our case being really proved beyond possibility of reasonable dispute'. Pistis, the goddess of good faith. She still did not even know who had brought the charges against her and Charles Bradlaugh. 'And yet we stand charged with a criminal offence before his lordship. Will you, I ask you gentlemen, give a verdict of guilty against me? You do not know very much of my life, it is true, and you may not be able to judge from it how far such a criminal charge is well- or ill-founded. I was not, as my co-defendant said he was, born among the poor – I have not the glory, I have not the honour of having risen from among them by sheer brain power and persistent labour, to stand here.'

If they sent her to prison, she promised that she would continue her campaigning among the wretched women who would receive her. 'You cannot give a verdict of guilty against me, guilty of intent to deprave – my whole life gives the lie to it.' Elpis, the goddess of hope. 'You cannot convict me, and so take from me whatever influence for good I may have won . . . You cannot convict me. Think for one moment upon all those who are watching this trial with the keenest anxiety . . . You cannot convict me if you think of the past and look forward to the future. Think of the juries in this great country who have over and over again stood between tyrannical Governments and the oppressed and helpless brought before the power of a court. Think what juries in this country have done. They have stayed the march of power against liberty, have widened freedom, and have protected discussion.'

Annie invoked the name of John Horne Tooke, an eighteenth-century political reformer charged with treason for criticising the king and Parliament. Jurors had only needed eight minutes to acquit him. 'Make them your examples,' she urged, 'and set us free today . . . But if, by some misdirection, some mismanagement of justice, you give a verdict against us, you will be doing what John Stuart Mill spoke of, you will be committing one of those crimes by which the men of one generation surprise and amaze posterity.'

It was a good line, and the would-be people's princess ended with a promise of their future. 'We appeal from you to the verdict of history, which shall judge us when we have all passed away – that history which shall bring us in not guilty, whatever the verdict may be today. History, that weighing us in the far-off tomorrow, shall say that this man and this woman who stood on their trial here, who, knowing the misery of their time, the sufferings of their fellows, the agony of the people of their day, joined their hands and their lives together to bring salvation to the homes of the poor, did good service in their day and in their generation – that history shall say to us, "Well done", whatever your verdict may be.'[2]

Pythia, the Oracle of Delphi. As Annie Besant, the high priestess of preventive checks of pregnancy resumed her seat, the audience applauded. But theirs was not the favour she needed to remain free.

After Charles Bradlaugh made a short address apologising if his previous recitation of medical facts had weakened the eloquent pleadings of his partner, Sir Hardinge Giffard rose to remind the jurors that no two people were 'more able to use words in a more fallacious sense than the two defendants who have addressed you'. *Fruits of Philosophy* was a harmless medical text? Humbug! With his black silk gown and piercing pouchy eyes, the Solicitor-General brimmed with the rectitude of Church and Crown.

'There is a policeman,' Sir Hardinge began, 'who is here as the prosecutor, in the ordinary sense of the term; but it appears to me that whoever the prosecutor may be that is quite immaterial to the issue before you. Whether it is a policeman, or the authorities that are behind the policeman, it is quite certain that if the persons who had challenged the prosecution had not been brought before you . . . they would have been entitled to say they were selling the book openly in the City of London, after having given notice to the authorities that they would do so.' The defendants had forced these men to choose: either prosecute, or agree that *Fruits of Philosophy* could be openly published and circulated.

'I say that this is a dirty, filthy book,' Giffard thundered, 'and the test of it is that no human being would allow that book to lie on his table; no decently educated English husband would allow even his wife to have it, and yet it is told to me, forsooth, that anybody may have this book in the City of London or elsewhere, who can pay sixpence for it!'

Fruits of Philosophy was obscene, he charged, because it 'enabled persons to have sexual intercourse, and not to have that which in the order of Providence is the natural result'. (He meant children, not orgasms.) The defendants, Sir Hardinge argued, had combed through science textbooks and could not produce a single line that taught these wicked methods of contraception, which depraved British morals, full stop. 'I submit to you that this is a matter to be dealt with, not on abstruse considerations, but with a little manly common sense. Let every man of common sense ask himself what is the inevitable result of disseminating such things among the common people?'

If the special jury exonerated the defendants, their steamy press would flood the country with *Fruits of Philosophy*. 'I cannot believe,' the Solicitor-General concluded, 'that any English jury, having any reverence for the marriage state, for the chastity and purity of their own wives and daughters, can do any such thing.'[3] The transcript shows that no applause greeted his speech.

The Lord Chief Justice began his summary of the trial by telling the jury that to his mind, 'A more ill-advised and more injudicious proceeding in the way of a prosecution was probably never brought into a court of justice.'

Looking severe under his square-fringe wig, Sir Alexander Cockburn disagreed with Sir Hardinge Giffard's contention that City police had to arrest Besant and Bradlaugh. 'I should very much like to know who are the authorities who are prosecuting, because that has not transpired. The Solicitor-General tells us it may have been the magistracy. I do not believe it. I do not believe it.' Deploring 'the rashness which set this prosecution going', Sir Alexander continued, the Court of Queen's Bench nevertheless had to treat the prosecution as though it had the sanction of the Crown – which, he mischievously told the special jury, 'I do not think it has.'

In fact, no one will ever be able to say, with certainty, who had brought the complaint. The following week, Charles Hastings Collette of the Society for the Suppression of Vice will threaten to sue a journalist for libelling him as the trial's instigator. Before dropping the charges, Collette will swear before a Bow Street magistrate that he had feared that arresting Besant and Bradlaugh would only increase their book's sales.[4] (Thinking it was the culprit, the best-selling Annie Besant had taken to calling his group the Society for the Promotion of Vice.)

That the Solicitor-General had been sent to prosecute, the Lord Chief Justice continued, signalled that powerful vested interests wanted to assure a conviction. The judge did not think it was warranted. There was no need to load the pamphlet with 'all the opprobrious epithets' Sir Hardinge Giffard had used. Sir Alexander said it only proved that the prosecution 'had half-studied the book'. Applause filled the courtroom.

Next the Lord Chief Justice read aloud Dr Knowlton's step-by-step instructions for douching with spermicide, and asked, 'Is that inconsistent with morality? There may be a certain degree of indelicacy in such a suggestion,' the judge allowed, but would it truly corrupt a person's morals? Clearly he thought not, and reminded the 12 men that if they also harboured a sliver of doubt they were bound to find the defendants not guilty.[5]

'The summing-up was a most masterly one,' Charles Bradlaugh wrote in the *National Reformer*, 'and was worthy of the high reputation of the judge who delivered it.' He praised 'The very thorough manner in which Sir Alexander Cockburn vindicated Dr. Knowlton's memory from the aspersion which some mean and cowardly rascals have suggested against it.'

'No two defendants,' Annie agreed in her own column,

> could have been treated with more courtesy, more fairness, more justice . . . Nor must the poor of this forget to mark and to remember the deep and earnest sympathy with their troubles shown by the Lord Chief Justice . . . His question whether it was immoral for a husband and wife to decide that they would not bring into the world more children than they could support and educate – all this, coming from one so high in the land as the Lord Chief Justice, will have an effect impossible to measure or over-estimate.

Sir Alexander had made the case so plainly to the special jurors, Annie 'was surprised to see them even leave the box'. She was not alone in presuming the high odds of an acquittal. 'I am told,' she wrote, 'that some of the more sporting among the barristers laid as much as 50 to 4 on a verdict of "Not guilty!"'[6]

'The jury had retired,' Hypatia Bradlaugh recounted, 'and everyone was so sure of a verdict for the defence, that my father thought we should like to hear it – for in spite of all his worries and anxieties, he could yet think of us at such a moment.'[7] For the first time, the girls followed him into the courtroom, where the crowd began to grow restless as the clock ticked on. The afternoon *Pall Mall Gazette* could not wait to go to press; its front page reported that 'a great battle has commenced' between Russian and Turkish forces, that the coaching club had met at Hyde Park, and that Mrs Besant had 'convincingly appealed to the jury' and received the spectators' applause. 'The verdict will be given in our next edition.'[8]

Finally, after one hour and thirty-five minutes of discussion, the special jury returned. The clerk asked, 'Gentlemen, have you agreed upon your verdict?'

The foreman replied that they had.

'Do you find the defendants guilty or not guilty of this charge?'

'We are unanimously of the opinion,' Arthur Walter intoned, 'that the book in question is calculated to deprave public morals, but at the same time we entirely exonerate the defendants from any corrupt motives in publishing it.'

'There was a general start of astonishment,' Annie reported, 'and I doubt if anyone was more surprised than the Chief himself.' As the audience showered the jurors with loud hisses, Sir Alexander Cockburn also did not hide his disdain, and disbelief. 'I am afraid, gentlemen,' he explained, 'I must direct you on that finding, to return a verdict of guilty. As I have already explained to you, the motive and intention of the defendants cannot in this case be taken into account at all.'

'There the verdict was, however,' Annie wrote, 'and it rivalled the celebrated one of "Not guilty, but don't do it again". "Guilty, but didn't do it" was the sapient conclusion arrived at, and on that, the Judge formally directed that a verdict for the Crown should be recorded.'[9]

The Times' scion bowed, and turned to his fellow jurymen. Some nodded, while others made to leave the box quickly, before the baying crowd could reach them.

Breaking precedent, the Lord Chief Justice set the convicted prisoners free until their sentencing, in a week's time. The Court then rose, and a large crowd which had gathered outside to learn the result heartily cheered the defendants as they passed to a waiting carriage.[10]

The next day, Annie would receive a signed letter from one of the six jurors who had voted to acquit. The men had expected to return to deliberations if the judge would not accept their jury-rigged verdict. Instead, 'the stupid men had not the sense to speak out at the right time, and the foreman had his way'. Two of the jurors had refused their guinea payment for serving, telling Annie to add it to her defence fund.

Little did she know that the past was not dead, nor even past: a day after Dr Charles Knowlton's convictions for publishing the same pamphlet, the American had written that a juror, 'and a steady hard-labour-looking man he was too, about forty years of age, came and said to me – "Well we brought you in guilty – we did not see how we could well get rid of it, still I like your book, and you must let me have one of them."'[11]

The next issue of the *National Reformer* was headlined with praise for Annie Besant. 'Here – while my hand is yet free to pen these lines,' Charles Bradlaugh wrote:

> let me record my deep sense of gratitude to the woman who has shared my fight, aided me by her help, encouraged me by her steadfastness, and strengthened me by her counsel. The brilliant eloquence, patient endurance, and sustained effort manifested for so many hours in the court – qualities displayed by Mrs. Besant, coupled with her great tact, won

repeated praise from the Lord Chief Justice, and congratu-
lations from almost the whole of the barristers who crowded
the court – so much of Mrs. Besant's work has been recorded
by most of the press in terms of the highest laudation.[12]

Even the *Sporting Gazette*, which less than two years ago
had dismissed her as a clergyman's wife, shrieking like a
drunken Cassandra, now singled Annie out for approval.
'The conduct of the defendants in this case,' its columnist
wrote, 'has been manly and straightforward, which is more
than I can say for the prosecution . . . Mrs. Besant spoke
remarkably well.' Her closing speech 'was, indeed, an admira-
ble one, and it was delivered with fire and energy which gave
it additional force'.[13]

Annie also noted the favourable coverage, including in the
newspaper owned by her jury foreman's family. 'The press, as
a whole, has been very fair to us,' she told readers in the
National Reformer.

> Our speeches have been read literally by millions, whom we
> could never have otherwise reached. *The Times* gave admir-
> able reports throughout, and I do not complain of its bitter
> hostility; it is the organ of British Philistinism, and reflects
> the feeling which howls a man down in one generation for
> doing what it will applaud in the next. The *Times* of 1900
> will praise us as heroes, and we must not grumble at the
> *Times* of 1877.

As for the special jurors, Besant wrote, the 12 men had
been 'very quiet, very attentive, very patient: the only explanation of their verdict is that they were also very stupid'.[14]

The defendants' knowledge that *The Times* scion Arthur
Walter had whipped the jury was borne out when the newspaper's coverage abruptly shifted, as media does, to back the

winning side. In a long unsigned editorial, *The Times* sarcastically called *Fruits of Philosophy* 'a present from America to this country', one which the defendants had believed to be the best gift to British women. 'Happily . . . we are glad to find that this pair are not held to have established a right to dictate new rules of action and new conditions of existence to a reluctant, and, as it feels, an insulted world.'[15]

That Sunday in Old Street, the convicts took the stage at a sold-out Hall of Science. *The Times* reported 600 attendees; Besant sniffed that the receipts showed that 1,418 people each had paid two pennies to enter. It was her rotten luck that the story appeared directly under one about the Master of the Rolls celebrating the marriage of his daughter at a London synagogue. If the UK's second-ranking judge, and head of its civil court, somehow had not yet heard of Annie Besant, he most likely had now.

At the freethinker's hall, copies of the birth control pamphlet 'sold by the hundred, young women and lads purchasing largely'. The crowd cheered as Annie announced that she would move for a new trial, demanding a clear verdict. 'She was as loyal to the cause as ever,' *The Times* recounted, 'and would not flinch from the struggle.'[16]

Like Annie Besant, the nineteenth-century German poet Heinrich Heine saw his work banned by his government; unlike her, today he is honoured by a statue in his country's capital. His bronze likeness in a lively Berlin neighbourhood park is captioned with his conviction that 'We don't catch hold of an idea, rather the idea catches hold of us and enslaves us and whips us into the arena so that we, forced to be gladiators, fight for it.'

Before her trial, Annie had promised her readers she would not lay down her sword until the battle was won. After the verdict, she swore never to sheathe it. 'I am going to strike with it again, and keep on striking until I have won.'[17]

At the sentencing hearing on 28 June, the Lord Chief Justice refused her and Charles Bradlaugh's request for a new trial, although he accepted her point that the special jury's finding had not actually included the word 'guilty'. What followed was an hour of wrangling that *Alice in Wonderland*'s Queen of Hearts might have enjoyed (*'Sentence first – verdict afterwards'*), as the three sides talked in circles around one another. Sir Hardinge Giffard failed to find any common law precedent for the conviction; instead he quoted from several American cases. Annie chided 'the learned Solicitor-General' for bringing a prosecution so weak that he was 'obliged to fall back upon cases cited from a foreign country'.[18]

Things looked promising for the convicts, until, after returning from lunch, Sir Hardinge stung back by handing the judge an affidavit from a journalist who had attended their defiant Hall of Science talk and purchased a copy of the *Fruits*. A newspaper clipping was attached to the document, which Annie Besant tried to convince the Lord Chief Justice had quoted her incorrectly. She did admit to telling her audience that 'one of the most highly-trained brains in England has declared in favour of our views'. If that description of the judge were 'a discourtesy to the Court, I can only apologise for it'. Sir Alexander Cockburn laughed here, at least. But then he upbraided Annie for continuing to sell a book that the jury had declared to be obscene.

'The matter assumes, then, a very serious aspect,' the Lord Chief Justice intoned. He had been prepared to show leniency, and, if the defendants had admitted they were in error and ceased their campaign, was prepared to release them. Yet here they only showed defiance of the law, a most grave and aggravated offence. He also correctly surmised that Annie

Besant would persist in publishing and promulgating birth control.

'The sentence is that you, Charles Bradlaugh, and you, Annie Besant, be imprisoned for the term of six calendar months.' Hypatia watched her father turn white. Furthermore, they each had to pay the princely sum of £200 to the queen (meaning state), as well as post a bond of £500 guaranteeing their good behaviour for the next two years. If they published another single copy of *Fruits of Philosophy*, they would forfeit the money, and serve the entirety of their time.

The cash could have purchased four middle-class houses in the northern London neighbourhoods around Holloway, the prison where the Lord Chief Justice was sending them. The crenelated brickpile would later jail suffragists – including Emmeline Pankhurst, an early admirer of the first-wave feminist Besant – but to Annie in 1877 its walls only meant separation from her daughter, and likely the loss of her custody.[19]

Charles Bradlaugh bowed to the judge, and the court officer moved to seize the condemned. 'In spite of all our vague fears,' Hypatia wrote:

I do not think we altogether realised what imprisonment could mean until the Judge pronounced the awful words. The whole Court seemed to fade away as I listened, and it needed the knowledge that my father relied upon me to do something for him to bring me to myself. I took his pocketbook from him as he had bidden me, and was with my sister mechanically following him from the Court when we were stopped by the Lord Chief Justice, his mild tones forming a contrast to the last sharply uttered words. It seemed, indeed, as though ages of agony had been lived through in those few minutes.[20]

Sir Alexander Cockburn decided to toss the defendants, still reeling from the shock, one final lifeline. As they stood framed by the right angles of the gallows-shaped courtroom door, he said that if they would pledge to cease publication before their appeal was heard, he would suspend their sentence. (*And a good judge, too!*)

Bradlaugh readily agreed; Besant remained defiantly silent. Martyrs do not bow. 'I wish you had taken this position sooner,' the judge replied. He released the pair on their own recognisances of £100 each. 'As a married woman,' Besant wrote, 'I was unable to give recognizances being only a chattel, not a person cognisable by law. The court mercifully ignored this – or I should have had to go to prison – and accepted Mr. Bradlaugh's sole recognizance as covering us both.'[21]

The Times reported that the case was thus concluded. Sir Alexander Cockburn now exits our stage, with less than three years on his life's clock. Sir Hardinge Giffard walked across Westminster Hall to weigh in on a debate about judges in the Raj being independent of checks by the Crown. (He was against this sort of check, too.) Douglas Straight appeared that afternoon at the Old Bailey to defend a victualler charged with the attempted murder of a barmaid on Shakespeare Road. He failed to impress the judge, who ignored the jury's plea for leniency due to drunkenness, and, unusually, sentenced the attacker to ten years of penal servitude.

More crimes and punishment against women filled the London police records that final Thursday in June. A stableman named Thomas Tobey assaulted his wife. Police pinched a rough-looking fellow for begging and cursing at women at Victoria station. A young mother, dressed in widow's weeds, appeared before a magistrate asking for public relief following the drowning of her husband and son, which left her with five young daughters, and no income. Also appearing in court was a man collared for selling pirated copies of *Fruits of Philosophy* in Trafalgar Square. He was released when the judge opened its covers and found a treatise on spiritualism. (*In the near future, you will be cheated.*) A constable hauled in two hawkers for flogging at Mansion House a pornographic parody titled *The Fruits of Adultery*. They were fined five shillings each, and released.[22]

In her diary, Queen Victoria began her 28 June entry by writing, 'My Coronation day'.[23] She had nothing further to add about that 1838 event, thirty-nine years before. The weather remained heavy and hot, and she breakfasted as usual at Frogmore. After a walk and drive, that night Victoria sat with friends until nearly 11pm, listening to the Grenadier Band play 'very well'. Time seemed to stop at Windsor.

In July, Annie lectured on birth control at the Hall of Science, which was 'crowded in every point', a London newspaper reported, 'a large portion of which consisted of young females, who appeared to fully endorse [her] opinions'.[24]

That same week, Victoria wrote to her namesake daughter, living in Berlin, to complain that British couples were suddenly commonly displaying 'intimacy' before marriage. 'Here now they have lost all modesty,' she brooded, 'for not only do they go about driving, walking, and visiting — everywhere alone, they have also now taken to go out everywhere in society — which till a year or so no young lady just engaged, ever did, and make a regular show of themselves.' Something had changed in this year of 1877. 'In short,' Her Majesty observed, 'young people are getting very American, I fear in their views and ways.'[25]

Decisions made in one's twenties take out mortgages against the decades to come. In the aftermath of her trial, Annie Besant did not play it safe, but felt emboldened to take further risks. 'Bunyan's little boy sang about the delights of sitting on the ground, and the happy security of such a position in regard to falling,' she wrote in the *National Reformer.* 'There is the same quiet kind of satisfaction in having received one's sentence: one knows the worst that can happen.'[26]

Before turning 30 that October, she lectured across Britain on behalf of the contraception-promoting organisation birthed by her and Charles Bradlaugh. Dr Charles Drysdale assumed its presidency, and Alice Vickery joined as a founding member. They called it the Malthusian League. How its namesake would have loathed them.

In Northampton, 'Hats, handkerchiefs and umbrellas were waved in the air' as Annie took the stage; crowds had to be turned away from sold-out speeches in Leeds and Glasgow. Edinburgh turned its brusque shoulder, however; one venue after another refused to rent to her, until at last the Oddfellows Hall acquiesced. The hisses that greeted the start of her talk by the end turned to cheers and laughter.[27] A news item running beside the report said that the queen was greatly opposed to the new fashion that saw ladies wearing pockets on their backs. The paper called it a 'Lead Us into Temptation' jacket, since pickpockets would feel an 'irresistible impulse' to rifle through its private recess.[28]

Annie Besant could not resist publishing two new pamphlets, poking at her sentence as it remained pending on appeal. In the first, she warned Britons that her prosecution threatened all dramatists and authors. Their works could be 'flung into the dusthole' and they could be thrown behind bars. She warned anyone selling or owning the Good Book to brace themselves, as under the law the Crown could also charge them with obscenity. She titled the pamphlet *Is the Bible Indictable?* Her satirical answer was yes.

'The story of Ruth is one which we should not like to see repeated by our daughters,' Besant wrote, 'for the virtue of a woman who should wait until a man is drunk, and then go alone at night and lie down at his feet, would, in our days, be regarded as problematical.'

She warned readers to keep their children away from the Book of Genesis (inebriation, indecency, swearing), Exodus and Leviticus (coarseness), and Judges (concubines). The story of David and Bathsheba and the sensual Song of Solomon were far more calculated to arouse the passions than anything Dr Charles Knowlton ever wrote. Sir Hardinge Giffard might faint if forced to read aloud Esther's search for young virgins.

Annie called on the police to apprehend the people who circulated such filth. 'If they will not do this, in common decency they ought to drop the prosecution against us for selling *Fruits of Philosophy*.' Its 'stupid and malicious' charges, she argued, were born of a fatal policy that 'buttresses up ignorance with prison and fines'.[29]

The second pamphlet further evinced her promise to keep up fighting. In sentencing, the Lord Chief Justice had made Annie promise to cease the publication and circulation of Knowlton's work, whose print run had ended at 185,000 copies. Following the letter of his law, Besant instead wrote and published her own book teaching birth control.

The Law of Population: Its Consequences, and Its Bearing upon Human Conduct and Morals recycled the American doctor's text in her own words. Its front-piece featured Annie's portrait, captioned defiantly, John Hancock-style, with a reproduction of her oversized signature. She dedicated the text 'To the Poor, in the Hope that it May Make Easier the Life of British Mothers'. The first edition contained little new material, save for a paragraph teaching that nursing an infant did not prevent further pregnancy, but in later editions she included interviews with obstetricians and gynaecologists, and added other methods to check pregnancy.

One doctor told her of something called a 'Tampon', which could be made into a contraceptive by first soaking it in quinine and smearing it in Vaseline. Annie endorsed the India-rubber pessary and sponge, directing readers where to buy them in London. 'The first,' she wrote, 'can be obtained from Mr. Rendell at the address given on the advertisement on page 47, the second from Messrs. Lambert and Son (see advertisement on page 48).' Rendell called his product 'The Wife's Friend'.

The devices promised to be reliable and safe, delivering 'sufficient power to destroy the life properties of the spermatic fluid without injury to the person'.[30] The illustrated ads for squeeze-bulb syringes and irrigators might look like they belonged in a dairy manual, but their publication – by a woman facing jail time, and using her own printing press – broke new ground.

Annie Besant's brazenness won her converts on the Continent, and in the furthest corners of the empire. Editions of *The Law of Population* appeared across Europe, and in India, Australia and New Zealand. In the Netherlands, it was being 'freely sold, and may be seen in booksellers' windows'.[31] One Dutch reader, Dr Aletta Jacobs, travelled to London to meet Annie; in 1880, back home in Amsterdam, she will open the world's first birth control clinic.

But Annie's rebellious actions also hardened critics, and created new ones. In December 1877, George Eliot's acolyte (and, if she's to be believed, lover) Edith Simcox confessed to the novelist that after attending a Besant and Bradlaugh lecture, she had shaken hands with the notorious woman. 'Of course she asked,' Simcox wrote of Eliot, 'how that

'Thoroughly cleansing the parts it is applied to.' Adverts for contraceptive devices in Annie Besant's *The Law of Population*.

might be – and of course, on the whole, all things well weighed, she wished me not to have my name printed in the same list with theirs.'

After defiantly continuing her scandalous relationship with the married George Lewes, Eliot presumably might have admired Annie Besant. But the 58-year-old, like many British women – including the editors of the *Women's Suffrage Journal*, who did not cover the obscenity trial – could not abide Annie's atheism.[32] Eliot warned Simcox that the 'dread of Pharisaism' could undermine her own work; in 1875, Simcox and the activist Emma Patterson had been the first women delegates at Britain's annual Trades Union Congress. George Eliot saw her own role as 'that of the aesthetic, not the doctrinal teacher ... It is one thing to feel keenly for one's fellow-beings; another to say, "This step, and this alone, will be the best to take for the removal of particular calamities."'[33]

Edith Simcox nonetheless returned to a gathering the next week at which Annie began organising the first meeting of the International Labour Union. Simcox found herself nominated to its leadership, alongside the feminist Harriet Law and the Anglican priest Stewart Headlam, freshly driven from his curacy in Bethnal Green for publicly supporting Besant and birth control. Due to George Eliot's warning, Simcox 'had grave doubts' of accepting the post. She refused, and never returned. 'I don't at all like being brought into any kind of relation with that type of woman,' she wrote. 'Though I confess it riles me a little to retreat – as I wasn't a match for any number of Besants.'[34]

The Crown was realising its impotence before her, too. In January 1878 – a month in which Prime Minister Disraeli ordered the British fleet to the Dardanelles, and London readers snapped up the serialisation of Thomas Hardy's bold depiction of illicit sex and furze in *The Return of the Native* – Annie Besant and her co-defendant appeared before a panel of three justices in the Supreme Court of Appeal. Technically, they could not contest their criminal sentence. They could, however, apply for a writ of error, proving that the charges against them had been filed incorrectly. Annie argued that they still did not know for what they had been condemned. 'We are simply told that the book "as a whole" is obscene,' she said, which left unclear which parts she could reprint, and which bits were forbidden. 'It is impossible to tell ... because it is not set out in the record.'[35]

Rather than order Besant and Bradlaugh to begin serving their sentence, the judges set a future hearing. More good news arrived the following week, when the trial against the bookseller Edward Truelove for selling *Fruits of Philosophy* fell apart after a single man on the common jury refused to agree to convict him. He had stood in the box and declared the pamphlet 'a good book and a useful one'.[36] In a separate victory, Charles Bradlaugh was granted the return of the 657 copies seized from Truelove's shop. 'We labelled the rescued pamphlets,' Annie wrote, with a stamp that inked RECOVERED FROM POLICE, 'and sold every one of them.'

On their return to the Supreme Court in February 1878, she and Bradlaugh listened as the panel of justices – 'majestically clad in ermine trimmed robes, and exceedingly large wigs' – lamented that the charges filed against them had not included the specific sentences in *Fruits of Philosophy* judged to be obscene. 'No passages are quoted on record.' That contravened precedent. The Solicitor-General may recently have had his wig re-curled, and looked stately in his 'very rustling glossy silk gown', but the only previous case that Sir Hardinge Giffard could cite as an example of punishing a publisher for sexual content involved the printing of pornographic pictures, not a book. Therefore, the judgment against them had to be vacated, and their sentence tossed out.[37]

On a technicality, Annie Besant and Charles Bradlaugh escaped prison and ruin.

Raised on the King James version of the Bible, Annie would have known the proverb about pride going before destruction, and a haughty spirit before a fall, but she could not resist a bit of gloating. Remember the recipe that began, 'First, catch your hare'? Her pursuers, she warned, would need 'fleet greyhounds for the task'.

Anyone plotting to arrest her for authoring and publishing

her own birth control pamphlet would take care to remember that her 'unknown prosecutors now have the pleasure of paying the whole of their own costs – which, with three counsel – come to a considerable sum'.[38]

Furthermore, the judges had made clear that future plaintiffs would have to read any allegedly offending words aloud in court, and into the public record. They would also, in these increasingly enlightened times, have to find a jury ready to convict her. 'Lastly,' Annie wrote in the *National Reformer*, 'they must be quite sure not to make any legal blunders, for they may be sure that such sins will find them out. Perhaps, on the whole, they had better leave us alone.'[39]

⁂

At February's end, Charles Bradlaugh led a peace rally to offset the pro-war demonstration marching 70,000-strong from Piccadilly to Marble Arch, singing 'Rule Britannia', and demanding entry into the Russo-Turkish War. 'As a Republican,' Annie had written earlier that month in the *National Reformer*, 'I rejoice to see Queen Victoria thus making hateful English monarchy and dragging the royal ermine into the mire of Turkish mis-rule, the mis-rule which she is preparing to water with the blood of our English sons.'[40]

At Hyde Park the two sides brawled. Speakers Corner clattered with pulled-up railings and thudded with bludgeons. Bradlaugh's head and arms met truncheons and jagged iron. He would be bedridden for 16 days. *The Times* blamed 'rowdies', but especially Bradlaugh's adherents for interrupting a patriotic day in the park. In a first, the park responded.

'My poor hyacinths and tulips,' read its letter to the newspaper (signed Hyde Park). 'My first flowers of spring, which I have been nursing the winter through for the delight of all

London, have been ruthlessly torn up and destroyed. My beds are trampled down and ruined.' Mr Bradlaugh's tailor may have welcomed the business coming his way, but the park 'would appreciate it if the organiser could defer' further demonstrations 'until its summer bedding out'.[41] At last acquiescing to Queen Victoria, Disraeli put the country on a war footing.

Annie Besant, meanwhile, found herself thrust into the fight she hoped would never come. 'Our readers will regret to learn,' Charles Bradlaugh reported in the *National Reformer*, 'that Mrs. Besant has received notice from the solicitor of the Rev. Frank Besant, of Sibsey, that an application is to be made to the Chancery Division of the High Court of Justice, to deprive Mrs. Besant of the custody of her daughter, on the ground that the conviction for publishing the Knowlton Pamphlet disqualifies Mrs. Besant from being the guardian of her own child.'[42]

She received her estranged husband's petition while nursing seven-year-old Mabel, dangerously ill with scarlet fever, at home in St John's Wood, at Oatlands. The father's case rested not on accusations of cruelty or neglect, but on the mother's public defence of birth control.

Unfortunately for Annie Besant, the hearing would be overseen by the Master of the Rolls, Sir George Jessel. The wattled 53-year-old had made history as the first Jewish person to sit on a British judicial bench and Her Majesty's privy council. He was also a wealthy, knighted Tory with five children. His curmudgeonly temperament could not have been improved by Sir Hardinge Giffard and Douglas Straight's failure that spring to convict the man who had attempted to assassinate him with a pistol shot as he stepped out of his hansom cab at the courthouse. The bullet missed; the jury found the defendant not guilty, on grounds of insanity.[43]

Unlike Sir Alexander Cockburn, Gilbert and Sullivan could not base a loveably dissolute character upon Sir George Jessel. 'The treatment I received at his hands on my first appearance in Court,' Besant recalled in her memoir, 'told me what I had to expect. After my previous experience of the courtesy of English judges, I was startled to hear a harsh, loud voice exclaim, in answer to a statement from Queen's Counsel, that I was appearing in person: "Appear in person? A lady appear in person? Never heard of such a thing! Does the lady really appear in person?"'

In disgust, Sir George declared her presence to be a 'shocking waste of time of the Court; it would be useless for the lady to attempt to argue the case, as it involved some very nice points of law'.

'After a variety of similar remarks,' Annie recounted, 'delivered in the most grating tones and with the roughest manner, Sir George Jessel tried to obtain his object by browbeating me directly:

"Is this the lady?"

"I am the respondent to the petition, my lord, Mrs. Besant."

"Then I advise you, Mrs. Besant, to employ counsel to represent you, if you can afford it, and I suppose you can." '[44]

Annie calmly replied that she would argue for custody of her daughter herself. The judge said that was within her rights, but that she must not expect to be shown any consideration – a dig, perhaps, at the Lord Chief Justice's handling of her previous trial. Sir George also frowned at the numerous women who had filled his courtroom to support her. Reverend Frank Besant had elected to remain in Sibsey, and let his two barristers do his fighting for him.

The Queen's Counsels came prepared, presenting the judge with copies of the 'indecent and obscene' birth control pamphlets Annie had published. The first, by Dr Knowlton, had been prosecuted. The second, by Mrs Besant, was 'rather more unpleasant than the other'. Sir George Jessel was only familiar with *Fruits of Philosophy*. 'The other book,' he said in surprise, 'I had never even heard of.'

Frank Besant's barrister summarised its contents, and argued, 'A woman or lady holding such views, and by disseminating such views is *ipso facto* unfit to have the care of young people.' The judge agreed. After listening to Knowlton's contraceptive advice read aloud, an offended Sir George said, 'What strikes me, quite independently of any other consideration, is the immense amount of mischief it might do, whether that is the intention of the writer or not, by getting into the hands of single women.'

'Just so,' replied the Queen's Counsel.

'It seems to me that this book is intended to be broadcast among the female population—'

'Precisely, my lord.'[45] Next he related that Mrs Besant had told Mabel's governess to avoid religious subjects, and to never say 'God bless you' after the seven-year-old sneezed. This disdain for morality and God proved, the barristers argued, that 'a girl brought up by such a mother must be shunned by respectable women and could expect no good either here or hereafter'.[46]

'I could have laughed,' Annie wrote, 'had not the matter been so terribly serious, at the mixture of Mrs. Grundy, marriage-establishment, and hell, presented as an argument for robbing a mother of her child.'[47]

'Grundyism' was Victorian slang for priggish righteousness. The only point Besant managed to score in this duel came when the reverend's barristers expressed their indignation that Annie had not allowed her daughter to read the New Testament due to its coarse sections. 'That is not true to say there are no passages unfit for a child's reading,'

Sir George interrupted, 'because I think there are a great many.'

Besant may have theatrically raised her eyebrow at this rebuke of her prosecutor, but her enjoyment was short-lived. 'With the exception of this little outburst of religious feeling against the book written by apostate Jews,' she wrote in her memoir, 'Jewish judge and Christian counsel were united in the hatred of the Atheist.' In the *National Reformer*, she added that 200 years earlier, Sir George's children would have been seized by the state for refusing to raise them as Christians. 'He now joins the persecuting majority, and deals out to the Atheist the same measure dealt to his forefathers by the Christians.'[48]

In the courtroom, Annie's explanation that she expected Mabel to make up her own mind about religion when the girl was older only fell on disbelieving ears, as did her contention that her writings explaining contraception were not immoral. She loved Mabel as only a mother could, and pleaded to keep her.

This really did appear to be a case of sentence before verdict, especially as Sir George Jessel held all the cards. From his bench he said that he was glad to see that Annie Besant had been kind and affectionate toward her daughter and cared for her welfare. 'But, unfortunately, since her separation from her husband, Mrs. Besant has taken upon herself not merely to ignore religion, but to publish and avow that non-belief.' Little Mabel would be harmed by remaining at Oatlands, since, he contended, her mother's conduct 'cut her off, practically, not merely from the sympathy of, but from social intercourse with, the great majority of her sex'.

Ignoring the room filled with her female supporters, judge Jessel further added that he had read both *Fruits of Philosophy* and Mrs Besant's own birth control pamphlet, and had found them to be 'lascivious and obscene', and 'a subversion of all public morality'. As a result, 'It was impossible to say that it would be beneficial for any young girl to be brought up and educated by such a mother.'[49]

He awarded custody to Reverend Frank Besant, who already had their son. Annie Besant had been prosecuted for wanting to limit the size of a family. That same legal system now reduced her own family down to none.

'My worst wish for Sir George Jessel,' Annie confessed in the *National Reformer*, 'is that the measure he has meted out to me may, before he dies, be measured out to him.'[50]

Her niece Freda Fisher described what happened next. Annie returned to Oatlands. The one family member who had never turned her back to her, her mother's sister, whom she called Aunt Co (for *cosy*), met Besant at the front door, anxious to hear the news. She saw the verdict written in her face. 'Gone against us,' Annie whispered.

> Then she said "They say I've got to give her up. Don't talk, bring Mabel here. My God, woman, don't wait to tidy her! I shall lose her if I'm not quick." Without a moment's hesitation she put her small grubby daughter, nursery pinafore and all, into the cab that was waiting and sent her off with Aunt Co to Charles Bradlaugh's house. On arrival there, the Bradlaugh girls told the maid that if anyone called she was to say that they were all out, a statement which Mabel, being a truthful child, contradicted firmly while being conducted to the top floor, and securely hidden. A policeman and a clergyman (presumably the child's father) called, and asked, first for Mrs. Besant, then for Mr. Bradlaugh, and being told that neither were there, went away.[51]

But soon they returned to claim the girl.

In her memoir's own retelling, Annie omitted her attempt to hide her daughter, but not the searing emotions of the judge's sentence made real. 'A messenger from the father came to my house,' she wrote, 'and the little child was carried away by main force, shrieking and struggling, still weak from the fever, and nearly frantic with fear and passionate resistance. No access to her was given me.' In early June, Annie told readers in the *National Reformer*, 'She is, I hear from one of my village friends, at Sibsey Vicarage, under the care of a Miss Robinson, who has taken up her abode with the Rev. Frank Besant. The law permits a father to take a child from the mother, and place it under the care of another woman, residing under his roof.'[52]

As the stress accumulated, Annie Besant realised that there were limits to her strength.

> The strain had been too great, and I nearly went mad, spending hours pacing up and down the empty rooms, striving to weary myself to exhaustion that I might forget. The loneliness and silence of the house, of which my darling had always been the sunshine and the music, weighed on me like an evil dream; I listened for the patter of the dancing feet, and merry, thrilling laughter that rang through the garden, the sweet music of the childish voice; during my sleepless nights I missed in the darkness the soft breathing of the little child; each morning I longed in vain for the clinging arms and soft, sweet kisses. At last health broke down, and fever struck me, and mercifully gave me the rest of pain and delirium instead of the agony of conscious loss.

One person remained by her bedside. 'Through that terrible illness, day after day, Mr. Bradlaugh came to me, and sat writing beside me, feeding me with ice and milk, and behaving more like a tender mother than a man friend; he saved my life, though it seemed to me for a while of little value, till the first months of lonely pain were over.' [53]

Earlier that summer, when she had exited Sir George Jessel's courtroom, Besant purportedly had said 'It's a pity there isn't a God. It would do one so much good to hate Him.'[54] On earth she had no shortage of other targets. Newspapers turned on her; one story began: 'No one is sorry for Mrs. Besant ... Let us hope we may hear no more of Mrs. Besant, her domestic convulsions, and her heresies against society.'[55]

As Annie remained confined in bed with rheumatic fever, a new action was brought against the bookseller Edward Truelove by an undeterred Charles Hastings Collette and his Society for the Suppression of Vice. This time Collette opted for the trial to be heard by a special jury, not the common type that had previously acquitted Truelove. Working alone as his attorney, Charles Bradlaugh could not save his friend. For selling books teaching contraception, the 68-year-old received a sentence of four months' hard labour, picking oakum in the Coldbath Fields Prison.

As the summer of 1878 dimmed into autumn, Annie reappeared in the pages of the *National Reformer* in September, thanking readers for their letters of 'such kindly feeling, adding an assurance that neither the illness, nor the trouble which produced it, has in any fashion lessened my determination to work for the Cause'. Below this notice, Charles Bradlaugh announced her return to the stage. 'Mrs. Besant will (we are glad to be able to state) lecture at the Hall of Science on Sunday evening. Her subject will be "The Late and Pending Struggles for the Freedom of the Press."'[56]

Earlier that summer, the British government had secretly promised the Ottoman Empire support in peace negotiations with Russia in exchange for the possession of Cyprus. To Her Majesty's delight, Prime Minister Disraeli related Otto von Bismarck's admiration. 'That is progress,' the German chancellor had said. 'His idea of progress is the acquisition of fresh countries.' Victoria laughed in glee.[57] In November, British Raj troops invaded Afghanistan. 'One step more,' Annie Besant wrote in the *National Reformer*, 'in the onward march of the British people towards a brutal and brutalizing imperialism.'[58] She was back to sounding like her old self.

In London, her estranged brother-in-law, the novelist Walter Besant, told a bewildered Thomas Hardy that he considered *The Return of the Native* – featuring deaths by adder-bite and weir – 'the most original the most virile and most humorous of all modern novels'.[59] He invited Hardy to join the Rabelais Club, a social group he founded to promote male sexuality in literature. Hardy demurred. That autumn, labourers erected the purloined Egyptian obelisk known as Cleopatra's Needle on the Victoria Embankment. Secreted into its pedestal was a time capsule that contained, among other sundries, several Bibles and a copy of John 3:16 (*Whosoever believeth in Him should not perish, but have everlasting life*) written in 215 languages. The Embankment's gas lamps were replaced by wired ones; for the first time, Londoners could walk beneath electric light.

A bulb went off above a rejuvenated Annie's head. Since her husband had never allowed them to divorce, why not simply return to Sibsey and resume life as his wife in their home? Her children could never be separated from her again. But Annie's legal attempts to undo her separation agreement and restore her conjugal rights proved futile; the Chancery court restrained Mrs Besant from 'annoying and molesting her husband'.[60] So much for the sanctity of marriage.

Chancery had been Charles Dickens's old stomping grounds, and had he been alive as the calendar turned to 1879, he would not have been shocked to see the screws of foolscap and sheafs of pages still forming ramparts of claims and counter-claims across the courtroom tables.

In a frankly Dickensian twist, Besant was extended a hand by the man who had torn Mabel from her arms. Sir George Jessel must have forgiven, or never saw, her depiction of him in the *National Reformer*, where she claimed he had 'the sneer of a Mephistopheles, mingled with a curious monkey-ish pleasure in inflicting pain'.[61] Or he suddenly believed in the rules of fair play. Alarmed to learn that Frank Besant was abrogating the terms of their separation by denying Annie her visitation rights, Sir George suggested that she formally file for divorce, on the grounds of her husband's cruelty.

At home and in her printshop, Besant dutifully wrote down a catalogue of her husband's insults and physical abuse. After reading the list, Frank Besant sent the judge his reply. If there had been any acts of cruelty, he averred, they had occurred 'in the heat of the moment', provoked by Mrs Besant's refusal to obey the reverend's 'reasonable request' that she forsake her writing, and fulfil her duties as mother and wife.

These emotionally exhausting wranglings spilled into the spring of 1879, when an appellate court upheld the absolute right of the father. Full custody to Frank Besant – who still refused to grant Annie a divorce, meaning that as long as he lived, she could not marry Charles Bradlaugh.

The law, she wrote, 'says to every woman: "Choose which of these two positions you will have: if you are legally your husband's wife, you can have no legal claim to your children;

if legally you are your husband's mistress, then your rights as mother are secure." [62]

In her memoir and *National Reformer* column, Annie called attention to the antiquated blasphemy statute that had originally empowered Sir George Jessel to take Mabel away. While she may have been the penultimate child that the Crown removed from its mother due to her religious belief (in 1883, it awarded custody to an Anglican father due to the mother's Catholicism), British women would not win fully equal custody rights with men over their children until passage of the Guardianship Act, in 1973. [63]

In a final hearing in his chambers in April 1879, Sir George Jessel surprised Annie by ordering that she be allowed her monthly access to Mabel and Digby in Sibsey, as well as three annual supervised weekly visits to London and the seaside. The children could send her one letter each week, and receive her reply. If it sounded like favours to a prisoner, that was how the arrangement felt to Annie. On their first trip to the beach, she wrote that their court-appointed guardians, a minister and his wife whose expenses she had to pay, 'treated me in their presence as though I were a dangerous animal from whom they were to be protected. I wished Mabel to have the benefit of sea-bathing, and was told that she could not be allowed to bathe with me, and this with a suggestiveness that sorely taxed my self-control'. [64]

That spring, while performing at a circus in Portsmouth, the human cannonball Zazel fell completely through her safety net, weakened by wear. 'No bones were broken,' reported *The Times*, 'but she was too severely injured to appear last evening.'[65] Her real name was Rossa Richter, and she vowed to climb back into the mortar's mouth.

After a few months of making the five-hour journey from London to Sibsey – requiring two trains and a hired cab, and leaving only three hours to see her children before making the return – Annie Besant realised how these intermittent arrivals and quick departures disturbed eight-year-old Mabel. The girl was 'in a continual state of longing and fretting for me'. Her husband's insults of Annie – *sinner, harlot* – in front of their children added further stress. As she had no further legal recourse, she made the most difficult decision of her life.

'I resolved neither to see nor write to my children,' Annie wrote, 'until they were old enough to understand and to judge for themselves. I know that I shall win my daughter back in her womanhood, though I have been robbed of her childhood.'[66]

When the bill for her daring feats came due, the Establishment took its payment in flesh. Every parent knows how quickly the years slip by; children are tumbling hourglasses, ceaselessly running out of sand. Officially, Annie Besant was not a criminal. But she must have felt like one. Her sentence was the violent reality of those missed, irreplaceable days, and the knowledge that she had been made a stranger to her children.

'Resolutely I turned my back on them,' she recounted, 'and determined that, robbed of my own, I would be a mother to all helpless children I could aid, and cure the pain at my own heart by soothing the pain of others.'[67]

'One pays dearly for immortality,' her contemporary Friedrich Nietzsche observed of an iconoclastic life. 'One has to die several times while alive.'[68]

As 1879 closed with the coldest winter since 1740, and the longest-ever fog shrouded London for five months, Zazel suffered another fall. This time, she missed the net completely. The audience recoiled from the horrifying plunge and percussive thud. 'I am killed!' she screamed. 'I am killed!' After an interval, however, the irrepressible aerialist emerged from behind the curtain to rousing applause. 'With her hands bandaged up,' a newspaper reported, 'and evidently suffering from great nervousness,' Zazel resumed her performance.[69] Later she would count her broken bones, but for now, bruised but unbowed, she summoned the strength to launch herself again.

PART III

'AT WAR ALL ROUND'

10

'SICK OF SEWING COAT TAILS'

The new decade began with new British battles against Afghans, Zulus and Boers, plus a shock defeat on the home front for Conservatives, who lost the 1880 general election. Annie Besant revelled in the Liberal victory, and the return of William Gladstone as prime minster. 'The Freethought party may well take credit to itself for having been the first in the field against the Tory policy,' she wrote. 'They did more than any other party in the country to create that force of public opinion which overthrew the Tory government.'

The only elected office that Annie or any British woman could stand for was the London School Board, so instead she had run Charles Bradlaugh's campaign in his fourth attempt to win a parliamentary seat as a Liberal in Northampton. After the polls closed, Annie knelt beside him at a hotel room window 'listening to the hoarse murmur of the crowd, knowing that presently there would be a roar of triumph or a howl of anger when the numbers were read out from the steps of the Town Hall'. The suspense ended when the crowd exploded into a cloud of thrown hats and handkerchiefs, cheering, 'Bradlaugh for Northampton!' At last he was in.

The next morning, as the weight of new responsibility fell upon her friend's broad shoulders, Annie watched women sobbing and men fighting to get near him as they made their way to the train station. 'Our Charlie!' they shouted, 'Our Charlie; we've got you and we'll keep you!' He was the first admitted atheist to be voted into the House of Commons.

'Ah me!' Annie sighed in her telling. 'We thought the struggle over, and it was only beginning; we thought our hero victorious, and a fiercer, crueller fight lay in front.' They were in their professional prime – in 1880 she would turn 33 and he 47 – but neither had an inkling of the toll to come. 'His life was to be the price of the winning,' she later wrote, 'the laurel-wreath was to fall upon a grave.'[1]

As she pined for Mabel – and made the questionable decision to sell a cabinet photograph that depicted the child, 'Deprived of her mother', as a martyr-in-training – Besant found a welcome diversion in studying for London University's entrance exams. Founded in 1836 as a secular alternative to Oxford and Cambridge, in 1878 it became Britain's first college to accept female degree candidates. In 1880 the school would award Bachelor of Arts degrees to four women. Annie Besant intended to add her name to that roll. 'And here let me say to anyone in mental trouble,' she advised, 'that they might find an immense relief in taking up some intellectual recreation of this kind.'[2]

With the same concentration she had once directed at the Bible and English case law, she now tackled physics and algebra. They proved to be more formidable opponents. Besant hired an exam tutor named Edward Aveling, who was two years younger than her, and had also grown up in Harrow. Upon graduating from the school, Aveling had won the top entrance scholarship to University College, London, in medicine, and earned medals in several physical sciences. Like Annie he had grown up in the Church. His father was a minister, and Aveling felt at home in the pulpit and on stage. He

MABEL EMILY BESANT.
DEPRIVED OF HER MOTHER, MAY 23, 1878,
BY ORDER OF SIR GEORGE JESSEL, MASTER OF THE ROLLS,
ON ACCOUNT OF THAT MOTHER'S HERESY.

Mabel Besant: 'Deprived of her mother
on account of that mother's heresy'

acted – once performing in a troupe with Henry Irving –
before becoming a well-liked teacher, starting at the North
London Collegiate School for Girls. His popularity was also
a product of charm and good looks – in photos, Aveling
appears to be lean, clean-shaven and earnest. He looked
like a man you would trust to take you boating.

George Bernard Shaw, however, sized up Edward Aveling
as an undersized reptile, with the eyes of a basilisk. The 24-
year-old writer, still searching for his footing in London, had
caught wind of Aveling swindling a group of female students
who had scraped together funds to pay for exam tutoring in
advance. 'The more fortunate ones,' Shaw recounted, 'got
nothing worse for their money than letters of apology for

breaking the lesson engagements. The others were seduced and had their microscopes appropriated.'[3]

Years later, Shaw will burn Aveling into infamy as the barely disguised bounder Dubedat in his play *The Doctor's Dilemma*. Like Aveling, Dubedat borrows money from anyone foolish enough to lend it to him, and seldom repays. In one scene, he is called a scoundrel and rascal before calmly putting his pencil down and saying, 'Look here. All this is no good. You don't understand. You imagine that I'm simply an ordinary criminal.'

'Not an ordinary one, Dubedat,' his cheated lender drolly replies. 'Do yourself justice.'

The play ends with his unmourned death. After a man surmises that Dubedat had passed into a new world, another replies, 'Borrowing his first five-pound note there, probably.'[4]

But all of this is in the future – as is the revelation that Edward Aveling was still legally married, to a woman who had fled him for cruelty.

In the summer of 1880, Aveling joined the National Secular Society and mooned over Annie Besant in book reviews, just as she had once couched her affection for Charles Bradlaugh. 'The loveliness of her face and form,' Aveling wrote in the *National Reformer*, 'make a new joy in the world. The loveliness of her mind increases that joy a thousandfold . . . Her tenderest smiles are reserved for my eyes only; her inmost thoughts are breathed to me alone.'[5] It may have sounded mawkish, but to Besant such flirtatious flattery was new. Frank Besant and Charles Bradlaugh had never proclaimed, as Aveling did, on stage before an audience, 'To read her book is a delight, but to hear the thoughts thereof spoken is like seeing a play of Shakespeare acted after having read it in the study.'[6]

Hypatia Bradlaugh felt a change as Annie and Aveling's

camaraderie deepened, calling it her father's 'first disappointment' in Mrs Besant. Hypatia sensed that his election and her
studies were leading them down different paths. Around this
time, she remembered her father stretching out his muscular
arm and telling her, 'I have not a passion that I could not
crush as easily as an egg within my hand if it were necessary
for the good of the cause I love.'[7]

In her memoir, the title Annie chose for the chapter sum-
marising this period was 'At War All Round'.

⁂

At first the attacks concentrated on the new Liberal MP
Charles Bradlaugh. In the weeks after his election, British
newspapers began wondering how this atheist could possibly
be seated when new members in the Commons were required
to swear the oath that ended 'so help me God'. Exceptions
had been made for non-Christians; Quakers could give an
affirmation, while the first elected Jewish MP, Lionel de
Rothschild, had endured winning four elections and the passage of 11 years before an 1858 act finally allowed him to
alter the vow to end 'so help me, Jehovah'.

Through each of the stages of their trial, Bradlaugh and
Besant had been permitted to affirm to tell the truth, rather
than swear to God. In all of England, only the House of
Commons still forbid this allowance. Conservatives defended
the rule, claiming that only a member who feared divine
(as opposed to electoral) retribution could feel the moral
accountability to vote in the national interest.

This was news to Britain's suffragists, and to Rossa Richter, whose cannonball act as Zazel was put to an end for
good that spring, after around 1,200 performances. A Tory
MP had introduced a bill prohibiting acrobats from being

launched more than six feet. A hard tackle by London's first professional football club – Fulham St Andrew's Church Sunday School – could launch someone further. Miffed that men had taken away her living, the human projectile took off for Anthony Comstock's vice-suppressive New York City, where male politicians still cared more about a woman's purity than her safety.

On 3 May 1880 in the House of Commons, after other new members had been sworn in, Charles Bradlaugh stood at the Table and announced that he would affirm his allegiance, rather than swear to a God he did not believe existed. Henry Brand had been Speaker for eight years and should have known to allow Bradlaugh his moment, and then ask a judge to rule if the new MP for Northampton had broken the law. Instead, the nonplussed Speaker ordered the atheist to withdraw from the House so its members could discuss its options.

The Conservative Lord Randolph Churchill seized his moment to make a name for himself free of his famous father the Duke of Marlborough, and of stories of sodden sinning that had made William Gladstone exclaim, 'God forbid that any great English party should be led by a Churchill!'[8] The pop-eyed 31-year-old gave a rousing speech, scored by cheers, quoting from Charles Bradlaugh's pamphlet denigrating the monarchy, and asking how the Commons could admit a man who professed no loyalty to either Church or Crown.

After the *hear-hears* died down, Bradlaugh's erstwhile prosecutor Sir Hardinge Giffard stood to announce that any member who supported the atheist's attempt to take his seat would be advising an illegal act. And so the House's select committee voted to bar Charles Bradlaugh from the Commons. In its editorial, *The Times* lamented that – three years after the prosecution of *Fruits of Philosophy* – the government was yet again popularising the ideas that it aimed to suppress, and making heroes of its enemies. The matter likely could have been settled if Charles Bradlaugh had followed Benjamin Disraeli's pithy maxim that in politics one should never complain or explain. Instead, on 21 May, he told the nation, via a long letter in *The Times*, that the oath to him included 'words of idle and meaningless character'. But for the sake of his constituents he would utter these 'sounds conveying no clear and definite meaning'.[9] He would swear the required oath.

A satirical newspaper was not that wide of the mark when it claimed that a secret band of Tories – sworn in on a copy of Hansard at midnight in St Stephen's crypt – planned to form a pile of bodies 17 deep to prevent him from reaching the House Bible.

In the full House of Commons that morning, Conservatives did leap up from their benches to protest the atheist's first move toward the Table. 'The Debate was hot,' Queen Victoria wrote in her diary, 'about that dreadful Bradlaugh's not taking his seat.'[10]

Her Majesty appealed to the 70-year-old granite-face Gladstone (a devout Christian, but also the prime minister she liked the least) to take care 'to prevent its being supposed (erroneously of course) that the Government sympathise with the opinions Mr. Bradlaugh is stated to hold'.[11] The Liberal leader had ignored entreaties to support Besant and Bradlaugh during their obscenity trial, but here he wrote to Queen Victoria that he believed that the duly elected member for Northampton was acting within his rights.[12] Sir Thomas Erskine May, the expert on parliamentary procedure, agreed. No precedent existed for barring an MP on the grounds of insincerity. Yet the prime minister remained silent as the opposition made political hay, even drawing to their side the usually rebellious Irish MPs who here feared upsetting their Catholic constituencies.

From her Fleet Street printing office, Annie Besant fired off one 'Special Extra Number' issue of the *National Reformer* after another, joining the front line after the Conservative MP Sir Henry Tyler insinuated in Parliament that she was an adulteress. Besant wondered how the Establishment press would react 'If Mr. Bradlaugh publicly and wantonly dragged the name of Sir Henry Tyler's wife or sister into an attack . . . Until now men have been content to attack their men opponents, without including a woman, but Sir Henry Tyler has set an example that if generally followed would scarcely add dignity to the House of Commons.'

In the same issue, she remembered her first moment of political awakening, standing outside the Salford gaol in 1867. The MP Charles Parnell, she wrote, 'and the better members of the Irish party, must have felt their cheeks burn when they heard Tories sneering at Mr. Bradlaugh's "honor and conscience," and remembered the days when the poor boy Allen was hanged at Manchester, and when the liberty and life of many an Irishman were committed fearlessly to that same "honor and conscience".'[13] (Did Annie also know that she and the MP shared a tie beyond their Irish heritage? Parnell's paramour Kitty O'Shea – née Wood – hailed from the aristocratic side of Annie's father's family. After leaving her husband, who refused to grant a divorce, O'Shea and Parnell would remain together for the rest of their lives, torpedoing his political career.)

Next Annie Besant organised a defence fund, and from podiums across England rallied supporters to Bradlaugh's side. She was a walking ultimatum; he was gaining support. *Vanity Fair* deemed Bradlaugh worthy to be sketched. The mainstream magazine captioned his portrait, simply, 'Icono-clast'. Behind the battlements of Windsor Castle, Queen Victoria simmered. 'There is great trouble about this horrid Bradlaugh,' she wrote in her diary on 25 May 1880. 'So many oppose his sitting, & Mr Gladstone & the Govt, only look at the legal question . . . Difficulties on all sides, are cropping up.'[14] Five days later, she added, 'Mr Gladstone's report, shows great annoyance, at the Bradlaugh Committee. He declares to loathe Mr Bradlaugh's horrible views, & that this is a merely technical question.'[15]

Yet Britain's elected minds could not resolve it. In June, a bitter but persuasive Sir Hardinge Giffard roused the oppos-ition to back his amendment preventing a court of law from deciding the outcome. Gladstone stood and disagreed. Sir Hardinge trumped him with a passionate intensity. 'The temper of the House does not improve,' the prime minister wrote to Queen Victoria, 'both excitement and suspicion appearing to prevail in different quarters.' The debate con-tinued past midnight; after the teller announced the vote, 'The excitement at this result was tremendous. Indeed, it was an ecstatic transport which exceeded anything that Mr. Glad-stone remembers to have witnessed.'[16]

When at last the din subsided, the speaker confirmed that enough Liberals had broken ranks to side with Tories uphold-ing the boycott of Bradlaugh. The next day, after the conclusion of lunchtime prayers, the unrepentant MP for Northampton strolled back to Table and yet again claimed his right to take the oath and be seated.

'Was much surprised to hear by telegraph,' Queen Vic-toria wrote that afternoon of 23 June, 'that there had been a most violent scene in the Hse of Commons, about Brad-laugh, which ended in his being taken up by the Sergeant at Arms!'[17]

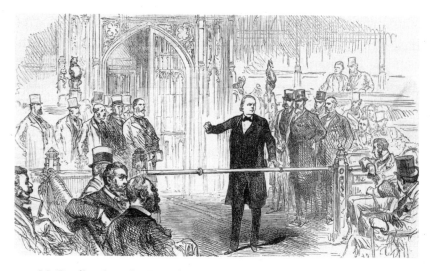

Mr Bradlaugh at the Bar of the House of Commons – *The Illustrated London News*, 3 July 1880

The Wednesday session had started with full benches on both sides of the House, and the Strangers' Gallery packed with Charles Bradlaugh's supporters. As loud cries of 'Withdraw!' rained down upon him, Bradlaugh demanded to be heard. 'At the Bar!' some MPs yelled. The Serjeant-at-Arms – a squat, white-haired former army captain dressed in silk stockings and knee-breeches – fastened the brass bar which placed Bradlaugh outside the Chamber. This, however, gave the atheist an arena stage of sorts. Instead of addressing the opposition from his side of the aisle, Bradlaugh faced all his peers.

'Do you tell me I am unfit to sit amongst you?' he shouted over the harrumphs and hoots. For 20 minutes, Charles Bradlaugh extemporaneously lectured the chamber on the hypocrisy of demanding a member pretend to be something he was not. If they would not allow him to argue before a judge, he would appeal to the court of public opinion. Would the Commons behave this way if his voters were standing at his back?

This only rankled his opposition, who, per the transcript, howled *Oh!*

Bradlaugh repeated his mentor John Stuart Mill's contention that if all mankind minus one person were of one opinion, mankind would be no more justified in silencing that one person than he, if he had absolute power, would be justified in silencing mankind. 'I beg you,' Bradlaugh continued, 'not in any sort of menace, not in any sort of boast, but as one man against six hundred, to give me that justice which on the other side of this Hall the judges would give were I pleading before them.'

Instead the members voted for his withdrawal. Bradlaugh defiantly stomped to the Table. 'I refuse to obey the orders of the House,' he told the Speaker, 'which are against the law.' The Speaker called for the Serjeant-at-Arms to remove the rebel. Bradlaugh towered over the portly Sir Ralph Gosset but at a light touch on the shoulder agreed to retreat behind the Bar.

As an audience would expect if this were a play, Bradlaugh then paused dramatically and made to turn. The mutton-chopped Gosset met his determined gaze but did not draw his sword. Launching himself like a cannonball, Bradlaugh dashed toward the Table. As the bow-legged Sir Ralph bounded after him, Bradlaugh thundered, 'I claim my right as a member of this House to come back. I admit the right of the House to imprison me, but I submit that it has no right to exclude me, and I refuse, Sir, to be excluded.'[18]

By a vote of 274 to 7 they opted to imprison him.

'Glad to see the feeling the House has shown on the subject,' Queen Victoria exulted in her diary.[19] Her prime minster,

"KICKED OUT." (?)

'Kicked Out': Bradlaugh as depicted in *Punch* magazine, 3 July 1880

however, wrote to tell her that Charles Bradlaugh's impressive speech to the House 'was that of a consummate speaker. But it was an address which could not have any effect unless the House had undergone a complete revolution of the mind. He challenged the legality of the act of the House, expressing hereby an opinion in which Mr. Gladstone himself, going beyond some other members of the minority, has the misfortune to lean towards agreeing with him.'[20]

The Serjeant-at-Arms led the criminal to the clock tower, and up the stairs to its 'prison room', built to hold a person removed from the Chamber. It may have been small, but it was better than the cold and damp cell beneath Guildhall where he and Annie Besant had lingered after their arrest for selling *Fruits of Philosophy*, three years before. Sir Ralph allowed visitors – including the Irish nationalist MP Charles Parnell, who had changed his mind and now supported the atheist. The Serjeant-at-Arms also permitted Bradlaugh to use his office telegraph to summon the one person he most needed beside him.

In the *National Reformer*, Annie Besant wrote, 'The man chosen by the Radicals of Northampton has been committed to prison. As this paper goes to press, I go to Westminster to receive from him his directions as to the conduct of the struggle with the nation into which the House of Commons has so recklessly plunged.'[21] She rushed to Big Ben.

Like the sweep of its clock hands, we have come full circle, to where this book began. For Charles Bradlaugh and Annie Besant it must have felt like old times. Once again the pair huddled against the Establishment in captivity. She plotted their public relations strategy and read aloud from the handfuls of telegrams the uniformed Sir Ralph continually carried in from off-stage. Perhaps for the first, and last, time in British history, correspondence was addressed, simply, to 'Clock Tower'. (But for new gold wallpaper and furnishings – and the removal of the bars that covered its tall windows – the prison's sitting room today looks little changed as a break area for the Houses of Parliament's Visitor Experience team. The small jail cell is now a modern kitchenette, undistinguishable but for Big Ben's thudding hammer strike followed by its perfect E-note toll that reverberates through a visitor's bones.)

The telegraphed slips of support came from as close as Clapham, and as far away as Dublin, Paris and Rome. 'The fools have put their foot in it,' wrote a man from Northampton. 'Now they make you a martyr.' A Liverpudlian offered £5 'to aid you in battling against the intolerance and bigotry of the imperial parliament'. Dr Fluery of Finsbury Square sent 'thanks for your unflinching resistance to the hypocritical bigots'. Others said that Bradlaugh's defeat would soon turn into a triumph, that he had lit a candle for England that could never be put out, that even if they disagreed with his atheism, he had struck a blow for civil and religious liberty. The Radical Reverend Stewart Headlam's message read, 'Accept my warmest sympathy. I wish you good luck in the name of Jesus Christ the emancipator whom so many of your opponent's blaspheme.'[22]

With their dinner in detention finished, Annie, joined by Alice, Hypatia and Edward Aveling, dashed back to the *National Reformer* office. 'After his visitors departed,' *The Times* reported, 'Mr. Bradlaugh spent some time on the terrace.'[23] *The Illustrated London News* added that the Serjeant-at-Arms treated him as a favoured guest. 'Never can there have been a courtlier gaoler, never a more comfortable prisoner ... Does not a meeting like this make amends for the cold-shoulder shown to Mr. Bradlaugh?'[24]

Annie Besant stayed up through the night, organising a Trafalgar Square demonstration that would, two days later (she would claim) gather 'the largest crowd – so say the papers – ever seen there'. Similar rallies took place in 200 towns across Britain. In Northampton, 6,000 protestors filled its Market Square to demand that Charles Bradlaugh be seated as their MP.

Though neither could know it then, this was the apotheosis of their union, their last shared fight and cause. 'Even in twenty-four hours the rising storm was heard so plainly,' Annie wrote, 'that the Tories shrank before its menace, and hurriedly released the man they had hurriedly imprisoned. Although they cried out that Parliament was defied, they released the defier without apology. They hoped to embarrass the Government; they only succeeded in making themselves ridiculous.'[25] Four thousand people, she reported, filled West-minster Hall to applaud his emergence from the clock tower's cell.

As Queen Victoria that summer enjoyed the delicious black cherries and strawberries ripening in Windsor Castle's kitchen garden, the pages of her diary became blighted with his name. 'The Bradlaugh business very disagreeable,' she wrote in her diary. 'Expressed my satisfaction at the conduct of the Majority of the Hse of Commons against this hor-rible, immoral Atheist.'[26] On Monday, 28 June, Her Majesty's entry began, 'My Coronation day.—Mr. Gladstone has written to say, that he would bring forward, a resolution, respecting Mr. Bradlaugh, proposing that he should be allowed to affirm.'[27] Four days later, the queen noted with distaste that the resolution 'has unfortunately carried. But he may be pro-ceeded against,—still it does much harm.'[28]

That morning, Charles Bradlaugh and Annie Besant walked through the cheers of the supporters crowding Palace Yard and into the Houses of Parliament. From the Ladies' Gallery she watched him stride to the Chamber's Table, quietly speak to the Clerk, and shake the Speaker's hand. To his mind, his affirmation had at last been accepted, and so, when the House of Commons divided to vote on a motion, Bradlaugh followed his Liberal peers to the Aye lobby.

A notorious Tory MP instructed a clerk to take note, cryp-tically adding, 'This may become the subject of enquiry hereafter.'[29] Before the sun could set on his triumphant day, Bradlaugh was served with a writ saying he was being sued for violating the 1866 Parliamentary Oaths Act. It fixed a £500 penalty for every vote, as well as every attended debate, by a member who had not been officially sworn in. If his opponents could not prevent him from sitting, they would bankrupt and ruin him forever.

The suit had been orchestrated by the memorably named Charles Newdigate Newdegate. The Conservative shared a nasty streak of righteousness with his ally the Archbishop of Canterbury, A.C. Tait. (Annie reminded her readers that in 1851, Newdegate had protested the election of Jews to Parliament, decrying the 'sitting in that House an individual who regarded our redeemer as an imposter'.)[30] Starting in 1880, the MP Newdegate mailed each of his printed attacks on Bradlaugh to Tait, who approved of his efforts to protect the Establishment. If the republican prevailed, Newdegate wrote, 'the Crown of these realms would be sold to some pawnbroker, and the Throne would be sent to some curiosity shop'.

As if that weren't enough cause to permanently expel Bradlaugh from Parliament, Newdegate continued, 'There is reason to believe that the obscene book, entitled the "Fruits of Philosophy", for the publication of which Mr. Bradlaugh and Mrs. Besant were condemned to imprisonment in 1877, is still in surreptitious circulation . . . What a comment upon the morality of the Atheism of which Mr. Bradlaugh is the exponent.' [31]

Bradlaugh of course dug in. As a conscientious representative of the bootmakers of Northampton he sat for every debate, voted on every motion, and introduced petitions (showing 251,332 signatures) to abolish the practice of perpetual pensions, rewarded to favoured gentry since Charles II. One of the largest beneficiaries of this royal prerogative happened to be Lord Randolph Churchill's family, who since Queen Anne's reign had received £4,000 annually for the past 170 years, along with Blenheim Palace.

As he kept turning up in the Commons, Bradlaugh's potential fine soared above £10,000. Next he filed a libel suit against a Tory MP – also a vice-admiral in Her Majesty's navy – who, newspapers reported, had made speeches calling Bradlaugh and Besant adulterers. In a public letter to Sir John Hay, Annie called for a retraction for the accusation 'of conduct which would entitle Mr. Besant to a divorce' on grounds that would denigrate her character.[32] Sir John remained silent.

Charles Bradlaugh, meanwhile, thanked *National Reformer* subscribers for their encouragement. He worried, he added, that the 'grave extra work' Mrs Besant was shouldering 'during the last few weeks of hard study [will] seriously interfere with her prospects of success at the forthcoming London University examination'.[33]

She passed the five-day test – and moreover, was rated 'First Class' – in botany, general biology, animal physiology, inorganic chemistry, theoretical mechanics, magnetism and electricity, and acoustics, light and heat. Plus maths. In the *Reformer*, a proud Bradlaugh told readers that Annie would be entering college.

She also left Oatlands – where Mabel's absence haunted the rooms – for a new house, also in St John's Wood, at 19 Avenue Road. The red-brick two-storey villa, just west of Primrose Hill at the northern edge of Regent's Park, remained close to Bradlaugh's rented rooms. (With its forecourt still giving it the appearance of a small Victorian train station, the home would be a more fitting, and accessible, site for Annie's Blue Plaque.) Edward Aveling rented his own room from her, drawing the two even closer together.

As the struggle to take his parliamentary seat consumed Bradlaugh, Annie sank into her studies. In the advanced botany class taught by T.H. Huxley – nicknamed 'Darwin's bulldog' for his strident defence of his friend's theory of evolution – Besant was the only student in 1881's national exam to pass with honours. Next she and Aveling, with

Bradlaugh's daughters, launched a free series of college entrance exam preparation classes at the Old Street Hall, plus courses in music, drama, and Alice and Hypatia's specialties, Latin and French.

What started as an act of goodwill towards London's working class was quickly assailed by a Tory MP. Sir Henry Tyler – an engineer who had traced the source of London's last great outbreak of cholera, and whose donation of railway artifacts had started the Science Museum – took umbrage at atheists working as teachers. Previously, he had slandered Besant as a supposed adulteress. Now, on the floor of the House, he raised a formal objection against Annie, Hypatia and Alice. Their classes, he fulminated, would undermine the Bible, since in a column Mrs Besant had asserted, 'God is left out of all calculations in science.'

'The Christian bloodhounds are loosed on the track of the heretics,' an unrepentant Annie wrote in the *National Reformer*. 'We have the spectacle of Sir Henry Tyler buying off god by keeping an insulting notice levelled against three women on the paper of the House for months, like the coward that he is.'[34]

Through his friends on its board, Sir Henry next moved to have Edward Aveling fired from teaching at the London Hospital. At the University of London, the Birkbeck Institute suddenly struck Annie's name from the list of students who had passed its course on electricity. The college feared that its donors would close their chequebooks if they learned the school had admitted her. Besant's application to use the Royal Botanical Gardens in Regent's Park also was refused. In a tone that suggested that he would like to toss her in the boating pond to see if she floated, the curator explained that his young daughters played amongst the plants, and he had to protect them. Upon hearing the news, the famous botanist J.D. Hooker sent Annie a pass to use Kew Gardens – but only before its gates opened, and the better-heeled ladies arrived.

Annie bristled at the divergence of her life's path from her co-defendant, four years after their trial. Bradlaugh's standing had improved; she had lost everything. He may have been branded a heretic, but he had also crammed his foot in the entrance door to the Establishment, adding legions of admirers who cheered on their working-class hero. She had become notorious, and felt the reverberating shock of those doors slamming in her face. Because a single chemistry examiner found her birth control teachings immoral and (three times) refused to pass her, Annie would never satisfy her degree requirements, ending her dream of a career in academia. The usually headstrong T.H. Huxley – a father of eight, who abhorred birth control – did not contest her exclusion from London University, or support her application to enrol at University College. Even the Somerville Club, a London social hall for working-class women named for an early feminist, refused to admit her.

There would be no *Vanity Fair* caricature. Victoria would not waste one pen stroke, nor one drop of ink, to set down her name. Charles may have pocked the pages of Her Majesty's diary ('how horrid & repulsive looking, Mr Bradlaugh was'), but in the 43,765 pages that survive, Annie did not warrant even a single mention.[35] She was being written out of history, even as she continued to make it. He was a man; she was a woman.

An editorial cartoon from this time showed her knitting and casting a baleful glance at the man she had boosted. Under her frowning visage, the caption read, 'Sick of sewing coat tails'.

'Mrs Besant – Sick of Sewing Coat Tails'

'Mr Bradlaugh – Sick of Inspector Denning', the Palace of Westminster's chief police officer

❧

'The Bradlaugh business, beginning again,' Queen Victoria lamented on 27 April 1881. Charles Newdigate Newdegate's ongoing suit meant that, by law, Bradlaugh was required to vacate his seat as if he had died. Following the by-election, 'He has been re-elected & has again been refused admittance to the House, & permission to swear.'[36] Two weeks later, Her Majesty noted 'Another disgraceful scene in the house, about Bradlaugh.'[37] After he had refused to leave the floor, MPs voted to bar his entry to the Commons, even as an observer in its gallery. The summer climaxed with Victoria's entry of 3 August: 'There was a most frightful scene this evening, in the Hse of C., on Mr Bradlaugh trying to force his way in, &

being ejected. Much violence was displayed, & Mr Bradlaugh got his clothes torn!'[38]

Once again he had tried to take his seat, and once again he had relied on Annie Besant to bring out the muscle. From Great George Street the pair had pushed through the throng of supporters she had summoned to Parliament Square. Annie, Alice and Hypatia used petitions defending Bradlaugh as their ticket to enter Westminster Hall, where they stood at the top of its stone stairs leading to the House. The Inspector of Police, commanding a force of one hundred officers that morning, escorted Bradlaugh to the Members' Lobby, where the forbidden MP burst through the door to the Chamber.

'Ah!' Annie wrote. 'We heard a crash inside, and listened, and there was sound of breaking glass and splintering wood.' The police dragged Charles Bradlaugh from the House and down the long hallway before at last shoving him into Palace Yard. There she found him 'standing, still and white, face set like marble, coat torn, motionless, as though carved in stone, facing the members' door'. One officer told her, 'Of all I have ever seen, I never saw one man struggle with ten like that.'

For a moment, Annie thought Bradlaugh was going to order his assembled supporters to attack their government. 'Injured,' she recounted, 'by the cruel wrenching of all his muscles – so that for weeks his arms had to be swathed in bandages – he was never greater than when he conquered his own wrath, crushed down his own longing for battle.' No man, he told her, would sleep in jail because of him, and no parent need worry about their child.

'Some hold their ideals lightly,' Annie continued, 'but his heart-strings were twined around his.'

He was a patriot, an Englishman, an adherent of law and liberty, and now, for the first time in England's long history, an elected representative who had been literally tossed out of Parliament. It was, Annie wrote with gathering steam, an 'outrage more worthy of a slum pot-house than of the great Commons House, the House of Hampden and Vane, the House that had guarded its own from Royal violence, and had maintained its privileges in the teeth of Kings'.

That morning, Annie Besant had witnessed the breaking of a heart. 'A wave of agony swept over his face,' she wrote, 'and from that fatal day Charles Bradlaugh was never the same man.'[39]

*　＊＊＊*

Still he continued to fight. In February 1882, as Charles Bradlaugh scrabbled through the judgments and appeals around Charles Newdigate Newdegate's lawsuit, he also refused to stop trying to claim his seat. At the start of the new parliamentary session, Bradlaugh managed to walk up to the House's Table, pull a New Testament from his pocket, and recite the official oath. An incensed Lord Randolph Churchill stood to question whether the book really was a Bible, 'for we have not the slightest guarantee that is not the *Fruits of Philosophy*'.[40] Bradlaugh was duly expelled, and again won the resultant by-election – his third Northampton victory in less than two years.

As sales of her birth control pamphlet *The Law of Population* passed 100,000 copies, Annie Besant turned her focus back to her own work. Her path to liberation from a Victorian housewife's cage had started only 14 years earlier, when she had sent unsolicited submissions to London publishers. Now she owned her own press, and no one could refuse her.

She wrote daily at 63 Fleet Street, penning pamphlets

protesting the British occupation of Egypt, and in favour of amendments to the Married Women's Property Act. After a decade of lobbying by her admirer Ursula Bright, the new law's passage that summer finally all but ended coverture. This 'Magna Carta for women' improved upon the previous law by not only allowing wives to own property and earn money independent of their husbands, but also to have their own legal identity.[41] It came too late to change Mrs Besant's standing, but for once she grew hopeful for Mabel's future. The judge who had taken the girl away from her would live just long enough to see the act come into effect at the start of 1883; that March, Sir George Jessel died at the age of 59, of a defective heart.

That year Annie Besant launched her own monthly magazine, called *Our Corner*. Each sixpence edition filled its 60-odd pages with features and reviews, ending with recurring columns from contributors. In the first issue's Political Corner, Charles Bradlaugh warned readers that 1883 had, 'politically, much menace for England'.[42] Although he would at last, via a final appeal to the House of Lords, dismiss the lawsuit accusing him of illegally voting in the Commons (after nearly three years, the fine had climbed to £350,000), within months the nation would be at war in Sudan, and London would tremble from bombs planted by Fenian terrorists agitating for Irish independence. One glass-shattering explosion reverberated in the House of Commons; an attempt to blow up *The Times* offices near Blackfriars failed when the dynamite did not ignite.[43]

Besant's personal life cratered around this time. Trawling the British Library Reading Room, the roué Edward Aveling met Karl Marx's youngest daughter by commissioning her to write an article about her father, who had died that spring. The beautiful and intelligent Eleanor Marx (who, in her translation of *Madame Bovary*, gifted to English the unchanged word *ennui*) was eight years younger than Annie Besant. She was also independently well-off, having inherited her father's £150 annuity (equivalent to £23,000 today) from his fellow communist Friedrich Engels.[44]

In December 1883 Besant told her readers in the *National Reformer*, 'My name is being used by a Miss Eleanor Marx . . . to give authority to a gross and scandalous libel.' 'Tussy', as Marx was known, allegedly had been telling people that the supposed Saint Annie had been Edward Aveling's lover. 'Warning should be given,' Annie continued, 'of strangers who try and creep into our movement with the object of treacherously sowing discord therein.'

After he started work on an English translation of Karl Marx's writings, Aveling announced that he was leaving the National Secular Society to join a socialist group. To her sister, Eleanor wrote that she found 'Mrs. Besant's chaste style' utterly absurd. Yet she took being assailed by the venerable speaker as 'the best compliment'.[45]

By the summer of 1884 Marx and Aveling were publicly presenting themselves as married, although not legally. This did not stop him from corresponding with Annie that autumn. In a rare letter giving a glimpse behind the dimity curtains drawn across her romantic life – and corroborating Eleanor Marx's suspicions – Aveling panted to Annie, 'I am so over worried and unstrung that I have not even written to you. How I miss & ache for you! When you come back,' he pleaded, 'may I come sometimes & just get what I always called & now more than ever call the <u>rest</u> of your presence? Help me – help me.' The scribbled note concluded, 'I do not write more to you as I can't tell if I am offending you. I have hurt you enough & I don't want to offend.'[46]

Time did not preserve her reply; the next letter in this

archival folder is, seriously, from a woman demanding Aveling return the microscope she had lent him. 'As a borrower of money and a swindler and seducer of women,' observed George Bernard Shaw, 'his record was unimpeachable.'[47]

Perhaps to avenge his treatment of Annie, Charles Bradlaugh sued Edward Aveling for failure to repay a number of small loans to cover living expenses that totalled £100. Aveling grovelled, promising that his translation of Karl Marx's '*The Kapital* is finished and two or three publishers are clamouring for it – so some money on that is coming.'[48] But even after its success, Aveling owed so many people that he only repaid Bradlaugh a single pound weekly, intermittently and across several years.

Edward Aveling will bleed Eleanor Marx's inheritance, and then take her heart. In 1898, after discovering that he had secretly married a new mistress under a false name, the 43-year-old will don her beloved white muslin dress, swallow cyanide and put herself to bed – a poisoning not unlike Madame Bovary's. The housekeeper will discover Marx's mottled indigo body too late. Karma can come quickly: Edward Aveling will die four months later, from kidney disease, at the age of 48. A mere six people will attend his funeral. The only notice that will appear in *The Times* will be from a solicitor, advising Aveling's many creditors not to delay in submitting their claims, as his estate was quite small.[49]

※

Annie Besant omitted mention of Edward Aveling in her 18 monthly columns telling her life story that ran in *Our Corner* from 1884 until summer of the following year. A half-century later in London, Virginia Woolf will write that Victorian biographies 'have a depressing similarity; very much overworked, very serious, very joyless, the eminent men appear to us to be, and already strangely formal and remote from us in their likes and dislikes'.[50] (A lone exception was Florence Nightingale's *Cassandra*, whose criticism of the dearth of roles for passionate and intellectual Victorian women 'is hardly writing,' Woolf noted, 'it is more like <u>screaming</u>.'[51]) She will urge her friends to write their life stories, as 'there's never been a woman's autobiography . . . Chastity and modesty I suppose have been the reason'.[52]

Like the rest of the smart set, Woolf will overlook Annie Besant's unorthodox memoir published in 1885 from a room of her own in Fleet Street. Compiled from her columns and printed by her Freethought press, *Autobiographical Sketches* was, one mainstream London magazine enthused, 'A touching account of the life of a singularly ill-used woman.' The reviewer hoped 'that her sufferings have not been in a vain, and that she will be the last in our own or any future generation to incur such a penalty for a matter of opinion'.[53] Besant did not need to veil her experiences or opinions; society had already done its worst. The book's events end in 1879 with the loss of Mabel, as did the author's life that she felt worth the telling. 'I live in the hope,' she concluded, 'that in her womanhood she may return to the home she was torn from in her childhood.'[54] Little did Annie suspect that, after what she called 'eleven years of strife', her life was again about to take a surprising turn towards new and greater renown.

Generations before Virginia Woolf and her friends claimed the name Bloomsbury as their own, a group of aspiring London socialists regularly met in the neighbourhood's Osnaburgh Street. Their Fabian Society – named for a Roman general credited as a progenitor of guerrilla warfare – became a magnet for progressive intellectuals after its founding in 1884.

In the next century, Mao Zedong will caution that a revolution is a not a dinner party. Many Fabians arrived at meetings wearing top hats and tails. The group aimed to erode the Establishment not by armed insurrection, but by educating the working class to vote and agitate for their interests, including the creation of a national school system, universal health care and a guaranteed minimum wage, along with suffragism and the abolishment of hereditary peerages.

Unlike Marxist communists, the Fabians didn't regard the word *bourgeoisie* as a term of reproach. It accurately described their leadership, including the founder Henry Mayers Hyndman (an estranged former student of Karl Marx), the academics Beatrice and Sidney Webb (founders of the London School of Economics) and William Morris (whose Oxford Street showroom sold the expensive textiles printed with his indigosaturated designs that decorated the era's upper-class homes). Oscar Wilde showed up to Fabian lectures wearing a large dahlia looking, as one chronicler noted, 'as ripe and enticing as a basket of fruit'.[55] Future Fabians will include H.G. Wells and Virginia Woolf.

In April 1884, the still-unseated Liberal MP Charles Bradlaugh agreed to debate the Fabian Henry Hyndman at Piccadilly's St James's concert hall on the topic 'Will Socialism Benefit the English People?' Two thousand spectators filled the building, among them Annie and, unknown to her, George Bernard Shaw and the future founders of the Labour Party, including Keir Hardie.

Bradlaugh's formal education ended when he was 12, and all his life he had followed his hero Emerson's instruction to remain self-reliant. Hyndman, in a top hat and gloves, was born into wealth and had graduated from Cambridge. Bradlaugh further defined their divide by telling the audience, 'We both recognise many social evils. He wants the State to remedy them, I want the individual to remedy them.' He dismissed Hyndman's sloganeering, and lack of a detailed plan to convince property owners to surrender their assets to the government. 'It is no use appealing in vague phrases to the future,' Bradlaugh chided. 'Take the broom and sweep one street clean by individual effort, and do not blow bubbles in the air.'[56]

The mainstream newspapers praised Bradlaugh for pulverising his opponent. 'Mr. Bradlaugh defending common sense and private property and private effort . . . is a pleasanter spectacle than the same person defying the House of Commons.'[57] At their Fleet Street printshop, Annie sold out the first 5,000 copies of the debate's transcript.

After the glow of her partner's triumph had dimmed, Annie studied what had been said on stage. Henry Hyndman, she wrote, 'kept me from Socialism for some time by his bitter and very unjust antagonism to Mr. Bradlaugh; but it was the debate at St. James's Hall that, while I angrily resented his injustice, made me feel that there was something more in practical Socialism than I imagined, especially when I read it over afterwards, away from the magic of Mr. Bradlaugh's commanding eloquence and personal magnetism.'[58]

At the start of 1885, the Fabians added the still-unpublished George Bernard Shaw to their ranks. The recruit's first assignment was to deliver a lecture advocating socialism to the London Dialectical Society. To his nervous chagrin, the 29-year-old learned that Annie Besant would be giving the rebuttal. Having watched her command the Court of Queen's Bench eight years earlier, Shaw knew that she would verbally destroy him.

'Rather in fear and trembling,' he later recounted to Besant's niece,

I got up to speak. I was very young then and Annie was a doughty speaker. Well, I finished my case, and when the discussion started, expected her to get up and rend me. To my amazement, and that of everyone else, she did not move. Some stranger rose to speak, and when he had finished opposing me, up got Annie, and flattened him out entirely in my favour, carrying off all the honours for the evening. Nothing was left of him, and my cause was made triumphant, but I regret to have to admit, more by Annie than by me.

'After the meeting,' Shaw continued, 'she asked me to nominate her for election to the Fabian Society, which of course I was only too pleased to do. From that time, she and I became friends, and although she continued to admire and revere Charles Bradlaugh, she never worked with him again.'[59]

Their professional break was sudden; their personal bond took longer to untie. The news of Annie joining the Fabians fell as a heavy blow. Bradlaugh had spent his entire life rising alone by hard graft. He was at this time exhausting himself in courtrooms, fighting off charges of libel and blasphemy while also attempting to claim his elected seat in the Commons. 'In truth,' Annie wrote in her memoir, 'I dreaded to make the plunge of publicly allying myself with the advocates of Socialism ... On his strong, tenacious nature, nurtured on self-reliant individualism, the arguments of the younger generation made no impression.'

He was 52 years old, she was 38. He spent his days in Westminster and Whitehall. She walked around Tower Hamlets and the wider East End. 'The cry of starving children was ever in my ears,' Annie recounted, 'the sob of women poisoned in lead works, exhausted in nail works, driven to prostitution by starvation, made old and haggard by ceaseless work. I saw their misery was the result of an evil system.'

British imperialism marched onward, pinning more geography to the Victorian map. In 1885, the empire would swallow tiny Bechuanaland and the vast swath of the Niger River basin. After decades of intermittent fighting, British troops finally seized Mandalay, and appended Burma to the Raj. Ireland continued to seethe. That winter, the ongoing Fenian terrorist campaign detonated bombs at the Tower of London and at Westminster Hall, killing two policemen, and shuttering the damaged building for four years. Annie's relative Evelyn Wood – recipient of the Victoria Cross for his role in suppressing the Indian Mutiny – was then commanding the occupying Egyptian Army. In 1885, in Sudan, Field Marshal Wood would lead the last battle fought by British forces wearing red coats.

If Annie knew her connection to Sir Evelyn, she never revealed it to her readers. Many were taking her embrace of socialism as a desertion. Annie Besant can probably claim the distinction of being the only person in our world's long history to be mocked as 'Saint Athanasius in petticoats'.[60] (Unlike that critic, she likely knew that the oft-exiled apostate priest had in the end been redeemed through martyrdom.) Her closest companion would not rebuke her, at least in public.

'Happily,' Annie wrote in her memoir, 'Mr. Bradlaugh was as tolerant as he was strong, and our private friendship remained unbroken; but he never again felt the same confidence in my judgment as he felt before, nor did he any more consult me on his own policy, as he had done ever since we first clasped hands.'[61]

Eight years after applauding her in court, George Bernard

Shaw turned up at her door on Avenue Road to belt out duets by her side at her piano. They made quite a pair. The impoverished Shaw that year had inherited £100 and bought a set of new clothes to replace his threadbare ones. He chose a Jaeger suit, a sort of undyed wool onesie patterned with a loud check. 'With his red hair and beige suiting,' a friend remarked, Shaw looked like 'a forked radish in a worsted bifurcated stocking.'[62]

George Bernard Shaw in 1888, looking rakishly unradish-like, and fun

Decades later, Shaw looked at Besant's niece from under his bushy eyebrows and in his thick brogue commended Annie as 'a very remarkable woman – a <u>very</u> – remarkable – woman'. Freda Fisher already knew this, 'but it pleased him to emphasize it as though it were news'. 'But she had one great defect,' Shaw continued. 'She was always so desperately in earnest, whereas I would regard everything with a heartless levity, and we disagreed almost to breaking point on several occasions.'

George Bernard Shaw cribbed from these quarrels and added them to his plays. Annie can be seen in the independent Mrs Clandon in *You Never Can Tell*, described as 'distinctly old fashioned for her age in dress and manners. But she belongs to the forefront of her own period (say 1860–80) in a jealously assertive attitude of character and intellect, and in being a woman of cultivated interests rather than passionately developed personal affections.'[63] Shaw said that he especially reproduced Annie in *Arms and the Man*'s proud Raina. In one exchange, all that's missing is a note for the actress to cock her eyebrow:

> **Raina**: *(staring haughtily at him)* Do you know, sir, that you are insulting me?
> **Captain Bluntschli**: I can't help it. When you strike that noble attitude and speak in that thrilling voice, I admire you; but I find it impossible to believe a single word you say.
> **Raina**: *(superbly)* Captain Bluntschli!
> **Captain Bluntschli**: *(unmoved)* Yes?
> **Raina**: *(standing over him, as if she could not believe her senses)* Do you mean what you said just now? Do you know what you said just now?
> **Captain Bluntschli**: I do.
> **Raina**: *(gasping)* I! I!! . . . *(He meets her gaze unflinchingly. She suddenly sits down beside him, and adds with a complete change of manner from the heroic to a babyish familiarity.)* How did you find me out?

Captain Bluntschli *(promptly)* Instinct, dear young
lady. Instinct, and experience of the world.
Raina: *(wonderingly)* Do you know, you are the first man
I ever met who did not take me seriously?
Captain Bluntschli: You mean, don't you, that I am
the first man that has ever taken you quite
seriously?[64]

Among her other forgotten achievements, Annie Besant
had been among the first to take the humorous George Bernard Shaw seriously. In 1885, his failure as a writer seemed a
better bet than his success. After a series of rejections and
low-paid assignments, Shaw received his first 'little less than
adequate' pay (as she said) from Annie Besant. Starting that
January, her monthly magazine *Our Corner* started serialising
Shaw's novel of an inequitable marriage, *The Irrational Knot*. It
was the first of his books to appear in print. Next, she serialised his second novel, *Love Among the Artists*. He would never
forget her habit of 'incorrigible beneficence'.[65]

His effect upon her was immediate. At first, she started
her letters 'Dear Mr Shaw', but soon switched to the more
intimate 'My dear Bernard'. Unfortunately only a handful
survive. One of the last notes, sent when both were entering
old age, picked up their playful banter from where it left off.
Acknowledging the receipt of his latest play, Annie replied,
'Many thanks for remembering me and for sending it. I am
glad it has been widely circulated – I always said you were
clever – and amused that, characteristically, you have made
no profit out of it.'[66]

'I could sometimes make her laugh at me,' George Bernard Shaw later reflected, 'but I could never make her stop
being generous.'[67]

In her correspondence with Shaw, Annie for the first time in her writing sounded like she was having fun. In the spring of 1885 she wrote to him from St Leonards-on-Sea: 'I am pretending to be ill and am down here to recover my usual liveliness . . . Consequently I am leading away others from the paths of virtue.' She had lured two fellow Fabians to the beach, and 'We are amusing ourselves muchly.'[68] Twenty years earlier, her holiday here had abruptly ended with Frank Besant's awkward marriage proposal, but that sad memory was not worth sharing. Now even her signature looked happy: the swoop she added beneath it made it look like the buoyant, unsinkable Annie Besant was surfing atop a gentle wave. Her memoir's description of this season shimmers with sunshine. 'Hatred,' she discovered then, 'ceases not by hatred at any time. Hatred ceases by love.'[69]

II

'WHEN SUCCESS COMES'

In the early days of Charles Bradlaugh's fight to be seated in Parliament, a satiric London weekly ran a bit of doggerel in his voice, addressed to the Chamber.

> By my shaggy locks behind,
> By my soul that's ill defined,
> By my coat tail run to waste,
> By my 'Fruits,' so sweet to taste,
> Tho' awhile I from thee go,
> I'll come back, I love thee so.
>
> House of Commons, when I come,
> Tremble, cowards, and be dumb;
> Tho' you kicked me from your door,
> Know I'll be your conqueror.
> Can I cease to pest thee so?
> Cease to be M.P.-iric? No![1]

The Victorian paper – affidavits, summons, petitions, newsprint, letters – piling up over his case could have fuelled the Guy Fawkes Night bonfires of November 1885. The general election held that month resulted in North-ampton voters returning their favourite atheist to the House for the fourth time, with his highest-ever vote total.

Five years and eight lawsuits after he had first been elected, Charles Bradlaugh again tried to enter the Commons in January 1886.

'We have assembled in a new Parliament,' the new Speaker, Arthur Peel, announced from the Chair. 'I know nothing of the Resolutions of the past. They have lapsed, they are void, they are of no effect in reference to this case.' Over the cheers and jeers, Peel said he had no authority, no right, to interfere with any member who wished to take the oath. And just like that, Charles Bradlaugh walked to the Table, picked up a Bible, recited the vow that ended 'so help me God', and kissed the book. The Clerk, perhaps suspecting trickery, required him to repeat the ritual a second time. Bradlaugh then shook hands with the Speaker, and took his rightful place on the Liberal side of the Chamber.

One of his first official acts was to avenge Annie's slanderous treatment by Sir Henry Tyler. On the House floor, Bradlaugh revealed the embarrassing fact that the righteous Tory MP's ironworks had been prosecuted and fined for illegally paying its labourers company scrip in lieu of cash wages.[2]

Entire volumes have been written on Charles Bradlaugh's litigious and bruising struggle to be seated in Parliament. Missing from them is the fate of the instigating antagonist, the irascible Lord Randolph Churchill. In her diary, Queen Victoria called him the Duke of Marlborough's 'strange troublesome son'.[3] He was 'so mad & odd, & also has bad health'.[4] After being elevated to Chancellor, in December 1886 Lord Randolph will shock Her Majesty with his 'audacity to write his letter of resignation from Windsor Castle — the night he dined!'[5] This protest of the government's refusal to make his recommended military spending cuts will end Churchill's political career. 'Newspapers full of anger & indignation,' Victoria will note, 'against Randolph Churchill & his unpatriotic conduct.'[6] When Her Majesty learns that Churchill had privately said that her mishandling of Russia had made him resign, she will fume (quite funnily): 'A monstrous lie! He never gave <u>that</u> as his reason, Sir E. Malet remarked, what could one say when people in such a position held such language. "In former years it would have been the Tower & the axe." '[7]

In fact, Lord Randolph does not have long to live. He will die, age 45, from a cocktail of maladies, likely including syphilis. In his dissipated life he had been an inattentive husband and absent father. When young Winston was a student at Harrow, he sent his father the train schedule, noting that it was only a 30-minute ride from London. But Lord Randolph never came. After Winston won admittance to Sandhurst, but only via the cavalry – whose expenses greatly thinned the competition – his father reproached him. 'You will become a mere social wastrel,' he told Winston, 'one of the hundreds of public school failures, and you will degenerate into a shabby unhappy & futile existence. If this is so you will have to bear all the blame for such misfortunes yourself.'[8]

From a distance that sounds like projection, but then Lord Randolph was never a strong judge of character, including his own. One man took great pleasure in reminding him. After Charles Bradlaugh had scored his late-round win and claimed his seat in Parliament, the Marquess of Queensbury – of boxing rules fame – gloated over having backed the right man.

'Dear Churchill,' he wrote in January 1886,

I expect shortly again to be leaving the shores of this Pagan country which still masquerades as a Christian one. I cannot resist reminding you of a letter I wrote you some two years ago. I don't know if you remember the bet I offered to lay to you. A thousand pounds to a sixpence I think it was on Mr. Bradlaugh. If you took it my sixpence looks <u>well</u>. But perhaps now you would like to hedge? As one who has made himself rather sore by tilting at the dying superstitions of Christianity, allow me once again to tender you my warmest <u>thanks</u> for the way you and the party to which you belong have helped to advertise the cause of free <u>thought</u> and so helped to still more dispel the mists and fog of a bygone <u>faith</u>. Which I hope some day to attend the funeral of. When a thing is dead, you know. You must bury it or cremate it otherwise it comes to <u>stink</u>.[9]

In the end, Churchill took the advice to heart, which is more than can be said of Queensbury, who, as the father of Lord Alfred Douglas, will later bait Oscar Wilde into suing him for libel, leading to the writer's ruinous imprisonment for homosexuality. In the summer of 1886, Lord Randolph unexpectedly granted Charles Bradlaugh's wish to form a Select Committee on Perpetual Pensions. (But not before Churchill redeemed his own for a windfall settlement of £107,780.) At MP Bradlaugh's instigation, the government finally abolished these lifelong hereditary gifts.

Next, Churchill convinced the Attorney-General to drop the residual cases against Charles Bradlaugh over the oath. 'For the first time in many years,' Bradlaugh told *National Reformer* readers, 'I am glad to say that I am free from the worry and painstaking strain of litigation. I am quite tired of the law which is costly in every way.'[10]

Lastly, in a letter to *The Times*, Lord Randolph surprisingly announced his endorsement of Bradlaugh's bill permitting MPs to affirm, rather than invoke God, upon their swearing-in to Parliament.[11] Only six years after being imprisoned by its members, Charles Bradlaugh was winning their support.

❦

His triumphs were solitary ones; by 1886, he and Annie mostly worked apart. While they still saw each other socially – after marrying in 1885, Hypatia and her husband rented rooms at Annie's house – the political fault-line widened between them.

In March 1886, Bradlaugh – on his way to passing a resolution to help protect workers by requiring the government to collect and publish labour statistics – drew laughter from the House benches at the expense of Annie's new cause. Socialism, he proclaimed, had 'no part in English thought or character. There were a few poets and a few idiots, and some to whom one could not apply as kindly words, who sought to make people believe that socialism was gaining ground in the country. It was not.'[12]

After hearing this, to her *Our Corner* magazine Annie added a new column she reported from the East End, called 'Socialist Notes'.

Much of what she then controversially called for – including an eight-hour workday and state-funded streetlighting – is now commonplace. As the calendar turned to 1887, Besant publicly demanded legislation banning the inheritance of capital. After an estimated 10,000 unemployed men marched down Pall Mall, only to be jeered from the windows of the Tories' Carlton Club and pelted with shoes and nail-brushes as they passed the Liberal Reform Club, Annie warned, 'Society must deal with the unemployed, or the unemployed will deal with Society.'[13]

Throughout that summer, Charles Bradlaugh lobbied for

and won passage of a strengthened Truck Act, increasing the Home Office's power to inspect and prosecute workplaces paying in scrip. Nevertheless, in October Annie resigned as editor of the *National Reformer*, telling readers that her belief in socialism made it impossible for the paper to maintain a unified voice. Bradlaugh hoped she would remain a contributor, and provide 'the efficient aid of her brain and pen'.

In her heart she knew their intimacy had ended. 'It was a wrench,' Annie wrote in her memoir, 'this breaking of a tie for which a heavy price had been paid thirteen years before', when she had left her husband and arrived in London as an unemployed single mother.

She also stepped down to protect her best friend. The man who had once published broadsides against the Establishment under the penname Iconoclast was now welcome into its clubs as a popular MP. Annie noted how Liberals and Conservatives who had formerly held Charles Bradlaugh at arm's length now sought his embrace. 'They looked upon me as a clog and a burden,' she wrote, 'and that were I less prominently with him his way would be the easier to tread. So I slipped more and more into the background, no longer went with him to his meetings; my use to him in public was over, for I had become hindrance instead of help. While he was outcast and hated I had the pride of standing at his side; when all the fair-weather friends came buzzing round him I served him best by self-effacement, and I never loved him better than when I stood aside.'[14]

One of the most bittersweet moments in Hypatia Bradlaugh's own memoir is her description of this 'new and deep division of opinion', which 'undoubtedly pained and depressed' her father. 'He was to find,' she wrote, 'as so many have found, that when success comes something is sure to go which leaves success a different thing from what was dreamt of.'[15]

᷍

In May 1887, one month before the Golden Jubilee would celebrate her 50 years on the throne, Queen Victoria journeyed by carriage down Mile End Road to open the People's Palace. The recreation hall for the working class, now part of Queen Mary University, had seen an influx of donations after Walter Besant's popular novel *All Sorts and Conditions of Men* superficially took readers into the 'utterly unknown town' of the East End. Had he really wanted to learn about the 2 million people who lived there, he could have asked his estranged sister-in-law, who knew its lanes and workers so well.

After returning to the safety of Windsor Castle, Victoria described to her prime minister, Lord Salisbury, a 'horrid noise (*quite* new to the Queen's ears)', he wrote, '"booing" she believes it is called'. Salisbury consoled her that 'all that is worthless, worn out, or penniless naturally drifts to London'.[16] In her diary, Victoria said that the noise had most certainly come from 'Socialists and the worst Irish'. They were 'very resentful men,' Lord Salisbury added, 'who would stick at nothing to show their fury.'[17]

That November, a woman would lead them. As jobless demonstrators continued to block central city traffic, London police closed Trafalgar Square. To protest this, as well as conditions in Ireland (the first Irish Home Rule Bill had failed to pass) and the arrest of a Fenian MP for starting a rent strike, Annie Besant and the Fabians organised a march to retake the square.

As her and William Morris's contingent prepared to set off from Clerkenwell, *The Times* correspondent embedded with them reported Annie's 'vigorous' speech declaring Trafalgar's closure an illegal, coercive act against the freedom of assembly. The MP Charles Bradlaugh, Annie told the crowd, had assured her that the law would be on their side. From strategic points around London, an estimated 10,000 people, flying green and red banners, waving Union Jacks draped in black crepe, and playing horns and drums, set off for Nelson's Column anticipating victory.

Instead it met violence. Two thousand police officers, backed by Life Guards with fixed bayonets, held the line against charges into Trafalgar Square. In what *The Times* called 'one of the most remarkable scenes enacted in modern times in the metropolis', the fighting spilled down Whitehall into New Palace Yard, outside Parliament. Mounted troops galloped into the mob with drawn staves; protestors fought back with sticks, fists and brass instruments. George Bernard Shaw fled the scene. 'Running hardly expresses our collective action,' he wrote. 'We *skedaddled,* and never drew rein until we were safe on Hampstead Heath.' Eleanor Marx, who had patched up her unpleasantness with Besant, noted, 'It was sickening to see the men run.'[18]

Annie had leaped from a horse cart and dashed from the Embankment towards the square, giving orders and plunging into the fray. A *Times* reporter 'witnessed several cases of injury to men who had been struck on the head and face by the police. The blood, in most instances, was flowing freely from the wound and the spectacle was indeed a sickening one.'[19]

Remarkably, on this 13 November – called 'Bloody Sunday' by the press – no one was killed, and Annie emerged unscathed. In the next edition of *The Times* MP Charles

Bradlaugh clarified 'that he was not only not associated with Sunday's attempt at a demonstration ... but that he thoroughly disapproves of any such efforts to oppose force'. A sharp-eyed reader might have cocked an eyebrow at this public disavowal from the man who had seen his own protests spiral into similar violence.

That winter, after organising another attempt to retake Trafalgar – resulting in the death of an unarmed demonstrator – Besant worked with the muckraking *Pall Mall Gazette* editor W.T. Stead to organise a bail fund to free arrested marchers from jail.

Annie choreographed the fallen man's funeral, which grew into the largest that London had seen since the Duke of Wellington's, 35 years earlier. With Stead, Annie served among the pallbearers, solemnly stepping slowly to the 'Dead March' past 100,000 people lining the capital's streets. It was a triumph of pageantry and messaging. The banner she draped across the coffin announced KILLED IN TRAFALGAR SQUARE. Annie knew how to make a martyr.

Writing in the *National Reformer*, Charles Bradlaugh called her brave, and praised her leadership and bail-raising. 'I wish to mark this the more emphatically,' Bradlaugh wrote, 'as my views and those of Mrs. Besant seem wider apart than I could have deemed possible.'[20] He recognised that they still struggled together, even when they stood on their own.

By that Christmas of 1887 something had changed. In a letter to W.T. Stead, Annie revealed that her usual routine of travelling back to St John's Wood with Bradlaugh's daughters after attending night class had been disrupted. 'Since I am boycotted,' Besant confided, 'I am left to wend my way home alone.'

The journalist saved a small packet of her correspondence – now held at Cambridge University Library – which provides a glimpse into Annie Besant's private life at this time. The 27 letters reveal a 40-year-old becoming overwhelmed by the forces arrayed against her. 'It is intolerably stupid of me,' she continued to Stead, 'but this sort of thing hurts me. I am afraid my mind gets bruised as readily as my skin. See what a baby a woman can be, who placidly walks into a business in which the most certainly sought bludgeon or arrest lay. I have been such an outcast since this fight began.'

Evoking the Greek philosopher who carried a lamp in broad daylight in search of an honest chap, Besant told W.T. Stead, 'Like Diogenes, I have been looking for "a man" for some time, and you seem to me the very one who has head and heart enough for the work.'[21]

As a child, William Thomas Stead had learned to read from the Bible of his father, a Congregational minister. Stead's social activist mother had campaigned against the Contagious Diseases Acts. After taking charge of the formerly staid *Pall Mall Gazette*, he became a progenitor of New Journalism, popularising the interview and chasing lurid scoops. After relief troops failed to reach Khartoum in time to save General Charles Gordon, in 1885 Stead ran the largest headline to that point in history, which bellowed:

TOO LATE!

That same year, Stead's exposé of London's trade in child prostitutes brought him infamy, and jail. Unbeknownst to the blockbuster story's readers, the journalist had staged its most sensational instalment. First he had paid an alcoholic mother £5 to place her 13-year-old daughter in a brothel. Next he had the child drugged with chloroform. Upon awakening and seeing W.T. Stead in the unfamiliar room, the girl screamed – evidence to the madame that her virginity had been taken – and then found herself bundled up and whisked to France into the care of an adoptive Salvationist family. After the girl's mother uncovered what had happened, Stead served three months in prison, for abduction. For him the ends justified the means: Parliament at last felt compelled to raise the age of consent from 13 to 16.

W.T. Stead was two years Annie's junior, and broodingly handsome, with a widow's-peak brow and tufted beard. He stepped into her life in the aftermath of George Bernard Shaw's rejection of the (since vanished) contract she had presented to the writer stating her terms for a romantic relationship. ('Good God!' Shaw had exclaimed. 'This is worse than all the vows of all the churches on earth. I had rather be legally married to you ten times over.'[22])Unlike Shaw, however, W.T. Stead was married to his childhood sweetheart, and the father of six children.

'My dear friend,' Besant wrote to him in January 1888. 'Your letter came late last night and was like the handclasp of a friend when one is weary.'[23] Later that week, she confessed, 'I am writing lightly because I am in a condition of extreme depression . . . Dear me. I am so tired and I am so troubled.'[24]

She signed the letter 'St. George'. Legend held that the patron saint of England would save the country from its enemies with his sword. Annie picked up her pen. She stopped attending Fabian meetings (Shaw grumbled to H.G. Wells that the all-male executive had made her feel like a 'fifth wheel'), ended *Our Corner* magazine, and with W.T. Stead launched *The Link*, a halfpenny newspaper promising to help the helpless and befriend the oppressed.[25] Regaining her past grandiloquence, Besant added that its editors also sought nothing less than 'the Temporal Salvation of the world'.[26]

The path of the righteous wended through the Docklands, where Annie went on strike with dockhands demanding a wage of four pence an hour. They won. Next she entered the East End schoolrooms where 'the child martyrs of the slums' were fed knowledge instead of meals. 'Society has only formulas, not food,' she protested. The children's parents scraped by on low pay for long hours processing meat and making items that they themselves could not afford to buy. Blaming the Establishment would only get you so far, Besant wrote. She called out London's unconscientious middle-class consumers who demanded low prices without considering the true cost of manufacturing goods. 'So much of our neighbour's labour has been put into the things we desire; if we will not yield him that fair equivalent, yet take his article, we defraud him.'[27]

She began feeling cheated herself, by W.T. Stead. 'I am <u>not</u> grateful for your formal "Many thanks for your letter",' Annie wrote in February 1888. She followed with a note telling him 'London is not as nice a place with you out of it; it feels chillier.' She missed his patient counsel. She would be, she signed the letter, always his.[28]

In March, as Lord Randolph Churchill threw his support behind Charles Bradlaugh's Oaths Act, Annie wrote to Stead that she imagined slipping her hand into his. No asterisks followed; the fantasy did not go farther, she assured him, than a wish for their 'political and spiritual marriage'.[29] His replies grew chillier.

'I have been so accustomed,' she wrote, 'these 14 years to

work with men, and not suffer from it, that I was not quite on my guard. But, let us be honest. I have not worked with any man in close intimacy brought by common work, who has not "fallen in love" with me; but I have managed, save in one case, to steer through it and keep my friend.' Presumably, the outlier had been Edward Aveling, but given their split, she may have, sadly, been referring to Charles Bradlaugh.

On 1888's All Fools' Day, W.T. Stead at last told her that he would not leave his wife. Annie chivalrously replied, 'I was not exaggerating when I told you that you were the best man I know. It was no idle phrase. And that fact is my only excuse for caring so much for you. We needs must love the highest when we see it.'

Two weeks later, Annie called him her anchor; her affection for him was her safeguard. 'I wish I did not suffer so much,' she concluded to Stead (who will drown in the frigid waters of the North Atlantic during the sinking of the *Titanic*). 'I do feel like the frog stoned by boys, that it is play to you and death to me.'[30]

Three months passed before her next surviving letter to him. In July she wrote to tell W.T. Stead that the Hyde Park rally she had organised had gone splendidly. She was back in fine fettle. 'A lot of the match girls came and were very vociferous,' she wrote.[31] The correspondence ends there, but Annie Besant's next pioneering act of defiance against the Establishment was about to kick off.

The Bryant & May match factory could not have looked more Victorian. Located in the East End near the west bank of the River Lea, its five-storey yellow-and-red-brick buildings lurked behind a wrought-iron fence flanked by cottage-like gatehouses. The water tower could have doubled as a defensive redoubt; the large clock facing Fairfield Road reminded workers to be on time. If a girl arrived late, she was shut out for half the day (that is, the first six hours of her shift), and lost five pence from her eight pence wage.

Other fines were just as ruinous. The mostly teenage female workers, who subsisted on diets of bread and butter and tea, were fined three pence for dirty feet and for talking. Putting a 'burnt' – a match that caught fire during work – on a bench drew a one-shilling penalty, equal to 18 hours of labour. One girl was forced to pay a shilling for jamming a cutting machine, instead of suffering a grievous injury. One of the foremen – part of the violent, clouting group that included Karl Marx's illegitimate son – yelled, 'Never mind your fingers!'

Worst of all for workers, the factory manufactured lucifer matches. Unlike safety matches, which had to be struck against the special surface on their box, lucifers could ignite against anything. They were tipped not by benign red phosphorous but the toxic white variety. Its effect on labourers was well known; in an 1852 article, Charles Dickens described a scrofulous match girl who began work at age nine. When the author met her 11 years later, she pulled back a veil to reveal 'that her lower jaw is almost entirely wanting; at the side of her mouth are two or three large holes. The jaw was removed at the Infirmary seven years ago,' when the girl had been only 13.[32]

She suffered from the condition called 'phossy jaw'. In addition to eroding the jawbone, its symptoms included abscesses in the mouth, gums that glowed in the dark and brain damage. Despite Dickens's warnings, factory owners continued to require their workers to dip matchsticks in vats of white phosphorous, whose inhaled fumes caused their

painful disfigurement. Still Victorians favoured the convenience of lucifer matches, even at the cost to their makers'
health.

Dickens would have recognised the miserly remaining
partner at Bryant & May as a descendent of *Hard Times*'
Josiah Bounderby, who grumbles that his ungrateful Coke-
town factory workers expected to be set up in a coach-and-six
and fed on turtle soup and venison with a gold spoon. All
that they really wanted was a living wage.

Bryant & May's match girls also wanted safer working
conditions, and the end of unfair fines. Many still fumed that
factory owner Theodore Bryant had forced them to donate
money to erect a statue of William Gladstone, after the prime
minister had scrapped a proposed tax on matches. (This
frock-coated bronze likeness stands in front of Bow Church,
gesturing with palms still regularly painted blood-red by vandals rumoured to be reminding us of its cost.)

Upon hearing the news that, after another highly profitable year, the windfall-tax-free Bryant & May was yet again
paying shareholders a 23 per cent dividend, Annie Besant
tromped down to its London factory 'to see how the money
is made'.

In June, her story – rather Steadishly headlined WHITE
SLAVERY IN LONDON – blazed from the front page of
The Link. It remains a fine piece of muckraking, blending
searing facts with outraged opinion. Besant described the
match cutters, fillers and boxers' working conditions, pay
structure, fines and mandatory contribution to London
statuary. In the eyes of factory-owners and capitalist bank-
ers, she had written the introduction of another dirty, filthy
book.

'But who cares for the fate of these white wage slaves?'
Besant asked readers of the mostly Irish and Jewish

immigrant workforce. 'Born in slums, driven to work while still children, undersized because underfed, oppressed because helpless, flung aside as soon as worked out, who cares if they die or go on the streets, provided only that the Bryant & May shareholders get their 23 percent, and Mr. Theodore Bryant can erect statues and buy parks?'[33]

At first, his only response to her came on the shop floor, where foremen bullied the youngest workers into revealing who had squawked. 'Cowards that they are!' Besant wrote in her follow-up story, accusing Bryant & May of being 'sweaters' (stewards of a sweat shop). 'Why not at once sue me for libel and disprove my statements in open court if they can, instead of threatening to throw these children into the streets?' Now she had been activated. 'A big meeting to protest against the White Slavery will be called.'[34]

In retaliation, on 5 July the factory fired a worker it accused of organising. In response, her fellow employee Sarah Chapman led approximately 1,400 workers out the factory's gate. A cry was raised to fetch Annie Besant, and the next day 200 of the women marched to the corner of Fleet and Bouverie Streets in the City. Only three of the group could fit inside her small printshop there. Chapman and two others told Annie how 'they had been asked to sign a paper certifying that they were well treated and contented, and that my statements were untrue; they refused. "You had spoke up for us," explained one, "and we weren't going back on you."'

Along with a fellow Fabian, Annie helped the women organise a strike committee, and became the public face of the campaign. 'If we ever worked in our lives,' Annie wrote, 'Herbert Burrows and I worked for the next fortnight.'[35] The Match Girls' Strike, as it became known, was not only one of the earliest industrial actions in British history, but the largest undertaken by women.

'Strike committee for the Matchmakers' Union.' Annie Besant holds the floor at the lectern. Immediately left of Herbert Burrows stands Sarah Chapman. Burrows was a co-founder of the Social Democratic Foundation, Britain's first socialist party.

The battle played out in familiar moves. In *The Times*, the owner of one of the country's wealthiest and most powerful firms blamed 'ringleaders', 'outside agitators' and 'Socialists'. On the streets, and at the Mile End wastes, nonviolent labour rallies collected money to replace the lost wages of the striking women, who comprised one of Britain's poorest and weakest workforces.

In the House, Charles Bradlaugh threatened to open an inquiry over Bryant & May's violation of wage laws, and welcomed an Annie-led delegation of 56 match girls into the Commons to be interviewed by MPs. In the popular *Pall Mall Gazette*, W.T. Stead ran daily stories in support of the strike; as it entered its second week, other mainstream papers – but never *The Times* – followed suit. (Queen Victoria, enjoying the attentions of her dashing new servant

Abdul Karim at Windsor Castle, said nothing about the stop-page in her diary.) With Eleanor Marx, Annie held strike meetings at Hanbury Hall in Spitalfields. On the sidelines, George Bernard Shaw cribbed notes about pious men who profited off underpaid women, driving the poorest into pros-titution. They would form the basis of his biting play, *Mrs Warren's Profession.*[36]

Before the strike could enter its third week, ownership gave in. For the first time in British history, a union of unskilled labourers had won the right to collective bargain-ing. A GREAT AND NOTABLE VICTORY announced the front page of the *Pall Mall Gazette*. 'There is nothing like letting in the light for stopping the cruelties that are done in the dark corners of the earth,' W.T. Stead wrote. 'It was the publication of the simple story in an obscure little halfpenny weekly paper which did the work.'

Eleven years after she had risked everything to publish *Fruits of Philosophy*, Annie Besant's defence of a free press had paid its own dividend. Bryant & May raised wages, abolished fines and allowed meals to be taken away from the work-bench, in a phosphorous-free room. (The manufacture of toxic lucifer matches continued. Another decade will pass before the government will inspect the factory, and finally fine Bryant & May for safety violations. Not until 1910 will Parliament ban the use of white phosphorous.[37])But in 1888, the fight felt finished. 'Of all women in London today,' the *Pall Mall Gazette* concluded at the strike's end, 'Mrs. Besant has most reason to feel proud.'[38]

The victors appointed her honorary secretary of their newly formed Union of Women's Match Makers, Britain's first female labour organisation. With Sarah Chapman and other match girls, Besant served as delegate to that year's International Trades Union Congress in London.

That autumn, as silver streaks began to lighten her chest-nut hair, the 41-year-old Annie Besant ran for the London School Board, still the highest elected office open to women. As she campaigned for the seat in Tower Hamlets, local clergy reminded the district's mothers of Mrs Besant's obscenity trial, even distributing 30,000 copies of a handbill accusing her of 'gross immorality'. With practised professionalism, she sued for libel, represented herself in court, and won.

Annie also took the election in a landslide. Her first of many successful acts required schools to purchase goods and services only from unionised providers. Another was to raise money to provide 36,000 school lunches, beginning a service now standard around the globe.

In 1878, Charles Bradlaugh and Annie Besant had nerv-ously waited before a judge to learn if their appeal of the ruinous sentence for selling a birth control pamphlet would send them to prison. Ten years later, they enjoyed parallel

1881: 'Tossed out'. 1888: 'Oaths Bill 100 Majority'

victories that once had seemed as improbable as the dissolution of their close-knit partnership.

In August, one month after the match girls' victory, enough Tories joined their Liberal counterparts to carry the third reading of Bradlaugh's Oaths Act across the line.[39] The law continues to permit any required oath to be affirmed, rather than sworn to God. After eight lawsuits, four elections and one night in Big Ben's tower, Charles Bradlaugh had single-handedly secularised Parliament.

Concurrently in 1888, Annie Besant had led a groundbreaking strike, and won her first election to public office. But her biggest win was about to come.

Her niece recalled the scene at 19 Avenue Road when Annie busily waved off the news that she had a visitor. 'But it is someone who loves you,' she was told, 'someone whom you have not seen for a long time – not for ten years.'

'My aunt looked up, and like a flash came "Is it the child?"' A nod was the only reply. 'So mother and daughter met again, and Mabel slept that night in her mother's arms.'[40]

Little Mabel, now an adult aged 19, had at last come home. Ignoring their father's threat to disown him, 21-year-old Digby soon followed. Later he would find the loving and longing letters from his mother that Frank Besant had hidden from the children across the past decade, contravening the court's conditions of their custody. A newspaper reporting the reunion of Annie with her children headlined the story: TIME DEFEATS BIGOTRY.[41]

But does it? Or do we have to continually keep winding the clock? Annie's crusading life evinces that progress and justice result from the unceasing, incremental acts of those who actively fight for change, rather than passively accept the status quo.

The easiest thing in the world is to do nothing. In her

memoir, Annie remembered the day maltreated match girls marched into her printshop and told her, 'It is time someone helped us.'

'I asked,' she wrote, '"Who will help?" Plenty of people wish well to any good cause; but very few care to exert themselves to help it, and still fewer will risk anything in its support. *"Someone ought to do it, but why should I?"* is the ever-re-echoed phrase of weak-kneed amiability. *"Someone ought to do it, so why not I?"* is the cry of some earnest servant of man, eagerly forward-springing to face some perilous duty. Between those two sentences lie whole centuries of moral evolution.'[42]

In this, Annie Besant was far ahead of her time, and our own benighted one, too.

Coda

'Our Annie'

That winter of 1888, the year's twin triumphs dimmed. In November Alice Bradlaugh contracted typhoid fever, coupled with meningitis. Hypatia moved her from the rooms at Circus Road to Annie's more commodious home. Forty-six years later, penicillin will be discovered in St Mary's Hospital a short walk from its front door, but Victorian medicine could offer little more than bed rest and compresses. Alice died two weeks later, only 32 years old.

Charles Bradlaugh had buried his infant son, and now he watched his eldest daughter be lowered into the ground. Of his family only Hypatia remained. And his relationship with Annie Besant frayed even further, due to a book review.

In early 1889, the *Pall Mall Gazette* editor W.T. Stead handed Annie two thick volumes of *The Secret Doctrine*. 'Can you review these?' he asked. 'My young men all fight shy of them, but you are quite mad enough on these subjects to make something of them.'

Like Hamlet after seeing his father's ghost, recent events had made Annie realise, she wrote in her memoir, that 'my philosophy was not sufficient; that life and mind were other than, more than, I had dreamed'.

The Secret Doctrine formed the central text of a new esoteric faith called Theosophy. 'As I turned over page after page the interest became absorbing,' she recounted, 'I was dazzled, blinded by the light in which disjointed facts were seen as parts of a mighty whole, and all my puzzles, riddles, problems seemed to disappear.'[1]

The book's author, Helena Petrovna Blavatsky, was a self-styled Russian mystic and naturalised American who claimed to channel the spirit world. Unlike Mary Baker Eddy – also attuned to that frequency, and founding Christian Science around this time – Madame Blavatksy, or H.P.B., as she was known, purported to have journeyed to Tibet and brought back ancient wisdom revealing the essential truth underpinning all science, religion and philosophy. (The first documented Westerners to enter Tibet will be British Indian Armed Forces invading in 1904. They will bring back looted artifacts and casualties.)

In 1889 Annie's favourable review of *The Secret Doctrine* appeared under the headline 'Among the Adepts'. Her follow-up essay was titled, 'Why I Became a Theosophist'.

'Dumfounded,' George Bernard Shaw recounted to her niece,

> I rushed round to the office and there I found Annie. "What do you mean by this?" I shouted at her. Quietly she replied that she had joined the Theosophical Society and was giving up all her other work. I argued with her, but it was all in vain. This time I could do nothing with her. The heavens had fallen, and I was powerless. All she said to me was that she had become a vegetarian, to which I could hardly object, seeing that I was one myself, and that possibly she was in consequence suffering from brain softening! I was undone! Annie had at last made a joke against herself.[2]

After meeting Madame Blavatsky, Shaw's fellow future Nobel laureate W.B. Yeats – a man who admitted that he saw fairies – will dismiss her as 'a sort of old Irish peasant woman with an air of humour and audacious power'.[3] James Joyce will make her a punchline in his own dirty, filthy book. 'That Blavatsky woman started it,' Joyce will write in *Ulysses*. 'She was a nice old bag of tricks . . . Mrs. Cooper Oakley once glimpsed our illustrious sister H.P.B's elemental . . . You naughtn't to look . . . when a lady's showing her elemental.'[4]

But to Annie, Madame Blavatsky was no joke. 'She had after many explorations,' George Bernard Shaw acknowledged, 'found her path and come to see the universe and herself in their real perspective.'[5]

When Annie called on Madame Blavatsky in Notting Hill, she experienced a moment of being seen that echoed her first meeting with Charles Bradlaugh. 'I was conscious of a sudden leaping forth of my heart,' she wrote, 'was it recognition?' At the end of their chat, Blavatsky looked at her with piercing eyes, and with a yearning throb in the voice, said, '"Oh, my dear Mrs. Besant, if you would only come among us!" I felt a well-nigh uncontrollable desire to bend down and kiss her.'[6]

Annie became Madame Blavatsky's disciple, co-editing the Theosophist journal named *Lucifer*. It punned on the popular matches, but also her favourite character from *Paradise Lost*, who decides that it is better to reign in Hell than to serve in Heaven.

Blavatsky moved into 19 Avenue Road, transforming part of Annie Besant's home into the lodge, or headquarters, of the British branch of the Theosophical Society. The agnostic became the gnostic. Annie ended old friendships, refused to stand for re-election to the London School Board and pulped her first autobiography, in which she had movingly recounted her prosecution for publishing *Fruits of Philosophy*.

Casual sex was out, too. Its 'holy mystery', Blavatsky wrote of intercourse, was a 'divine gift' only to be used for procreation, for bringing forth the re-embodiment of another soul. Annie smashed the printing plates of her birth control book. 'I refused to reprint *The Law of Population*,' she wrote, 'or to sell the copyright, giving pain, as I sadly knew, to all the brave and loyal friends who had so generously stood by me in that long and bitter struggle, and who saw the results of victory thrown away on grounds to them inadequate and mistaken!'

Yet, as we shall see, the movement she had helped popularise was bigger than one person, and would continue to grow without her.

In the confused moment, Charles Bradlaugh felt compelled to answer the letters questioning readers sent to the *National Reformer*. 'I very deeply regret,' he wrote in June 1889, 'that my colleague and co-worker has, with somewhat of suddenness, and without any interchange of ideas with myself, adopted as fact matters which seem to me to be as unreal as it is possible for any fiction to be. My regret is greater as I know Mrs. Besant's devotion to any course she believes to be true.'[7]

In December 1890, the *National Reformer* announced, 'With the closing down of 63 Fleet Street, the partnership between Annie Besant and Charles Bradlaugh under the title of the Freethought Publishing Company, is dissolved by mutual consent.'[8]

The following month, Bradlaugh caught a chill walking in the clinging London fog and retired to his bed in 20 Circus Road. Weakened by heart and kidney disease, he looked aged beyond his 57 years. His daughter Hypatia rebuffed visitors – with one exception. Sitting at his bedside as he had once comforted her, Annie Besant listened to her old friend's mighty voice now sounding low and broken as it lamented that no one remained who could continue his new cause of advocating home rule for Hindustan. After his recent return from a fact-finding journey to the Raj, independence activists began lauding Bradlaugh as the 'MP for India'.

He died on 30 January 1891. Earlier that week, Parliament voted to expunge its 1880 resolution that had first forbidden him to take his elected seat. *The Times* did not behave so gallantly. Its long, rather begrudging obituary reported that by the time the news of the House's apology had arrived at Circus Road, 'Mr. Bradlaugh had already passed into unconsciousness.' The paper reminded readers that 'he and Mrs. Besant were indicted for publishing an obscene book', avoiding prison only due to his skill at 'pushing technicalities to extremes'. Charles Bradlaugh was neither a John Wilkes nor a Danton, the paper of record concluded, but 'a remarkable figure of a somewhat obsolete type'.[9]

In his own commemoration, George Bernard Shaw marvelled at his novelty. Although Bradlaugh had preached the gospel of Rationalism, Shaw told a gathering of old colleagues, he had throughout his life acted in the most irrational manner. Instead of choosing the line of least resistance – the order by which Darwin had taught them the whole world had been produced – Bradlaugh had taken the line of greatest resistance. And when in his work he encountered one of the Establishment's idols (including men 'in robes and an absurd wig' that we called 'justice', and men in 'a sort of collar that opened at the back' that we called 'religion'), instead of taking off his hat and filling his pockets – the sensible, rational thing to do – he hit the idol as hard as he could, and very often he knocked it down. The next time a person tries to convince you of a religious miracle, Shaw added, tell them 'Look at Charles Bradlaugh; explain that miracle.'[10]

Three special trains departing London's Necropolis railway station (located next to Waterloo) carried mourners to the funeral at Woking's Brookwood Cemetery. Most of them, including a 21-year-old law student named Mohandas (today known as Mahatma) Gandhi, honoured Charles Bradlaugh's instruction to avoid the trappings of mourning. In lieu of black armbands, his admirers flashed hatbands and rosettes of bright white, mauve and green, the colours of his election campaigns. Unsurprisingly, Annie Besant disobeyed, and arrived wearing a black dress and veil. But his would-be widow did adhere to his wish that no one make a speech, or say even a word. Silence, punctuated with muffled weeping and birdsong, followed the atheist into the grave.

He was laid next to his daughter Alice. Hypatia will join them, although not until 1935, when she will die at the age of 77, leaving behind a loving husband and a son named Charles Bradlaugh Bonner. Nearby will rest his friends and courtroom defenders, the doctors Charles Drysdale and Alice Vickery. Per his wishes, Bradlaugh's epitaph reads only THOROUGH. Later, friends will garland the stone with a bronze wreath and bust. Vandals will steal them in 1968. Following a fundraising campaign, in 2021, National Secular Society members will unveil their replacements. In an emotional address to an audience of 60 gathered around his grave, a speaker will call Charles Bradlaugh 'a man of the people, and a man for the people'.[11]

In 1894, an estimated 20,000 people cheered the unveiling of Bradlaugh's oversized stone likeness in Northampton's Abington Square. Today the statue's cold gaze remains fixed on a Paddy Power betting shop, and a pub named the Black Prince. After his death, the owner of 20 Circus Road long refused to allow a plaque or any other memorial to be affixed to Bradlaugh's longtime residence. Today the St John's Wood public library sits upon the site. But look closer: outside on its pavement, a sign taped to a cart of mouldering texts reads: INDIAN ART & HISTORY BOOKS £5. Flip to the index in *The*

History and Culture of the Indian People. At 20 Circus Road, between the musty covers of *Volume X: British Paramountcy and Indian Renaissance*, Charles Bradlaugh and Annie Besant are at this moment still together, making 'important contributions to the growth of Indian nationalism'.

☙☙

Even after the dissolution of their partnership, he had left his last will and testament unchanged. Bradlaugh had few assets; to distribute his entire estate he needed to write only 31 lines. Fourteen were about Annie. 'I appeal to Freethinkers,' he instructed, 'to rally round my loyal friend and brave co-worker Annie Besant and this to repay to her some of the sacrifice and devotion she has made and shown for me . . . I have nothing to leave to the true good woman who has stood side by side with me and borne calumny and slander.' To A.B., C.B. left his 'tenderest love and most earnest hope'.[12]

A little over three months later, on 8 May 1891 – a date Theosophists commemorate as White Lotus Day – Madame Blavatsky also died, of influenza. In her will she appointed Annie Besant the Theosophical Society's Chief Secretary of the Inner Group of Esoteric Section and Recorder of the Teachings. Soon she would rise to become its president.

In 1893 Annie visited the group's headquarters in India for the first time. She would remain for nearly 40 years. Her India decades fill other books, but to complete the circle of this one, in Madras (present-day Chennai), the seat of British power in the colonial southern Raj, she waged her last great fight against Victorianism. After rebelling against the Church of England, against legal restrictions of the freedom of speech, against the social taboos of talking about sex and contraception, against the conditions of the working class, and against the absence of women's labour unions, her final idol to smash was imperialism.

In Britain Annie had been rejected by universities; in Varanasi she founded her own. Central Hindu College – along with its residential girls' school – has since grown into Banaras Hindu University. Its alumni include Jawaharlal Nehru. After the school granted Annie an honorary degree, many Indians knew her as Dr Besant.

She also bought a defunct newspaper and renamed it *New India*. 'It was a rag, but it will be a power,' Annie promised. And so it was, becoming a forum for native nationalist writers calling for Home Rule. The old flame sparked to life. 'Queen Mary thought she was blowing out candles when she burned her heretics,' Besant wrote. 'She blundered; she was lighting them.' [13]

Soon she was back on the lecture circuit, rallying Indians to demand democracy over dependency. In her life's final act, like Lucifer cast out from the kingdom, she again took on the throne. A regal portrait from this time showcased her white hair, snowy robes, and icy confidence, the inverse of the vacant-eyed Empress Victoria, ever swaddled in black. In the photo Annie looks sanctified, as if she had broken clean through.

Recalling her secular hymnbook, she composed an Indian national anthem. Set to the tune of 'God Save the King', the lyrics for 'God Save Our Ind' may not have been memorable, but the song planted a symbolic flag for what Besant was now calling 'the Motherland'.

In 1917, the British Raj put her under house arrest, threatening to charge her with sedition. Annie warned that she had been in politics her entire life, and had worked with Charles Bradlaugh. As the colonial authorities debated deporting her, public demonstrations only increased her public support. 'India is determined to be free,' she told the British

Lucifer on her throne

viceroy, 'and if you do not meet her, you will be up against a Nation.'[14] His administration sentenced her to three months of home confinement. Upon her release, voters chose Annie Besant as the first woman president of the independence movement's political party, the Indian National Congress.

It would prove to be the apogee of her political life. She quickly fell out with Mahatma Gandhi over his *satyagraha* campaign of passive resistance, which was siphoning away her adherents. 'You little realise,' she wrote to him in 1919, 'how you have led young men of good impulses but thoughtless, to break their most solemn pledges by inducing them to take your vow.'[15]

'I do not want to strive with you,' Gandhi responded. 'I shall continue to think of the Mrs. Besant whom from my youth I had come to regard as a great and living illustration of fearlessness, courage and truth.'

Calling him 'Mr. Gandhi' (not, pointedly, his honorific Mahatma, meaning great-souled), Annie replied, 'It is a pity that both you & I have lost our ideal of each other. Time will tell which of us has been the more faithful to India & to Freedom.' [16]

❋

Annie's other misstep in these years haphazardly resulted in a small but enduring legacy in the United States. In 1909 she celebrated a fellow member's 'discovery' of an unassuming 14-year-old from Madras named Jiddu Krishnamurti as the reincarnation of the One, sent to earth to become the World Teacher. After an unseemly custody battle with the boy's father, Annie became Krishnamurti's legal guardian. Later, when lobbying for his acceptance at Oxford, she told the president of Magdalen, 'My ward is a very special person. I don't want to stress it, but he does happen to be the Son of God.'

'Madam,' he replied drolly, 'we have the sons of many distinguished people in this college.'[17]

The story is likely apocryphal, since Krishnamurti had failed the entrance exam. Instead he moved to a lush valley in coastal Ojai, California, where Annie envisioned building an educational centre to nurture spiritual and intellectual growth. Major donors to the land's purchase included the grandson of her old London University botany professor, T.H. Huxley – the *Brave New World* author Aldous Huxley.

In 1929, Krishnamurti would renounce his role as a Messiah and resign from the Theosophists, denouncing organised belief. 'Truth,' he said, 'was a pathless land.' ('The Coming had gone wrong,' shrugged the sect.[18]) The 520 idyllic acres that Annie purchased in southern California's Topatopa mountains is now home to a coeducational high school. Around 100 students from 17 countries board and learn at the Besant Hill School of Happy Valley. Its website does not mention its namesake's trailblazing trial and advocacy for birth control. It does, however, inform visitors that the school's motto is Aún Aprendo, 'I am still learning'.

Victorian censors never understood that the more stridently they attempted to put out the fire that Annie Besant had kindled, they only fanned its flames. In 1887, a Leeds doctor named H. Arthur Albutt had been struck off the medical register for publishing a sixpence edition of *The Wife's Handbook*, which explicitly explained contraception. Over the next 25 years, the undaunted Albutt printed 45 editions of his pamphlet, selling 430,000 copies.[19]

Even after she stopped her presses, editions of *Fruits of Philosophy* and Annie's own *The Law of Population* continued to circulate, at home and throughout the British Empire. In 1888, a bookseller was arrested and fined in Australia for selling her text teaching birth control. Overturning the conviction, a Supreme Court of New South Wales justice wrote:

> As pointed out by Lord [Chief Justice] Cockburn in the case of the "Queen v. Bradlaugh and Mrs. Besant", all prosecutions of this kind should be regarded as mischievous, even by those who disapprove the opinions sought to be stifled, inasmuch as they only tend more widely to diffuse the teaching objected to. To those, on the other hand who desire its promulgation, it must be a matter of congratulation that this, like all attempted prosecutions of thinkers, will defeat

its own object and truth, like a torch – "the more it's shook it shines."[20]

Sales of the Australian edition of Annie's book surpassed 100,000. 'The birth-rate of New South Wales,' one of the era's best-known demographers observed in 1931, 'dropped sharply in 1889 following the trial, and through the next ten years fell off by nearly one-third.'

A similar rapid decline, James Alfred Field continued:

> began to show itself over the greater part of western Europe in the late seventies and early eighties. In England particularly, as several careful studies have shown, the drop appears suddenly about 1878. The coincidence of this change with the propaganda called forth by the Bradlaugh-Besant trial is too significant to be ignored . . . The falling birth-rate would have come, no doubt, in its own time, had the *Fruits of Philosophy* never been protested. But the ill-starred prosecution gave to slow-gathering forces instant and overwhelming effect.

('Perhaps in the course of time,' the University of Chicago professor added, 'Americans also will learn the lesson that mere denunciation of birth control characteristically defeats its object.' He hoped that on the subject of reproductive health his countrymen could stop being so 'consistently medieval'.[21] As this book went to press, American lawmakers were threatening to invoke the long-forgotten, but never repealed, 1873 Comstock Act to prohibit the mailing of contraceptive devices, birth control pills and the emergency-contraceptive drug mifepristone.)

The *Oxford History of England* puts the start of the continuous reduction of British family size at 'the year 1877, when a prosecution of Bradlaugh and Mrs. Besant for publishing a

Malthusian pamphlet served to give methods of birth control their first really wide advertisement in England.'[22] Yet the nationwide adoption of contraception did not suddenly occur in 1877, any more than sexual intercourse began in 1963 (after the 'Chatterly' ban and before the Beatles' *Please Please Me*, as the poet Philip Larkin put it.[23]) Nor did Annie Besant ever claim that credit. The quantum leap she made was legitimising contraception as worthy of public discussion, and morally permissible to practise at home.

The deeper causes of the declining birth rate was rooted in the late Victorian era's changing social conditions, including the passage of laws forbidding child labour and ones mandating schooling (making children not potential economic providers but costly 'burdens'); women aspiring to roles beyond child-bearing (including teaching in the new state schools); and rising household incomes (and a desire to defend against downward social mobility).[24] As demand for contraception increased, its quality and availability quickly improved, too.[25]

Annie could even exult that the Church, whose authority over households was waning, belatedly moved with the times she had nudged forward. In 1893, she wrote:

> we find the *Christian World*, the representative organ of orthodox Christian Protestantism, proclaiming the right and the duty of voluntary limitation of the family. In a leading article, it said: "There are certain easily-understood physiological laws of the subject, the failure to know and to observe which is inexcusable on the part either of men or women in these circumstances." Thus has opinion changed in sixteen years, and all the obloquy poured on us is seen to have been the outcome of ignorance and bigotry.[26]

The vituperation had not been eradicated – it just found

new targets, including suffragists advocating for the right to vote, and pacifists refusing to serve in the charnel trenches along the Western Front. But after the First World War ended, the right to access birth control would again come under fire in Britain's highest court.[27]

In 1914, Margaret Sanger fled New York City after being indicted under the Comstock Act, for her 'obscene, lewd, and lascivious' booklet, *The Woman Rebel*, in which she merely suggested when a woman might want to avoid pregnancy, such as during a sickness. After arriving in London, Sanger met Marie Stopes at a Fabian Society lecture on birth control, and offered her advice on the writing of *Married Love*, which frankly discussed women's sexual desire. Upon its publication in 1918, the book sold 165,000 copies. Letters to Stopes poured in, asking her for advice on contraception. In 1921, she opened Britain's first birth control clinic, in Holloway, north London. (Her Blue Plaque, identifying her as a 'Promoter of sex education and birth control' – conveniently omitting 'and eugenics' – hangs on her former home near Crystal Palace Park in south London, a 15-minute walk from Annie Besant's vine-obscured official marker.)

In 1923, Stopes sued a Scottish physician for libel after he asserted that she was not a medical doctor (*true*), and that the Crown should shutter her immoral clinic, since it was offering an abortifacient called the 'gold pin' (*false*, although she did promote sterilisation). The Lord Chief Justice and a special jury took their seats in the Court of King's Bench (George V being the regent), and heard that Marie Stopes was 'a lady who in fact has committed a crime worse than that of Charles Bradlaugh'.

'Of course your Lordship will remember the charge against Bradlaugh, of publishing an obscene libel,' added the

King's Counsel. Britain's top judge said he did not remember the case.[28]

On the stand, Stopes admitted that she had read *Fruits of Philosophy*, and did not find it to be obscene. Throughout the proceedings, the defence asserted that Charles Bradlaugh had been sentenced to six months in prison for 'having indiscriminately distributed information on contraceptives'. The unchallenged assumption was that he had served that time.[29]

Annie's name only came up glancingly in the six-day trial, once when a barrister called her Charles Bradlaugh's co-defendant, and 'as clever a woman, perhaps, as Mrs. Stopes'.[30] He did not mean it flatteringly. If, after repudiating birth control, Annie had hoped that her pioneering role in the fight for reproductive rights would be forgotten, her wish was coming true.

Karl Marx observed that history repeats itself, first as tragedy, and second as farce. Forty-six years after Annie's obscenity trial, the special jury ruled against Marie Stopes. She won her appeal, but then lost again when that decision was heard in the House of Lords. A familiar voice sent his condolences. 'The decision is scandalous,' the 67-year-old George Bernard Shaw wrote to Stopes, 'but I am not surprised at it; the opposition can always fall back on simple taboo. The subject is obscene: no lady would dream of alluding to it in mixed society: reproduction is a shocking subject, and there's [the] end of it ... The taboo is impregnable. [T.H.] Huxley had to leave reproduction out of his textbook on physiology; and you are as helpless as Huxley ... And WHAT has this business cost you?'[31]

Marie Stopes's trial damages were repaid many-fold through her subsequent increase in book sales. In the year following the trial, visitors to her family planning clinic more than doubled. The court actions, she crowed, 'roused so much more enthusiasm for me than simple success would have done that I cannot regret it.'[32] The Establishment will turn its back; *The Times* will even refuse to print the birth announcement of her son. But in 1974, 16 years after her death from breast cancer, the National Health Service will implement her suggestion, first made in 1921, to freely provide contraception to all women, regardless of marital status.

Annie Besant died in Chennai in 1933, just shy of her eighty-sixth birthday. Mahatma Gandhi – in a year of fasting, arrest, and leading a nation-building civil disobedience campaign against the British – sent his condolences. 'So long as India lives,' he wrote, 'the memory of the magnificent services rendered by Dr. Besant will also live. She had endeared herself to India by making it the country of her adoption and dedicating her all to her.'[33]

Wrapped in silk, Annie's body was cremated on a pyre beside the Adyar River. Back in her birthplace of London, the *Times'* obituary was shorter than Charles Bradlaugh's, but much more respectful. She had, after all, long outlived her enemies. The notice, which accurately praised her 'no slight literary talent', said that her husband Frank had died in 1917. The story neglected to mention her trial, as well as her bravery in publishing pamphlets promoting birth control. It did, however, thoughtfully note that this 'champion of neo-Malthusianism was deprived by the Courts of the custody of her little daughter, but both children when they grew up returned to her'. The official paper of record's account of this remarkable life ended with the fact that Mrs Besant's son was 'a distinguished actuary'.[34]

The Times did not think to remark upon her daughter.

Mabel by then had married and divorced Ernest Scott, an Australian journalist-turned-historian who continued the tradition of Besant-adjacent men being knighted, while the women soldiered on.[35] Mabel had left Melbourne with their daughter Muriel and returned to live in London.

In her unpublished memoir, Annie's niece Freda Fisher recalled the day Mabel brought a photograph of her mother into an East End shop to have it framed. The city was then suffering through the Great Depression that made the 1930s known as the Devil's Decade. One world war was over; another was about to begin. *The Times* ran letters from Britain's National Birth Control Association (today's Family Planning Association) extolling 'the rapidly spreading contraception'.[36] Meanwhile, over in Nazi Germany, one of Adolph Hitler's first acts had been to outlaw all forms of birth control. In the Third Reich, a woman's place was pregnant in her Sieg Heil-ing home.

At the framing shop counter, a gruff, stolid man stared at the portrait and told Mabel, 'That's Annie Besant.'

'Yes,' she nodded. Mabel watched the man look down at the photo he held tenderly in a liver-spotted hand. He raised his gaze from a memory and studied the woman in her sixties who stood before him.

'You're very like 'er,' he said at last. 'You're not by any chanst 'er daughter, are yer?'

Mabel said that she was.

'Well I never!' exclaimed the old man. 'Our Annie's daughter.' Noticing the confusion on Mabel's face, the East Ender flashed an embarrassed grin. ''Scuse me, Miss,' he explained, 'but we allus called 'er Our Annie.'[37]

They didn't use her husband's name, but the one she had made on her own.

Acknowledgements

Librarians and archivists are essential, frontline workers in the defence of an open society. As someone who reported for over a decade in China, I am always amazed by and appreciative of the preservation of primary sources and the access afforded to them in a democracy. We are lucky that the Victorians were inveterate recorders of their world, and that so much of it remains in print. This book would not have been possible without the patient assistance of people who really deserve to be paid more. They scanned pages when the research began during lockdown, welcomed me into the archives when their doors reopened – and then scanned some more until we all could be together again. Like the superb Times Archive and British Newspaper Archive websites, Annie was great company then, as was Nigel Taylor at the National Archives in Kew; Frank Bowles and Hannah James at the Cambridge University Library's Churchill Archives Centre; Francesca Tate at the Middle Temple Library; Melissa Harrison at the Lambeth Palace Library; Jim Gerenscer at Dickinson College; the Wellcome Collection's Victoria Sloyan; and the Special Collections Team at the Bishopsgate Institute, whose hallway is guarded by an illuminated portrait of Charles Bradlaugh, looking like a revivalist preacher with his shoulder-length hair topped by a grey gambler hat. The photo is captioned with his belief that 'The word heretic ought to be a term of honour.'

I was also greatly assisted by the staff at the British Library, starting in the Manuscript Reading Room, which holds Freda Fisher's unpublished manuscript about her aunt, Annie. It was amusing to peruse George Bernard Shaw's letters there while a bust of the playwright smirked down from a shelf upon me. In the Newsroom, I read accounts of the trial seated in front of a blown-up image of the 1977 *Daily Mirror* front page featuring the Sex Pistols, headlined THE FILTH AND THE FURY, which inspired the book's title, after Sir Hardinge Giffard's flaccid accusation. Annie's trial was to birth control writing what the Pistols' Lesser Free Trade Hall show was to the formation of new bands.

Speaking of busts, a rather large one of Charles Bradlaugh watched me read bound copies of the *National Reformer* held at Conway Hall's library in London's Red Lion Square. I am grateful to Olwen Terris for finding everything I was looking for, and more. In addition to displaying a copy of Annie's 'Secular Song & Hymn Book', this Freethought library also features a small desk whose plaque identifies it as 'The favorite writing table and fellow prisoner for more than nine years of Richard Carlile during his struggle to obtain the freedom of the Press 1816 to 1834.' Touching that wood, and turning those newspaper pages, delivered a tangible connection to the past. Conway Hall's Sunday concert series and speaker events continue the legacy of the South Place Ethical Society, where Annie's ally Moncure Conway once served as minister.

A big thank you, too, to Lord Filkin CBE (or Geoff, to me) who connected me with Matthew Hamlyn CBE, Strategic Director of the Chamber Business Team at the House of Commons, who took me and my history-buff 11-year-old son backstage at the Palace of Westminster and into the former prison cell and sitting room. You created a lifelong memory, Matthew. (Benji named his souvenir stuffed Speaker Bear 'Sir Humphrey'.) Benji also introduced me to Charles Dickens, Jr.'s wonderful guide to London, pages of which he read reproduced in a Sally Lockhart mystery, by Philip

Pullman, whose books have never failed to teach him – and me – something new. Thanks to Benji for being such a curious bookworm, and for understanding so young the pleasure of finding things out. And equal thanks to my wife Frances for urging me on as always, especially when morale was low and we were far from home. Who knew that National Taiwan University's library held such a trove of Victorian texts? 我爱你!

I also appreciate the help of Dr Mark Collins, Estates Historian and Archivist at the Houses of Parliament, who found the image of the sitting room that appears in the Preface, and patiently answered my queries about arcana, such as what the 'R' in the wallpaper represented. (It's likely the designer Augustus Pugin's tribute to Richard II, who commissioned some of the most important surviving bits of the old Palace, including the great roof of Westminster Hall.)

I must gladly acknowledge the permission given by His Majesty King Charles III to quote freely from Queen Victoria's diary, including the many entries appearing here in print for the first time. You can peruse the entirety of her surviving journals online at the easy-to-use www.queenvictoriasjournals.org. It's a good read.

The book benefited from camaraderie and conversations at Pitt with William Lychack (cheers, Bilford), and while I was a 2021–22 fellow at the University of Oxford Centre for Life-Writing. Special thanks to its founder Dame Hermione Lee, along with Dr Kate Kennedy, Ian Hembrow, Mary Black and Rebecca Gowers, who introduced me to the wider world of Sir Douglas Straight. After becoming a judge in India, he returned to London and worked as the editor of the *Pall Mall Gazette*. Today Straight rests a short walk away from Charles Bradlaugh in Brookwood Cemetery. I am also grateful to the University of Pittsburgh's Momentum Fund, whose support enabled me to overturn every last scrap of paper I sought in the recesses of London.

The final document found me. After returning to my rented flat in Bayswater's Hallfield Estate, I bent down to see what had been slipped under the door. I picked up the paper and read 'THEOSOPHY: Ageless Wisdom for Modern Life.' The pamphlet's front page listed the times for Queen's Gardens study sessions of *The Secret Doctrine*. Shortly before Annie's death, the *New York Times* (calling her a 'highly cultured Irishwoman') reported her illness under the sub-headline 'Says Work in this Life Is Done, but Promises to Return'. Holding the pamphlet in a dark hallway as a chill raced down my spine, I laughed at ever doubting her. It's been a pleasure to spend these years with you, A.B.

This time has been made even more enjoyable by the Ebury team cheering, cajoling, and improving the text from behind the scenes. Thanks to Miranda Ward for an incisive copy edit, and Amanda Waters for several rounds of line edits, queries, and suggested improvements. Amanda, you made every page better. The remaining mistakes are my own.

Lastly, three cheers for the indefatigable Georges Borchardt, still finding the right homes for books since 'Waiting for Godot.' Georges, along with Cora, Anne and Valerie in New York, and everyone at Abner Stein in London: thank you for connecting this project with Jamie Joseph, a publisher who saw the importance of Annie's activism, and her relevance to our own time. I appreciate the patience, Jamie, and your excitement to reintroduce and reanimate her voice for readers today. In the end, this is Annie's story; we just got her back on contemporary bookshelves, where she belongs.

Bibliography

Archival material

A.C. Tait letters. Lambeth Palace.

Charles Bradlaugh papers. Bishopsgate Institute.

Freda Muriel Fisher. 'Autobiographical Memoir of Freda Muriel Fisher'. Unpublished manuscript, circa 1935–1939. British Library.

G.B. Shaw Papers. British Library.

Lord Randolph Churchill Papers. Cambridge University.

National Archives record group KB6/4 (Trinity 1877), arrest warrant and depositions.

Queen Victoria's Journals. Royal Archives, Windsor Palace. RA VIC/ MAIN/QVJ.

W.T. Stead Papers. Cambridge University.

Newspapers

Banbury Advertiser
Barnsley Chronicle
Bradford Observer
Colonial Standard and Jamaica Despatch
Court and Fashion—Belfast News-Letter
Derby Mercury
Echo (London)
Edinburgh Evening News
Household Words
Kingston Daily Gleaner
Moonshine
Morning Post (London)
Reynolds's Newspaper

Sheffield Independent
St. James's Gazette
The Era (London)
The Illustrated London News
The National Reformer
The New York Times
The Pall Mall Gazette
The Scotsman
The Sporting Gazette
The Times
Truth
Western Morning News
Women and Work: A Weekly Industrial, Educational, and Household Register for Women

Published material

Acton, William. *Functions and Disorders of the Reproductive Organs, in Childhood, Youth, Adult Age, and Advanced Life.* London: Churchill. 1862.

Agate, Peter. *Sexual Economy as Taught by Charles Bradlaugh.* London: W. Stewart & Co. [c.1877.]

Arnstein, Walter. *The Bradlaugh Case.* Oxford: Clarendon Press. 1965.

Baird, Julia. *Victoria: The Queen.* New York: Random House. 2016.

Banks, J.A. and Banks, Olive. 'The Bradlaugh-Besant Trial and the English Newspapers'. *Population Studies.* 8(1): July 1954.

Barnes, Julian. *The Man in the Red Coat.* New York: Knopf. 2020.

Bedford, Sylvia. *As It Was.* London: Sinclair-Stevenson. 1990.

Benson, Christopher Arthur and Viscount Reginald Baliol Brett Esher (eds). *The Letters of Queen Victoria, Volume III, 1854–1861.* Project Gutenberg eBook. 2009.

Besant, Annie.
An Autobiography. London: Freethought. 1893.
Auguste Comte. London: Freethought. 1875.
Autobiographical Sketches. London: Freethought. 1885.

Is the Bible Indictable? London: Freethought. 1877.

Marriage: A Plea for Reform. London: Freethought. 1879.

On the Political Status of Women. London: Trubner & Co. 1874.

The Law of Population. London: Freethought. 1877. Later edition, 1887.

The Secular Song and Hymn Book. London: Freethought. 1876.

'White Slavery in London'. *The Link.* 23 June 1888.

Bonner, Hypatia Bradlaugh and Robertson, J.M. *Charles Bradlaugh: A Record of His Life and Work. Vols. I–III.* London: T. Fisher Unwin. 1908.

Box, Muriel (ed.). *Birth Control and Libel: The Trial of Marie Stopes.* New York: A.S. Barnes and Company. 1968.

Browne, Janet. *Charles Darwin. Vol. I, Voyaging.* London: J. Cape. 1995.

Buckle, George Earle (ed.). *The Letters of Queen Victoria 1862-1878. Vol. 1-3.* London: John Murray. 1926.

Caldwell, John. 'The Delayed Western Fertility Decline: An Examination of English-Speaking Countries'. *Population and Development Review.* 25(3): September 1999. pp. 479–513.

Carlile, Richard. *Every Woman's Book.* London: Self-published. 1828.

Chandrasekhar, Sripati. *'A Dirty, Filthy Book'.* Berkeley: University of California Press. 1981.

Darwin, Charles. *The Descent of Man.* Vol. 2. London: John Murray. 1871.

Davis, Tracy C. *George Bernard Shaw and the Socialist Theatre.* Westport: Greenwood Press. 1994.

Dickens, Charles.
A Christmas Carol. Open Books Edition. 2007.
The Pickwick Papers. London: Penguin. 2003.

Dickens, Charles, Jr. *Dickens's Dictionary of London.* London: Charles Dickens and Evans. 1879.

Dinnage, Rosemary. *Annie Besant.* Harmondsworth: Penguin. 1986.

Disraeli, Benjamin. *Sybil, or The Two Nations.* Oxford: Oxford University Press. 1998.

Doyle, Arthur Conan. *A Study in Scarlet.* Project Gutenberg eBook. Chapter 1. *c.*1887.

Eekelaar, John. 'The Emergence of Children's Rights'. *Oxford Journal of Legal Studies*, Vol. 6, No. 2 (Summer, 1986), pp. 161–182.

Eliot, George. *Middlemarch*. New York: Penguin. 1994.

Elwin, Verrier. *The Tribal World of Verrier Elwin*. New York: Oxford University Press. 1964.

Ensor, Robert C.K. *England 1870–1914*. Oxford: Oxford University Press. 1980.

Ferguson, Niall. *The Cash Nexus*. New York: Basic. 2001.

Field, James Alfred. *Essays on Population*. Chicago: University of Chicago Press. 1931.

Fulford, Roger (ed.). *Dearest Child: Letters between Queen Victoria and the Princess Royal, 1858–1861*. New York: Holt, Rinehart and Winston. 1964.

Fulmer, Constance M. and Barfield, Margaret E. (eds). *A Monument to the Memory of George Eliot: Edith J. Simcox's Autobiography of a Shirt-maker*. New York: Taylor & Francis. 1998.

Garrigan, Kristine Ottesen (ed.). *Victorian Scandals*. Athens: Ohio University Press. 1992.

Geddes, Patrick and Thomson, J. Arthur. *The Evolution of Sex*. London: Walter Scott. 1889.

Gibbs, A.M. *Bernard Shaw*. Gainesville: University Press of Florida. 2005.

Goldman, Emma. *Living My Life*. New York: Knopf. 1931.

Goodman, Ruth. *How to Be a Victorian*. New York: Liveright. 2015.

Gordon, Linda. *The Moral Property of Women: A History of Birth Control Politics in America*. Third edition. Champaign: University of Illinois Press. 2007.

Gowers, Rebecca. *The Scoundrel Harry Larkyns*. London: Weidenfeld & Nicolson. 2020.

Griffin, Emma. *Breadwinner*. New Haven: Yale. 2020.

Guha, Ramachandra. *Rebels Against the Raj*. New York: Knopf. 2022.

Haight, Gordon S. (ed.). *Selections from George Eliot's Letters*. New Haven: Yale University Press. 1985.

Hanly, Conor. 'The Decline of Civil Jury Trial in Nineteenth-Century England'. *The Journal of Legal History*. 26(3): December 2005. pp. 253–278.

Heffer, Simon. *The Age of Decadence*. London: Windmill Books. 2017.

Hewitt, Martin (ed.). *The Victorian World*. London: Routledge. 2012.

Hibbert, Christopher. *Queen Victoria*. New York: Basic. 2000.

Himes, Norman E. 'Jeremy Bentham and the Genesis of English Neo-Malthusianism'. *Economic History*. 3(11): 1936. pp. 267–276.

Holmes, Rachel.
Eleanor Marx. New York: Bloomsbury. 2014.
Sylvia Pankhurst. London: Bloomsbury. 2020.

Horn, Kate. 'Women's Rights'. New York: Horace Waters. 1853.

Hughes, Kathryn. *Victorians Undone*. Baltimore: Johns Hopkins University Press. 2018.

Johnson, Diane. *The True History of the First Mrs Meredith*. New York: New York Review of Books. 2020.

Joyce, James. *Ulysses*. New York: Knopf. 1997.

Kalsem, Kristen Brandser. 'Law, Literature, and Libel: Victorian Censorship of "Dirty Filthy" Books on Birth Control'. *William & Mary Journal of Women and the Law*. 10: April 2004. pp. 533–568.

Keane, Angela. 'Richard Carlile's Working Women: Selling Books, Politics, Sex and the *Republican*'. *Literature & History*. 15(2): 2006. pp. 20–33.

Knowlton, Charles.
A History of the recent excitement in Ashfield. 1834. No publisher identified. See: https://access.bl.uk/item/viewer/ark:/81055/vdc_100054799934.0x000001
Fruits of Philosophy. London: Freethought Publishing. 1877.

Larkin, Philip. 'Annus Mirabilis'. In *Collected Poems*. London: Marvell Press. 1988.

Lawrence, D.H. *Lady Chatterley's Lover*. London: Penguin. 2009.

Lee, Hermione. *Virginia Woolf*. New York: Knopf. 1997.

Longford, Elizabeth.
Queen Victoria. New York: Harper & Row. 1965.
Victoria R.I. London: Weidenfeld & Nicolson. 1961.

Lutyens, Mary. *Krishnamurti: The Years of Awakening*. New York: Avon. 1975.

MacPherson, Myra. *The Scarlet Sisters*. New York: Twelve. 2014.

Mackay, Carol Hanbury. 'A Journal of Her Own: The Rise and Fall of Annie Besant's Our Corner'. *Victorian Periodicals Review*. 42(4): Winter 2009. pp. 324–358.

Manvell, Roger. *The Trial of Annie Besant and Charles Bradlaugh*. London: Elek. 1976.

Marcus, Sharon. *Between Women*. Princeton: Princeton University Press. 2007.

Martin, Sir Theodore. *Queen Victoria as I Knew Her*. Edinburgh: William Blackwood and Sons. 1902.

Marx, Karl and Engels, Frederick. *Marx and Engels in Ireland*. Moscow: Progress Publishers. 1971.

Mayhew, Henry. *London Labour and the London Poor*. London: Penguin. 1985.

McCarthy, Fiona. *William Morris. A Life for our Time*. London: Faber and Faber. 1994.

Mill, John Stuart.
Autobiography. London: Penguin. 1989.
On Liberty. London: John W. Parker and Son. 1859.

Morley, John. *The Life of William Ewart Gladstone*. Vol. 3. Project Gutenberg eBook. 2010.

Nietzsche, Friedrich. *Ecce Homo*. Harmondsworth: Penguin. 1979.

Nethercot, Arthur H.
The First Five Lives of Annie Besant. Chicago: University of Chicago Press. 1960.
The Last Four Lives of Annie Besant. Chicago: University of Chicago Press. 1963.

Niblett, Brian. *Dare to Stand Alone*. Oxford: Kramedart Press. 2010.

Nightingale, Florence. *Cassandra*. New York: The Feminist Press. 1979.

Oldham, James C. 'The Origins of the Special Jury'. *The University of Chicago Law Review*. 50(137): 1983. pp. 137–221.

Peters, Sally. *Bernard Shaw*. New Haven: Yale. 1996.

Picard, Liza. *Victorian London*. New York: St Martin's Griffin. 2005.

Pooley, Sian. 'Parenthood, child-rearing and fertility in England, 1850–1914'. *The History of the Family*. 18(1): March 2013. pp.83–106.

Purdy, Richard Little and Millgate, Michael (eds). *The Collected Letters of Thomas Hardy, Vol. 1: 1840–1892.* Oxford: Oxford University Press. 1978.

Ricks, Thomas E. *Churchill & Orwell.* New York: Penguin. 2017.

Rosenbaum, S.P. (ed.). *Women & Fiction: The Manuscript Version of a Room of One's Own.* Glasgow: The Shakespeare Head Press. 1992.

Sappol, Michael. 'The Odd Case of Charles Knowlton: Anatomical Performance, Medical Narrative, and Identity in Antebellum America'. *Bulletin of the History of Medicine.* 83(3): 2009. pp. 460–498.

Schnucker, Robert V. 'Elizabethan Birth Control and Puritan Attitudes'. *The Journal of Interdisciplinary History.* 5(4): 1975. pp. 655–667.

Shanley, Mary Lyndon. *Feminism, Marriage, and the Law in Victorian England, 1850–1895.* London: Bloomsbury Academic. 2021.

Shannon, R.T. *Gladstone and the Bulgarian Agitation 1876.* London: Thomas Nelson and Sons. 1963.

Shaw, George Bernard.

   Arms and the Man. New York: Penguin. 2006.

   Pygmalion and Three Other Plays. New York: Barnes & Nobel Classics. 2004.

   You Never Can Tell. New York: Brentano's. 1913.

Showalter, Elaine. *A Jury of her Peers.* New York: Knopf. 2009.

Sreenivas, Mytheli. 'Birth Control in the Shadow of Empire: The Trials of Annie Besant, 1877–1878'. *Feminist Studies.* 41(3): Gendering Bodies, Institutional Hegemonies (2015). pp. 509–537.

Steinbach, Susie. *Women in England 1760–1914.* New York: Palgrave Macmillan. 2004.

Sterne, Laurence. *The Life and Opinions of Tristram Shandy, Gentleman.* London: Penguin Books, 2003.

Strachey, Lytton. *Queen Victoria.* New York: Harcourt, Brace and Company. 1921.

Straight, Douglas. *Harrow Recollections. By an old Harrovian (Sidney Daryl).* London: George Routledge and Sons. 1867.

Summerscale, Kate. *Mrs Robinson's Disgrace.* New York: Bloomsbury. 2012.

Taylor, Anne. *Annie Besant.* Oxford: Oxford University Press. 1992.

The Ecclesiastical Observer. London: Arthur Hall and Co. XXV: 167–170. April 1, 1872.

The Queen v. Charles Bradlaugh and Annie Besant. London: Freethought. 1877.

Tomalin, Claire. *Thomas Hardy*. New York: Penguin. 2007.

Tribe, David. *President Charles Bradlaugh, M.P.* London: Elek. 1971.

Tyson, Brian (ed.). *Bernard Shaw's Book Reviews*. Vol. 2. University Park: Penn State Press. 1996.

Urol, Indian J. 'The Story of the Condom'. *Indian Journal of Urology*. 29(1): January–March 2013. pp. 12–15.

Vendler, Helen (ed.). *Dickinson*. Cambridge: Harvard University Press. 2010.

Weintraub, Stanley. *Uncrowned King*. New York: Free Press. 1997.

Wilde, Oscar. *The Importance of Being Earnest*. Leipzig: Bernhard Tauchnitz. 1910.

Williams, Gertrude Marvin. *The Passionate Pilgrim*. New York: Coward-McCann. 1931.

Williams, Holly. 'The cross-dressing gents of Victorian England'.www.bbc.com/culture/article/20160608-the-cross-dressing-gents-of-victorian-england. 8 June 2016.

Wilson, A.N. *The Victorians*. New York: Norton. 2004.

Worsley, Lucy. *Queen Victoria*. New York: St. Martin's Press. 2019.

Wynne, Deborah. 'Reading Victorian Rags: Recycling, Redemption, and Dickens's Ragged Children'. *Journal of Victorian Culture*. 20(1): 1 March 2015. pp. 34–49.

Notes

Prelude: 'This battle must be won'

1 RA VIC/MAIN/QVJ (W). 25 June 1880 and 13 January 1881 (Princess Beatrice's copies).

2 Fisher, Freda Muriel. 'Autobiographical Memoir of Freda Muriel Fisher'. Unpublished manuscript, circa 1935–1939. British Library. Vol. 2, ff. 159, p. 106.

3 Banks, J.A. and Banks, Olive. 'The Bradlaugh-Besant Trial and the English Newspapers'. *Population Studies.* 8(1): July 1954. p. 22.

4 *National Reformer.* 1 July 1877.

5 Williams, Gertrude Marvin. *The Passionate Pilgrim.* New York: Coward-McCann. 1931. p. 77.

6 *National Reformer.* 17 June 1877.

7 Besant. Ibid., 8 July 1877.

8 Nightingale, Florence. *Cassandra.* New York: The Feminist Press. 1979. p. 25

9 Fisher. Vol. 2, p. 78.

10 Nethercot, Arthur H. *The Last Four Lives of Annie Besant.* Chicago: University of Chicago Press. 1963. p. 349.

11 Rosenbaum, S.P. (ed.). *Women & Fiction: The Manuscript Version of A Room of One's Own.* Glasgow: The Shakespeare Head Press. 1992. p. 184.

12 Heffer, Simon. *The Age of Decadence.* London: Windmill Books. 2017. p. 160., and Wilson, A.N. *The Victorians.* New York: Norton. 2004. p. 551.

13 Marcus, Sharon. *Between Women.* Princeton: Princeton University Press. 2007. p. 17.

14 Hall, Rachel. 'Access to contraception has got harder in England, top doctor says.' *Guardian.* 5 June 2023. The story quotes Prof

Lesley Regan, a gynaecologist appointed women's health ambassador for England in 2022.

15 *National Reformer.* 17 June 1877.

Chapter 1: The times of London

1 Picard, Liza. *Victorian London.* New York: St. Martin's Griffin. 2005. p. 21.

2 'The London Main-Drainage Works', *The Illustrated London News*, 21 May 1864. p. 501.

3 Fulford, Roger (ed.). *Dearest Child: Letters between Queen Victoria and the Princess Royal, 1858–1861.* New York: Holt, Rinehart and Winston. 1964. p. 115.

4 For a chilling gallery of prepubescent Victorian mugshots, see https://rarehistoricalphotos.com/victorian-child-criminals-mugshots/

5 Dickens, Charles, Jr. *Dickens's Dictionary of London.* London: Charles Dickens and Evans. 1879. p. 234.

6 Dickens, Charles. *The Pickwick Papers.* London: Penguin. 2003. p. 24.

7 Johnson, Diane. *The True History of the First Mrs Meredith.* New York: New York Review of Books. 2020. p. 47.

8 W.T. Stead, 'The Maiden Tribute of Modern Babylon'. *Pall Mall Gazette*, 6 July 1885.

9 'Overcrowding', *The Times*, 6 April 1877, p. 11.

10 RA VIC/MAIN/QVJ (W). 6 April 1877 (Princess Beatrice's copies).

11 Doyle, Arthur Conan. *A Study in Scarlet*, Chapter 1. 1887.

Chapter 2: Iconoclast – Charles Bradlaugh

1 Carlile, Richard. *Every Woman's Book.* London: Self-published. 1828. p. 39.

2 Goodman, Ruth. *How to Be a Victorian.* New York: Liveright. 2015. p. 419. Goodman relates how she attempted to make sheep-gut condoms, and the complexity of the process.

3 Steinbach, Susie. *Women in England 1760–1914*. New York: Palgrave Macmillan. 2004. p. 122.

4 Urol, Indian J. 'The Story of the Condom'. *Indian Journal of Urology*. 29(1): January–March 2013. pp. 12–15.

5 Wilson, A.N. *The Victorians*. New York: Norton. 2004. p. 288.

6 Royal Shakespeare Company. 'Slang and Sexual Language', using examples compiled by Heloise Senechal. www.rsc.org.uk/shakespeare/language/slang-and-sexual-language

7 Schnucker, Robert V. 'Elizabethan Birth Control and Puritan Attitudes'. *The Journal of Interdisciplinary History*. 5(4): 1975. pp. 655–667.

8 Himes, Norman E. 'Jeremy Bentham and the Genesis of English Neo-Malthusianism'. *Economic History*. 3(11): 1936. pp. 267–276.

9 Dickens, Charles. *A Christmas Carol*. Open Books Edition. 2007. p. 12.

10 Browne, Janet. *Charles Darwin. Vol. I, Voyaging*. London: J. Cape. 1995. p. 398.

11 Picard, Liza. *Victorian London*. New York: St. Martin's Griffin. 2005. p. 265.

12 Shanley, Mary Lyndon. *Feminism, Marriage, and the Law in Victorian England, 1850–1895*. London: Bloomsbury Academic. 2021. p. 157.

13 Keane, Angela. 'Richard Carlile's Working Women: Selling Books, Politics, Sex and the *Republican*.' *Literature & History*. 15(2): 2006. pp. 20–33.

14 Wynne, Deborah. 'Reading Victorian Rags: Recycling, Redemption, and Dickens's Ragged Children'. *Journal of Victorian Culture*. 20(1): 1 March 2015. pp. 34–49.

15 Dickens, Charles, Jr. *Dickens's Dictionary of London*. London: Charles Dickens and Evans. 1879. p. 102.

16 Mayhew, Henry. *London Labour and the London Poor*. London: Penguin. 1985. p. 107.

17 Sappol, Michael. 'The Odd Case of Charles Knowlton: Anatomical Performance, Medical Narrative, and Identity in Antebellum America'. *Bulletin of the History of Medicine*. 83(3): 2009. pp. 460–498.

18 Tribe, David. *President Charles Bradlaugh, M.P.* London: Elek. 1971. p. 173. Quoting from Summons to H. Cook, 9 Walter St., Bristol. Bradlaugh Collection, National Secular Society.

19 Bonner, Hypatia Bradlaugh and Robertson, J.M. *Charles Bradlaugh: A Record of His Life and Work. Vol. I.* London: T. Fisher Unwin. 1908. pp. 33–34.

20 Dickens, Jr. p. 269.

21 Fulford, Roger (ed.). *Dearest Child: Letters between Queen Victoria and the Princess Royal, 1858–1861.* New York: Holt, Rinehart and Winston. 1964. pp. 209 and 251. The cleric was Dr Pusey, of Oxford. Not atypically for her era, the novel put the blame for the heroine's demise on inciteful Catholics and Jews. Its author Charles Kingsley was a broad church Anglican priest.

22 Bonner, pp. 137–139.

23 Ibid., p. 149.

24 RA VIC/MAIN/QVJ (W). 2 April 1873 (Princess Beatrice's copies).

25 Niblett, Bryan. *Dare to Stand Alone.* Oxford: Kramedart Press. 2010., p. 75.

26 Bonner, p. 381.

27 Ibid., p. 384.

28 Nethercot, Arthur H. *The First Five Lives of Annie Besant.* Chicago: University of Chicago Press. 1960. p. 66.

29 Bonner, pp. 389–390.

Chapter 3: Ajax – Annie Besant

1 Bonner, Hypatia Bradlaugh and Robertson, J.M. *Charles Bradlaugh: A Record of His Life and Work. Vol. II.* London: T. Fisher Unwin. 1908. p. 16.

2 Besant, Annie. *On the Political Status of Women.* London: Trubner & Co. 1874. p. 3.

3 Nethercot, Arthur H. *The First Five Lives of Annie Besant.* Chicago: University of Chicago Press. 1960. p. 402.

4 Besant, Annie. *An Autobiography.* London: Freethought. 1893. p. 12.

5 Fisher, Freda Muriel. 'Autobiographical Memoir of Freda Muriel Fisher'. Unpublished manuscript, circa 1935–1939. British Library. Vol. 1. p. 32.

6 Eliot, George. *Middlemarch*. New York: Penguin. 1994. pp. 70–71.

7 Besant, Annie. *An Autobiography*. p. 22.

8 Showalter, Elaine. *A Jury of her Peers*. New York: Knopf. 2009. p. 173.

9 Williams, Gertrude Marvin. *The Passionate Pilgrim*. New York: Coward-McCann. 1931. p. 23, quoting Stead.

10 RA VIC/MAIN/QVJ (W). 23 November 1867. (Princess Beatrice's copies).

11 Engels, Frederick. Letter of 24 November 1867 Engels to Marx. *Marx and Engels in Ireland*. Moscow: Progress Publishers. 1971.

12 Besant. *An Autobiography*. pp. 22–23.

13 RA VIC/MAIN/QVJ (W). 10 February 1840. (Lord Esher's typescripts).

14 Ibid., 11 February 1840.

15 Ibid., 12 February 1840.

16 Ibid., 13 February 1840.

17 Besant, *An Autobiography*. London: Freethought. 1893. p.27.

18 Nethercot, p. 31.

19 Martin, Sir Theodore. *Queen Victoria as I Knew Her*. Edinburgh: William Blackwood and Sons. 1902. pp. 69–70.

20 Besant. *An Autobiography*. p. 28.

21 Ibid., p. 31.

22 Ibid., p. 37.

23 Vendler, Helen (ed.). *Dickinson*. Cambridge: Harvard University Press. 2010. p. 184. (Poem 407.)

24 Besant. *Autobiography*. p. 42.

25 Shanley, Mary Lyndon. *Feminism, Marriage, and the Law in Victorian England, 1850–1895*. London: Bloomsbury Academic. 2021. p. 49, quoting Cobbe's 1862 essay 'Celibacy v. Marriage'.

26 Fulford, Roger (ed.). *Dearest Child: Letters between Queen Victoria and the Princess Royal, 1858–1861*. New York: Holt, Rinehart and Winston. 1964. p. 254.

27 Garrigan, Kristine Ottesen (ed.). *Victorian Scandals*. Athens: Ohio University Press. 1992. p. 294.

28 Fulford, p. 44.

29 Besant. *An Autobiography*. p. 43.

30 Fisher, p. 84.

31 Besant, Annie. *Autobiographical Sketches*. London: Freethought. 1885. p. 84.

32 Besant. *An Autobiography*. p. 49.

33 Arnstein, Walter. *The Bradlaugh Case*. Oxford: Clarendon Press. 1965. p. 14.

34 Hewitt, Martin (ed.). *The Victorian World*. London: Routledge. 2012. pp. 522 and 627.

35 Arnstein, p. 50.

36 Eliot, George. *Middlemarch*. New York: Penguin. 1994. p. 392.

37 Besant. *An Autobiography*, p. 64.

38 Ibid., p. 66.

39 Geddes, Patrick and Thomson, J. Arthur. *The Evolution of Sex*. London: Walter Scott. 1889. p. 287.

40 Martin, pp. 89–90.

41 Besant, Annie. *On the Political Status of Women*. pp. 5–11.

42 Bonner, p. 16.

43 Besant. *An Autobiography*. p. 66.

Chapter 4: The fruits of their philosophy

1 Besant. *An Autobiography*. p. 70.

2 Dinnage, Rosemary. *Annie Besant*. Harmondsworth: Penguin. 1986. p. 31.

3 Besant. *An Autobiography*. p. 70.

4 Baird, Julia. *Victoria: The Queen*. New York. Random House. 2016. p. 369.

5 Strachey, Lytton. *Queen Victoria*. New York: Harcourt, Brace and Company. 1921. p. 349.

6 Baird, p. 380.

7 Strachey, p. 352.

8 Hughes, Kathryn. *Victorians Undone*. Baltimore: Johns Hopkins University Press. 2018. p. 249.

9 Besant, Annie. 'The Legalisation of Female Slavery in England'. *National Reformer.* 4 June 1876.

10 MacPherson, Myra. *The Scarlet Sisters.* New York: Twelve. 2014. p. 186.

11 *Women and Work: A Weekly Industrial, Educational, and Household Register for Women.* London. 24 July 1875.

12 Picard, Liza. Victorian London. New York: St. Martin's Griffin. 2005. p. 86.

13 Wilson, A.N. *The Victorians.* New York: Norton. 2004. p. 427. See also: www.ons.gov.uk/peoplepopulationandcommunity/personal andhouseholdfinances/incomeandwealth/bulletins/ distributionofindividualtotalwealthbycharacteristicingreatbritain/ april2018tomarch2020

14 Besant, Annie (ed.). *The Secular Song and Hymn Book.* London: Freethought. 1876. p. 83.

15 Besant, Annie. *Auguste Comte.* London: Freethought. 1875. p. 16.

16 Besant. *An Autobiography.* pp. 64–65.

17 Picard, p. 309.

18 Purdy, Richard Little and Millgate, Michael (eds). *The Collected Letters of Thomas Hardy, Vol. 1: 1840–1892.* To Mary Hardy, 19 February 1863. Oxford: Oxford University Press. 1978.

19 Dickens, Charles, Jr. *Dickens's Dictionary of London.* London: Charles Dickens and Evans. 1879. p. 103.

20 Barnes, Julian. *The Man in the Red Coat.* New York: Knopf. 2020. p. 47.

21 Nethercot, Arthur H. *The First Five Lives of Annie Besant.* Chicago: University of Chicago Press. 1960. p. 102.

22 Besant. *An Autobiography.* p. 73.

23 Nethercot, p. 101.

24 Besant. *Autobiographical Sketches.* London: Freethought. 1885. pp. 100–101.

25 Weintraub, Stanley. *Uncrowned King.* New York: Free Press. 1997. p. 99.

26 Besant, Annie. *Marriage: A Plea for Reform.* London: Freethought. 1879. pp. 13–14.

27 Acton, William. *Functions and Disorders of the Reproductive Organs, in Childhood, Youth, Adult Age, and Advanced Life.* London: Churchill. 1862. pp. 101–102.

28 Besant. *Marriage: A Plea for Reform.* p. 59.

29 'Demonstration in Hyde Park'. *The Times.* 19 July 1875.

30 *The Sporting Gazette*, Vol. XIII, Issue 708, 4 December 1875.

31 The Shady Old Lady's Guide to London. www.shadyoldlady.com/location/2826

32 For more on Mary Ellen, see Diane Johnson, and George's sonnets at poetryfoundation.org. More than 150 years later the opening poem in *Modern Love* remains searing: 'By this he knew she wept with waking eyes/That, at his hand's light quiver by her head,/The strange low sobs that shook their common bed/Were called into her with a sharp surprise,/And strangled mute, like little gaping snakes,/Dreadfully venomous to him. She lay/Stone-still, and the long darkness flowed away/With muffled pulses . . . Like sculpted effigies they might be seen/Upon their marriage-tomb, the sword between;/Each wishing for the sword that severs all.'

33 Bonner, Hypatia Bradlaugh and Robertson, J.M. *Charles Bradlaugh: A Record of His Life and Work. Vol. II.* London: T. Fisher Unwin. 1908. p. 31.

34 'Unjust Judgments on Subjects of Morality'. *The Ecclesiastical Observer.* London: Arthur Hall and Co. XXV: 167–170. 1 April 1872. The unsigned review of a Josephine Butler lecture quotes her use of the term.

35 Tribe, David. *President Charles Bradlaugh, M.P.* London: Elek. 1971. p. 179.

36 Ibid., p. 180.

37 Besant. *An Autobiography.* p. 15

38 Barnes. p. 165.

39 Williams, Gertrude Marvin. *The Passionate Pilgrim.* New York: Coward-McCann. 1931.p. 70. A bit of doggerel explained that the Besant name did not rhyme with *decent* or *crescent*, but *pant* and *can't*: Besànt. 'Nor are things a whit more pleasant, when fellow creatures call me Bésant.' Nethercot, pp. 20–21.

40 Tribe, p. 173.

41 Knowlton, Charles. *Fruits of Philosophy*. London: Freethought Publishing. 1877. p. 54.

42 Niblett, Brian. *Dare to Stand Alone*. Oxford: Kramedart Press. 2010. p. 105.

43 Hibbert, Christopher. *Queen Victoria*. New York: Basic. 2000. p. 362.

44 Shannon, R.T. *Gladstone and the Bulgarian Agitation 1876*. London: Thomas Nelson and Sons. 1963. p. 47. The speaker is the Liberal reformer James Fitzjames Stephen.

45 Longford, Elizabeth. *Victoria R.I.* London: Weidenfeld & Nicolson. 1961. p. 411.

46 Tribe, p. 174. Quoting 'Mrs. Watt's Reply to Mr. Bradlaugh's Representations'. February 1877.

47 Tribe, p. 175.

48 Bonner, Vol. II. p. 17.

49 Tribe, p. 177.

50 Old Bailey Proceedings. 5 February 1877. p. 468. Online: www.old-baileyonline.org/browse.jsp?name=18770205

51 *National Reformer*. 17 March 1878.

52 RA VIC/MAIN/QVJ (W). 21 January 1866 (Princess Beatrice's copies).

53 Mill, John Stuart. *Autobiography*. London: Penguin. 1989. p. 71.

54 Mill, John Stuart. *On Liberty*. Introductory paragraph. London: John W. Parker and Son. 1859. p. 7.

55 Besant. *Autobiographical Sketches*. p. 118.

56 *National Reformer*. 25 March 1877.

57 Bonner. Vol. II. p. 33.

58 *Times of London*, 26 March 1877. p. 8.

59 Besant. *Autobiographical Sketches*. p. 125.

60 RA VIC/MAIN/QVJ (W). 27 March 1877. (Princess Beatrice's copies).

61 *The National Reformer*. 29 July 1877.

62 Bonner. Vol. II. pp. 33–34.

63 Besant. *Autobiographical Sketches*. p. 129.

64 Warrant arrest deposition. DC William Simmonds. 29 March. National Archives KB6/4 (Trinity 1877).
65 Besant. *Autobiographical Sketches*. p. 130.
66 *Pall Mall Gazette*. Friday 6 April 1877.

Chapter 5: 'Oh, they are a stiff-necked people'

1 Straight, Douglas. *Harrow Recollections. By an old Harrovian (Sidney Daryl)*. London: George Routledge and Sons. 1867. p. 26.
2 Ibid., pp. 16–17.
3 Shanley, Mary Lyndon. *Feminism, Marriage, and the Law in Victorian England, 1850–1895*. London: Bloomsbury Academic. 2021. p. 161. Also 3 Hansard 211, 6 May 1872, p. 285.
4 Hansard 215. pp. 477–479. The bill was named the 'Seduction Laws Amendment'.
5 Gowers, Rebecca. *The Scoundrel Harry Larkyns*. London: Weidenfeld & Nicolson. 2020. pp. 100–101.
6 Williams, Holly. 'The cross-dressing gents of Victorian England'. www.bbc.com/culture/article/20160608-the-cross-dressing-gents-of-victorian-england. 8 June 2016.
7 *Morning Post* (London). 18 April 1877.
8 *Derby Mercury*. 18 April 1877.
9 Knowlton. *Fruits of Philosophy*. London: Freethought Publishing. 1877. pp. 38–39.
10 Fulford, Roger (ed.). *Dearest Child: Letters between Queen Victoria and the Princess Royal, 1858–1861*. New York: Holt, Rinehart and Winston. 1964. pp. 77–78.
11 RA VIC/MAIN/QVJ (W). 12 April 1877. (Princess Beatrice's copies).
12 Worsley, Lucy. *Queen Victoria*. New York: St. Martin's Press. 2019. p. 1.
13 *Derby Mercury*. 18 April 1877.
14 Horn, Kate. 'Women's Rights'. New York: Horace Waters. 1853. See: www.protestsonglyrics.net/Women_Feminism_Songs/Womans-Rights.phtml. A similar song has also been attributed to Fanny Fern.

15 RA VIC/MAIN/QVJ (W). 14 April 1877. (Princess Beatrice's copies).

16 *National Reformer*. 29 April 1877.

17 Ibid.

18 *The Times*. 20 April 1877.

19 Knowlton, Charles. *A History of the Recent Excitement in Ashfield*. p. 18. 1834. [Publisher not identified. Accessed at the British Library, Digital Store 4183.bb.35]

20 Besant's Statement. 19 April. National Archives KB6/4 (Trinity 1877).

21 Knowlton, Charles. *A History of the Recent Excitement in Ashfield*. p. 23.

22 Shannon, R.T. *Gladstone and the Bulgarian Agitation 1876*. London: Thomas Nelson and Sons. 1963. p. 238.

23 *National Reformer*. 29 April 1877.

24 Ibid., 6 May 1877.

25 *Banbury Advertiser*. 19 April 1877.

26 *The Times*. 27 April 1877.

27 *Court and Fashion—Belfast News-Letter*. 21 April 1877.

28 RA VIC/MAIN/QVJ (W). 18 July 1895. (Princess Beatrice's copies).

29 Knowlton. *A History of the Recent Excitement in Ashfield*. p. 23.

30 Shannon, p. 229.

31 Longford, Elizabeth. *Queen Victoria*. New York: Harper & Row. 1965. p. 412.

32 Buckle, George Earle (ed.). *The Letters of Queen Victoria 1862–1878*. *Vol. 3*. London: John Murray. 1926. pp. 37–38.

33 Ferguson, Niall. *The Cash Nexus*. New York: Basic. 2001. p. 27.

34 RA VIC/MAIN/QVJ (W). 18 April 1877. (Princess Beatrice's copies).

35 Ibid., Sunday 22 April 1877.

36 Ibid., Tuesday 24 April 1877.

37 *Pall Mall Gazette*. Friday 27 April 1877.

38 Baird, Julia. *Victoria: The Queen*. New York. Random House. 2016., p. 379.

Chapter 6: Trial by Jury

1 Dickens, Charles, Jr. *Dickens's Dictionary of London*. London: Charles Dickens and Evans. 1879. p. 129.

2 RA VIC/MAIN/QVJ (W). 2 May 1877. (Princess Beatrice's copies).

3 Original indictment. National Archives. KB12/127, No. 1.

4 *National Reformer*. 6 May 1877.

5 Agate, Peter. *Sexual Economy as Taught by Charles Bradlaugh*. London: W. Stewart & Co. c. 1877. p. 59.

6 *National Reformer*. 17 June 1877.

7 *Barnsley Chronicle*. Saturday 26 May 1877.

8 *National Reformer*. 1 July 1877.

9 Bonner, Hypatia Bradlaugh and Robertson, J.M. *Charles Bradlaugh: A Record of His Life and Work*. *Vol. II*. London: T. Fisher Unwin. 1908. p. 34.

10 *National Reformer*. 17 June 1877.

11 Darwin, Charles. *The Descent of Man*. Vol. 2. London: John Murray. 1871. pp. 328–329.

12 Darwin, Charles. To Charles Bradlaugh. 6 June 1877. Darwin Correspondence Project. Darwin Correspondence Project, 'Letter no. 10988'. www.darwinproject.ac.uk/letter/?docId=letters/DCP-LETT-10988.xml

13 *The Times*. Tuesday 15 May 1877.

14 *Echo* (London). Monday 14 May 1877.

15 RA VIC/MAIN/QVJ (W). 15 May 1877. (Princess Beatrice's copies).

16 *The Times*. 15 May 1877. The response, from Lord John Manners, was reported in the 17 May edition of the paper.

17 *Echo* (London). Friday 25 May 1877.

18 *The Times*. 14 May 1877.

19 *The Era* (London). Sunday 20 May 1877.

20 *The Times*. 23 May 1877.

21 RA VIC/MAIN/QVJ (W). 17 May 1877. (Princess Beatrice's copies).

22 Ibid. 24 May 1877. (Princess Beatrice's copies).

23 Ibid. 27 May 1877. (Princess Beatrice's copies).

24 Bonner. Vol. I. p. 51.

25 *National Reformer*. 20 May 1877.

26 *The Times*. 2 June 1877.

27 Summerscale, Kate. *Mrs Robinson's Disgrace*. New York: Bloomsbury. 2012. p. 167.

28 Ibid., p. 44.

29 Ibid., p. 205.

30 *The Times*. 22 November 1880.

31 RA VIC/MAIN/QVJ (W). 11 April 1875. (Princess Beatrice's copies).

32 *Kingston Daily Gleaner*. 24 October 1874.

33 Benson, Christopher Arthur and Viscount Reginald Baliol Brett Esher (eds). *The Letters of Queen Victoria, Volume III, 1854–1861*. Project Gutenberg eBook. Viscount Palmerston to Queen Victoria. 13 November 1856. p. 215.

34 Buckle, George Earle (ed.). *The Letters of Queen Victoria 1862–1878*. *Vol. 1*. London: John Murray. 1926. Sir Charles Phipps to Earl Granville. 3 March 1865. p. 257.

35 Ibid., Queen Victoria to Viscount Palmerston. 13 March 1865. p. 261.

36 'Chief-Justice Cockburn Dead'. *The New York Times*. 22 November 1880.

37 *National Reformer*. 10 June 1877.

Chapter 7: Day One

1 Oldham, James C. 'The Origins of the Special Jury'. *The University of Chicago Law Review*. 50(137): 1983. pp. 137–221.

2 Hanly, Conor. 'The Decline of Civil Jury Trial in Nineteenth-Century England'. *The Journal of Legal History*. 26(3): December 2005. pp. 253–278.

3 RA VIC/MAIN/QVJ (W). 18 June 1877. (Princess Beatrice's copies).

4 *Pall Mall Gazette*, 18 June 1877.

5 Fisher, Freda Muriel. 'Autobiographical Memoir of Freda Muriel Fisher'. Unpublished manuscript, circa 1935–1939. British Library. Vol. 1. p. 93. Shaw won his Academy Award for Best Adapted Screenplay, for *Pygmalion*. He and Bob Dylan are the only two people to win both prizes.

6 *National Reformer.* 10 June 1877.

7 *The Queen v. Charles Bradlaugh and Annie Besant.* London: Freethought. 1877. p. 6.

8 Ibid., p. 18.

9 Ibid., pp. 20–22.

10 Fisher. Vol 2. p. 13.

11 *National Reformer.* 6 May 1877.

12 Disraeli, Benjamin. *Sybil, or The Two Nations.* Oxford: Oxford University Press. 1998. p. 66.

13 *The Queen v. Charles Bradlaugh and Annie Besant.* pp. 27–28.

14 Ibid., p. 32.

15 Ibid., p. 35.

16 Ibid., p. 43.

17 *Echo* (London). Monday 18 June 1877.

18 Sterne, Laurence. *The Life and Opinions of Tristram Shandy, Gentleman.* London: Penguin Books, 2003. p. 466.

19 Griffin, Emma. *Breadwinner.* New Haven: Yale. 2020. pp. 98–102.

20 *The Queen v. Charles Bradlaugh and Annie Besant.* p. 44.

21 Bedford, Sylvia. *As It Was.* London: Sinclair-Stevenson. 1990. pp. 164–165.

22 Fisher, p. 94.

23 Ibid.

24 *The Queen v. Charles Bradlaugh and Annie Besant.* p. 50.

25 Ibid., p. 59.

26 *Sheffield Independent.* 19 June 1877.

Chapter 8: 'For us women'

1   *The Times.* 22 June 1877.

2   *The Queen v. Charles Bradlaugh and Annie Besant.* p. 89.

3   Bonner, Hypatia Bradlaugh and Robertson, J.M. *Charles Bradlaugh: A Record of His Life and Work. Vol. II.* London: T. Fisher Unwin. 1908. pp. 35–36.

4   Worsley, Lucy. *Queen Victoria.* New York: St. Martin's Press. 2019. p. 151.

5   Baird, Julia. *Victoria: The Queen.* New York. Random House. 2016. pp. 157-158.

6   Worsley, p. 156.

7   Ibid., p. 159.

8   Fulford, Roger (ed.). *Dearest Child: Letters between Queen Victoria and the Princess Royal, 1858–1861.* New York: Holt, Rinehart and Winston. 1964. p. 166.

9   Worsley, pp.171–172.

10   *Western Morning News.* 19 June 1877.

11   *The Queen v. Charles Bradlaugh and Annie Besant.* p.126.

12   Ibid., p. 135.

13   Fulford, p. 182.

14   *The Queen v. Charles Bradlaugh and Annie Besant.* 1877. p. 142.

15   Fisher. p. 94.

16   *The Queen v. Charles Bradlaugh and Annie Besant.* p. 152.

17   *Pall Mall Gazette,* 20 June 1877.

18   RA VIC/MAIN/QVJ (W). 20 June 1877. (Princess Beatrice's copies).

19   Bonner. Vol. II. p. 35.

20   *The Queen v. Charles Bradlaugh and Annie Besant.* p. 202.

21   Ibid., p. 213.

22   *The Times.* 21 June 1877.

23   *The Queen v. Charles Bradlaugh and Annie Besant.* pp. 215–220.

24   *London Daily News.* Friday 22 June 1877.

25 See www.english-heritage.org.uk/visit/blue-plaques/charles-vickery-drysdale/

26 *The Queen v. Charles Bradlaugh and Annie Besant.* pp. 223–225.

27 Ibid., p. 227.

Chapter 9: Sentence first – verdict afterwards

1 *Truth.* Thursday 28 June 1877.

2 *The Queen v. Charles Bradlaugh and Annie Besant.* pp. 239–243.

3 Ibid., pp. 250–255.

4 *Bradford Observer.* Friday 29 June 1877.

5 *The Queen v. Charles Bradlaugh and Annie Besant.* pp. 255–267.

6 *National Reformer.* 1 July 1877.

7 Bonner, Hypatia Bradlaugh and Robertson, J.M. *Charles Bradlaugh: A Record of His Life and Work. Vol. II.* London: T. Fisher Unwin. 1908. p. 35.

8 *Pall Mall Gazette.* 21 June 1877.

9 *National Reformer.* 1 July 1877.

10 *The Queen v. Charles Bradlaugh and Annie Besant.* pp. 267–268.

11 Knowlton, Charles. *A History of the recent excitement in Ashfield.* p. 19.

12 *National Reformer.* 1 July 1877.

13 Ibid., 8 July 1877.

14 Ibid., 1 July 1877.

15 *The Times.* 22 June 1877.

16 Ibid., 25 June 1877.

17 *National Reformer.* 8 July 1877.

18 *The Queen v. Charles Bradlaugh and Annie Besant.* p. 305.

19 Holmes, Rachel. *Sylvia Pankhurst.* London: Bloomsbury. 2020. p. 55.

20 Bonner. Vol. II. p. 36.

21 Besant. *Autobiographical Sketches.* London: Freethought. 1885. p. 147.

22 *The Times.* 29 June 1877.

23 RA VIC/MAIN/QVJ (W). 28 June 1877. (Princess Beatrice's copies).

24 *Reynolds's Newspaper.* 22 July 1877.

25 Hibbert, Christopher. *Queen Victoria*. New York: Basic. 2000. p. 246.

26 *National Reformer*. 8 July 1877.

27 *The Scotsman*. Friday 28 September 1877.

28 *Colonial Standard and Jamaica Despatch*. 4 September 1877.

29 Besant, Annie. *Is the Bible Indictable?* London: Freethought. 1877. pp. 10–14.

30 Besant, Annie. *The Law of Population*. London: Freethought. 1877. Later edition, 1887. pp. 32 and 47–48.

31 *National Reformer*. 17 November 1877.

32 Sreenivas, Mytheli. 'Birth Control in the Shadow of Empire: The Trials of Annie Besant, 1877–1878'. *Feminist Studies*. 41(3): Gendering Bodies, Institutional Hegemonies (2015). pp. 509–537.

33 Haight, Gordon S. (ed.). *Selections from George Eliot's Letters*. New Haven: Yale University Press. 1985. pp. 592 and 597.

34 Fulmer, Constance M. and Barfield, Margaret E. (eds). *A Monument to the Memory of George Eliot: Edith J. Simcox's Autobiography of a Shirtmaker*. New York: Taylor & Francis. 1998. No page number; 12 December 1877.

35 *The Times*. 30 January 1878.

36 *National Reformer*. 10 February 1878.

37 *The Times*. 13 February 1878.

38 *National Reformer*. 24 February 1878.

39 Ibid., 3 March 1878.

40 *National Reformer*. 3 February 1878.

41 *The Times*. 27 February 1878.

42 *National Reformer*. 20 January 1878.

43 The accused was Henry John Dodwell. The case was heard 11 March 1878. See: www.oldbaileyonline.org/browse.jsp?id=def1-365-18780311&div=t18780311-365#highlight

44 Besant. *Autobiographical Sketches*. p. 160 and *National Reformer*, 12 May 1878.

45 *National Reformer*. 26 May 1878.

46 *The Times*. 20 May 1878.

47 Besant. *Autobiographical Sketches*. p. 161.

48 *National Reformer*. 26 May 1878.

49 *The Times.* 20 May 1878.

50 *National Reformer.* 26 May 1878.

51 Fisher, Freda Muriel. 'Autobiographical Memoir of Freda Muriel Fisher'. Unpublished manuscript, circa 1935–1939. British Library. Vol. 1. p. 88.

52 *National Reformer.* 9 June 1878.

53 Besant. *An Autobiography.* p. 80.

54 Dinnage, Rosemary. *Annie Besant.* Harmondsworth: Penguin. 1986. p. 47.

55 *Bradford Observer.* 10 April 1879.

56 *National Reformer.* 15 September 1878.

57 Longford, Elizabeth. *Victoria R.I.* London: Weidenfeld & Nicolson. 1961. p. 414.

58 *National Reformer.* 20 October 1878.

59 Tomalin, Claire. *Thomas Hardy.* New York: Penguin. 2007. p. 176. In 1884, Walter Besant was a founder and first chairman of the Society of Authors, a guild that transformed how publishers paid writers, advocating for royalties.

60 *The Times.* 5 November 1878.

61 *National Reformer.* 26 May 1878.

62 Besant, Annie. *An Autobiography.* p. 80.

63 Eekelaar, John. 'The Emergence of Children's Rights. Oxford Journal of Legal Studies, Vol. 6, No. 2 (Summer, 1986), p. 169. The 1883 case was *Agar v. Ellis.* The 1886 Guardianship of Infants Act stipulated that the welfare of the child should be taken into consideration, giving a divorced mother a broader remit over her child, but full equality of custodial rights was not achieved until 1973.

64 Besant. *Autobiographical Sketches.* p. 168.

65 *The Times.* 13 May 1879.

66 Besant. *Autobiographical Sketches.* p. 168.

67 Besant. *An Autobiography.* p. 80.

68 Nietzsche, Friedrich. *Ecce Homo.* Harmondsworth: Penguin. 1979. p.105.

69 *Edinburgh Evening News.* Thursday 18 December 1879.

Chapter 10: 'Sick of sewing coat tails'

1   Besant. *An Autobiography*. London: Freethought. 1893. p. 93.

2   Ibid., p. 90.

3   Dinnage, Rosemary. *Annie Besant*. Harmondsworth: Penguin. 1986. p. 51.

4   Shaw, George Bernard. *Pygmalion and Three Other Plays*. New York: Barnes & Noble Classics. 2004. pp. 317 and 343.

5   Nethercot, Arthur H. *The First Five Lives of Annie Besant*. Chicago: University of Chicago Press. 1960 p. 154.

6   Ibid., p. 159.

7   Ibid., p. 150.

8   Wilson, A.N. *The Victorians*. New York: Norton. 2004. p. 485.

9   *The Times*. 21 May 1880.

10 RA VIC/MAIN/QVJ (W). 22 May 1880. (Princess Beatrice's copies).

11 Heffer, Simon. *The Age of Decadence*. London: Windmill Books. 2017. p. 341.

12 Morley, John. *The Life of William Ewart Gladstone*. Vol. 3. Project Gutenberg eBook. 2010. p. 19.

13 *National Reformer*. 4 July 1880.

14 RA VIC/MAIN/QVJ (W). 25 May 1880. (Princess Beatrice's copies).

15 Ibid. 30 May 1880. (Princess Beatrice's copies).

16 Morley, p. 19.

17 RA VIC/MAIN/QVJ (W). 23 June 1880. (Princess Beatrice's copies).

18 *The Times*. 24 June 1880.

19 RA VIC/MAIN/QVJ (W). 23 June 1880. (Princess Beatrice's copies).

20 Morley, p. 20.

21 *National Reformer*. 4 July 1880.

22 Charles Bradlaugh papers. Bishopsgate Institute. Items 676–714.

23 *The Times.* 24 June 1880.

24 *The Illustrated London News.* 3 July 1880.

25 *National Reformer.* 4 July 1880.

26 RA VIC/MAIN/QVJ (W). 25 June 1880. (Princess Beatrice's copies).

27 RA VIC/MAIN/QVJ (W). 28 June 1880. (Princess Beatrice's copies).

28 Ibid. 2 July 1880. (Princess Beatrice's copies).

29 Niblett, Brian. *Dare to Stand Alone.* Oxford: Kramedart Press. 2010. p. 176.

30 *National Reformer.* 4 July 1880.

31 A.C. Tait letters, Lambeth Palace. *The Press and St. James's Chronicle.* 4 February 1882.

32 Nethercot. p. 165.

33 *National Reformer.* 4 July 1880.

34 Williams, Gertrude Marvin. *The Passionate Pilgrim.* New York: Coward-McCann. 1931. p. 134.

35 RA VIC/MAIN/QVJ (W). 13 January 1881. (Princess Beatrice's copies). Queen Victoria wrote in her diary for nearly 69 years, filling 141 volumes. The bulk of these were transcribed in longhand by her daughter Beatrice, who after Victoria's death spent 39 years copying 111 volumes – omitting material deemed offensive – before destroying the originals. Only 13 volumes of the queen's original journal, dating from 1832 to 1836, survive. See 'Queen Victoria's Journals', http://qvj.chadwyck.com/marketing/about.jsp

36 Ibid. 27 April 1881. (Princess Beatrice's copies).

37 Ibid. 11 May 1881. (Princess Beatrice's copies).

38 Ibid. 3 August 1881. (Princess Beatrice's copies).

39 Besant. *An Autobiography.* pp. 98–99.

40 Niblett, p. 220.

41 Shanley, Mary Lyndon. *Feminism, Marriage, and the Law in Victorian England, 1850–1895.* London: Bloomsbury Academic. 2021. p. 103.

42 Mackay, Carol Hanbury. 'A Journal of Her Own: The Rise and Fall of Annie Besant's Our Corner'. *Victorian Periodicals Review.* 42 (4): Winter 2009. p. 328.

43 *The Times*. 16 March 1883.

44 Tyson, Brian (ed.). *Bernard Shaw's Book Reviews*. Vol. 2 University Park: Penn State Press. 1996. p. 149.

45 Holmes, Rachel. *Eleanor Marx*. New York: Bloomsbury. 2014. pp. 215–216.

46 Charles Bradlaugh papers. Bishopsgate Institute. Edward Aveling to Annie Besant. 22 September 1884. Item 1158.

47 Nethercot. p. 130.

48 Charles Bradlaugh papers. Edward Aveling to Charles Bradlaugh. 3 March 1886. Item 1249.

49 *The Times*. 19 August 1898.

50 Lee, Hermione. *Virginia Woolf*. New York: Knopf. 1997. pp. 13–14.

51 Rosenbaum, S.P. (ed.). *Women & Fiction: The Manuscript Version of A Room of One's Own*. Glasgow: The Shakespeare Head Press. 1992. p. 184. In her masterful biography *Virginia Woolf*, Hermione Lee notes (p. 17) that Woolf struck this critical observation from the final version of her famous essay.

52 Lee, Hermione. *Virginia Woolf*. New York: Knopf. 1997. pp. 13–14.

53 Mackay. p. 336.

54 Besant. *Autobiographical Sketches*. p. 169.

55 McCarthy, Fiona. *William Morris. A Life for our Time*. London: Faber and Faber. 1994. p. 522.

56 Niblett. pp. 266–267.

57 *St. James's Gazette*. 18 April 1884.

58 Besant. *An Autobiography*. p. 111.

59 Fisher, Freda Muriel. 'Autobiographical Memoir of Freda Muriel Fisher'. Unpublished manuscript, circa 1935–1939. British Library. Vol. 2. p. 4.

60 Besant. *An Autobiography*. p. 116.

61 Ibid., p. 112.

62 Davis, Tracy C. *George Bernard Shaw and the Socialist Theatre*. Westport: Greenwood Press. 1994. p. 50.

63 Shaw, George Bernard. *You Never Can Tell*. New York: Brentano's. 1913. p. 16.

64 Shaw. *Arms and the Man*. New York: Penguin. 2006. p. 51.

65 Fisher. Vol. 2. p. 4.

66 G.B. Shaw Papers: Series I. Vol XXII (ff. 59–67. Annie Besant). Item 65. 6 August 1902.

67 Fisher. Vol. 2, p. 6.

68 G.B. Shaw Papers. Item 59. 24 March 1885.

69 Besant. *An Autobiography*. p. 117.

Chapter 11: 'When success comes'

1 'Mr. Bradlaugh Poses as Ajax'. *Moonshine*. 20 August 1881.

2 Hansard. HC Deb 11 March 1886 vol 303 c435.

3 RA VIC/MAIN/QVJ (W). 10 July 1883. (Princess Beatrice's copies).

4 Ibid. 25 July 1883. (Princess Beatrice's copies).

5 Ibid. 23 December 1886. (Princess Beatrice's copies).

6 Ibid. 24 December 1886. (Princess Beatrice's copies).

7 Ibid. 16 January 1887. (Princess Beatrice's copies).

8 Ricks, Thomas E. *Churchill & Orwell*. New York: Penguin. 2017. pp. 6 and 9.

9 Lord Randolph Churchill Papers. Cambridge University. Letter from Lord Queensbury. 1/13/86.

10 Niblett, Brian. *Dare to Stand Alone*. Oxford: Kramedart Press. 2010. p. 295.

11 *The Times*. 16 May 1887.

12 Hansard. HC Deb 2 March 1886 vol 302 C1772.

13 Besant. *An Autobiography*. London: Freethought. 1893. p. 118.

14 Ibid., p. 119.

15 Bonner, Hypatia Bradlaugh and Robertson, J.M. *Charles Bradlaugh: A Record of His Life and Work. Vol. II*. London: T. Fisher Unwin. 1908. p. 383.

16 Wilson, A.N. *The Victorians*. New York: Norton. 2004. p. 508.

17 Hibbert, Christopher. *Queen Victoria*. New York: Basic. 2000. p. 303.

18 Holmes, Rachel. *Eleanor Marx*. New York: Bloomsbury. 2014. p. 299.

19 *The Times*. 14 November 1887.

20 Besant. *An Autobiography*. p. 121.

21 W.T. Stead Papers. Correspondence B, Part 4, 1887–1888. Letter from Annie Besant. 20 December 1887.

22 Peters, Sally. *Bernard Shaw*. New Haven: Yale. 1996. p. 131.

23 W.T. Stead Papers. Correspondence B, Part 4, 1887–1888. Letter from Annie Besant. 20 December 1887.

24 Ibid., 19 January 1888.

25 Gibbs, A.M. *Bernard Shaw*. Gainesville: University Press of Florida. 2005. p. 653.

26 Nethercot, Arthur H. *The First Five Lives of Annie Besant*. Chicago: University of Chicago Press. 1960. p. 253.

27 Besant. *An Autobiography*. London: Freethought. p. 123

28 W.T. Stead Papers. Correspondence B, Part 4, 1887–1888. Letter from Annie Besant. 22 February 1888.

29 Ibid., 4 March 1888.

30 Ibid., 17 April 1888. Coincidentally, the next item in the sheaf of this file's letters is from Walter Besant, writing to Stead from Frognal Gardens.

31 Ibid., 23 July 1888.

32 Charles Dickens. *Household Words*. Vol. 5. 1852. p. 152.

33 Besant, Annie. 'White Slavery in London'. *The Link*. 23 June 1888.

34 Ibid., 30 June 1888.

35 Besant. *An Autobiography*. p. 124.

36 After Anthony Comstock banned the play from appearing on Broadway, Shaw said, 'It confirms the deep-seated conviction of the Old World that America is a provincial place, a second-rate country-town civilization after all.' See MacPherson, Myra. *The Scarlet Sisters*. New York: Twelve. 2014. p. 204.

37 Hansard. HC Deb 7 June 1898 vol 58 cc861–864.

38 *Pall Mall Gazette*. Wednesday 18 July 1888.

39 Hansard. HC Deb 9 August 1888 vol 330 cc128–137. On its third reading, the bill passed with a majority of 87.

40 Fisher, Freda Muriel. 'Autobiographical Memoir of Freda Muriel Fisher'. Unpublished manuscript, circa 1935–1939. British Library. Vol. 1. p. 90.

41 Charles Bradlaugh papers. Item 1775. No date given on clipping, although other papers reported the news in 1890. Digby's discovery of the letters indicates that Annie broke her vow not to write to her children during their years apart.

42 Besant. *An Autobiography*. p. 124.

Coda: 'Our Annie'

1 Besant. *An Autobiography*. London: Freethought. 1893. pp. 127–128. Annie did not cite Shakespeare, but in Act I of *Hamlet*, the titular prince tells Horatio, 'There are more things in Heaven and Earth/ Than are dreamt of in your philosophy.'

2 Fisher, Freda Muriel. 'Autobiographical Memoir of Freda Muriel Fisher'. Unpublished manuscript, circa 1935–1939. British Library. Vol. 2, p. 17.

3 Wilson, A.N. *The Victorians*. New York: Norton. 2004. p. 551.

4 Joyce, James. *Ulysses*. New York: Knopf. 1997. p. 277.

5 Nethercot, Arthur H. *The First Five Lives of Annie Besant*. Chicago: University of Chicago Press. 1960. p. 283.

6 Besant. *An Autobiography*. p. 128.

7 Ibid., p. 132.

8 *National Reformer*. 21 December 1890.

9 *The Times*. 31 January 1891.

10 Charles Bradlaugh papers. Bishopsgate Institute. Item 2975.

11 'Secularists celebrate restoration of Charles Bradlaugh's grave'. 18 October 2021. www.secularism.org.uk/news/2021/10/secularists-celebrate-restoration-of-charles-bradlaughs-grave

12 Charles Bradlaugh papers. Item 1093. 30 January 1884.

13 Guha, Ramachandra. *Rebels Against the Raj*. New York: Knopf. 2022. pp. 17 and 33.

14 Ibid., p. 45.

15 Ibid., p. 52.

16 Ibid., pp. 52–53.

17 Elwin, Verrier. *The Tribal World of Verrier Elwin*. New York: Oxford University Press. 1964. p. 27.

18 Lutyens, Mary. *Krishnamurti: The Years of Awakening*. New York: Avon. p. 277.

19 Heffer, Simon. *The Age of Decadence*. London: Windmill Books. 2017. p. 415.

20 *The New South Wales Law Reports*. Vol. 9. Sydney: Charles F. Maxwell. 1888. p. 528, quoting Justice Windeyer.

21 Field, James Alfred. *Essays on Population*. Chicago: University of Chicago Press. 1931. p. 225.

22 Ensor, Robert C.K. *England 1870–1914*. Oxford: Oxford University Press. 1980. p. 103.

23 Paraphrasing Philip Larkin's 'Annus Mirabilis'. In *Collected Poems*. London: Marvell Press. 1988. p. 167.

24 Pooley, Sian. 'Parenthood, child-rearing and fertility in England, 1850–1914'. *The History of the Family*. 18(1): March 2013. pp. 83–106.

25 Caldwell, John. 'The Delayed Western Fertility Decline: An Examination of English-Speaking Countries'. *Population and Development Review*. 25(3): September 1999. pp. 479–513.

26 Besant. *An Autobiography*. p. 82.

27 In *The Moral Property of Women: A History of Birth Control Politics in America*, the historian Linda Gordon helpfully notes that 'in different historical periods there are specifiable hegemonic and resistant meanings and purposes to reproduction control ... and that they express the (unstable) balances of political power between different social groups.' Third edition. Champaign: University of Illinois Press. p. ix.

28 Box, Muriel (ed.). *Birth Control and Libel: The Trial of Marie Stopes*. New York: A.S. Barnes and Company. 1968. p. 51. The defendant was the Catholic doctor Halliday Sutherland.

29 Ibid., p. 242.

30 Ibid., p. 203.

31 Ibid., p. 38.

32 Kalsem, Kristen Brandser. 'Law, Literature, and Libel: Victorian Censorship of "Dirty Filthy" Books on Birth Control'. *William & Mary Journal of Women and the Law*. 10: April 2004. pp. 533–568.

33 Guha, p. 177.

34 *The Times*. 21 September 1933. Digby would receive his own *Times* obituary, on 30 April 1960. Mabel's passing in 1952 would not be noted by the paper.

35 As in so many aspects of his life, George Bernard Shaw was the exception, having refused both a knighthood and the Order of Merit.

36 *The Times*. 29 October 1936.

37 Fisher. Vol. 2. p. 9.

Illustration credits

p. 2 'Bradlaugh Incarcerated', 'The Prison in the Clock-Tower of the Palace of Westminster' © Mary Evans Picture Library

p. 15 'Zazel Shot From a Gun', newspaper image © The British Library Board. All rights reserved. With thanks to The British Newspaper Archive (www.britishnewspaperarchive.co.uk)

p. 29 Courtesy of Bishopsgate Institute

p. 51 Courtesy of Archives and Special Collections, Dickinson College, Carlisle, PA

p. 109 Courtesy of The National Archives (UK)

p. 116 Sir Douglas Straight ('Men of the Day. No. 199.') by Sir Leslie Ward, published in *Vanity Fair* 10 May 1879 © National Portrait Gallery, London

p. 118 'Mrs. Besant', newspaper image © The British Library Board. All rights reserved. With thanks to The British Newspaper Archive (www.britishnewspaperarchive.co.uk)

p. 119 Courtesy of Conway Hall Ethical Society

p. 151 Alexander Cockburn © The Honourable Society of Middle Temple, 2023

p. 166 Hardinge Stanley Giffard, 1st Earl of Halsbury, by Alfred Bryan, late 19th century © National Portrait Gallery, London

p. 174 'Annie Besant' by Rischgitz/Stringer © Hulton Archive/Getty Images

p. 183 Victorian postcard © Wikimedia commons, public domain

p. 190 Charles Knowlton © Wikimedia commons, public domain

p. 213 Carte-de-visite of Alice Drysdale Vickery (1844–1929), photograph by Bradshaw & Sons, New York Academy of Medicine, Carte de Visite Collection, Creative Commons Public Domain Mark 1.0

Index

Note: page numbers in **bold** refer to information contained in captions.